Politics and Development in Contemporary Africa

Published by one of the world's leading publishers on African issues, 'Politics and Development in Contemporary Africa' is an exciting new series that seeks to provide accessible but in-depth analysis of key contemporary issues affecting countries within the continent. Featuring a wealth of empirical material and case study detail, and focussing on a diverse range of subject matter – from conflict to gender, development to the environment – the series is a platform for scholars to present original and often provocative arguments.

Editorial board:

Already published

Mobility between Africa, Asia and Latin America: Economic Networks and Cultural Interactions, edited by Ute Röschenthaler and Alessandro Jedlowski

Agricultural Development in Rwanda: Authoritarianism, Markets and Spaces of Governance, Chris Huggins

Liberia's Female Veterans: War, Roles and Reintegration, Leena Vastapuu and Emmi Nieminen

Forthcoming titles

Kakuma Refugee Camp: Humanitarian Urbanism in Kenya's Accidental City, Bram Jansen

Development Planning in South Africa: Policy Challenge in the Eastern Cape, John Reynolds

South Africa, AIDS and the Shadow of Biomedicine, Isak Niehaus

Infrastructure and Hybrid Governance in the Democratic Republic of Congo, edited by Kristof Titeca and Tom De Herdt

Slum Africa: Life and Governance at the Margins in Accra, Paul Stacey

About the author

For over thirty years, **Susanne Jaspars** has researched the social and political dynamics of food security, livelihoods and nutrition in situations of conflict, famine and humanitarian crises. Susanne first worked in Darfur, Sudan, from 1989 to 1990 when she managed Oxfam's nutritional surveillance programme. She continued her engagement with Sudan throughout the 1990s and 2000s, including in Darfur for Oxfam, the World Food Programme and as a Research Fellow at the Overseas Development Institute's Humanitarian Policy Group. Susanne also has extensive experience in other parts of the Horn and East Africa, and has published a number of books, academic articles and policy reports. She recently completed a PhD at Bristol University, examining the history and politics of food aid in Sudan, on which this book is based. Susanne is currently a Research Associate at the Food Studies Centre in SOAS, University of London and at the School of Sociology, Politics and International Studies of the University of Bristol. She is on the editorial board of *Disasters* journal and on the board of the *International Humanitarian Studies Association*.

Food Aid
in Sudan

A History of Power, Politics and Profit

Susanne Jaspars

ZED

Food Aid in Sudan: A History of Power, Politics and Profit
was first published in 2018 by Zed Books Ltd,
The Foundry, 17 Oval Way, London SE11 5RR, UK.

www.zedbooks.net

Typeset in Plantin MT by seagulls.net
Index by Rohan Bolton
Cover design by Keith Dodds
Cover photo © William Daniels/Panos

A catalogue record for this book is available from the British Library

ISBN 978-1-78699-209-3 hb
ISBN 978-1-78699-208-6 pb
ISBN 978-1-78699-210-9 pdf
ISBN 978-1-78699-211-6 epub
ISBN 978-1-78699-212-3 mobi

Contents

List of tables and illustrations

Abbreviations

ABS	Agricultural Bank of Sudan
AC	Area Council
AMIS	African Union Mission in Sudan
APU	Agricultural Planning Unit
AU	African Union
CBO	Community-based organisation
CMAM	Community-based management of acute malnutrition
CPA	Comprehensive Peace Agreement
COVA	Commission for Voluntary Agencies
CSI	Coping Strategies Index
DD	Dietary diversity
DDPD	Doha Document for Peace in Darfur
DFID	Department for International Development (of the UK government)
DPA	Darfur Peace Agreement (signed in May 2006)
FAC	Food Aid Convention
FAO	Food and Agriculture Organization (of the United Nations)
FCS	Food Consumption Score
FEA	Food Economy Approach
FRC	Food Relief Committee
GDP	Gross domestic product
HAC	Humanitarian Aid Commission
ICC	International Criminal Court
ICRC	International Committee of the Red Cross
IDP	Internally displaced person
INGO	International non-governmental organisation
JEM	Justice and Equality Movement

IMF	International Monetary Fund
LJM	Liberation and Justice Movement
MoA	Ministry of Agriculture
MoF	Ministry of Finance
MoH	Ministry of Health
MT	Metric tonne
NCP	National Congress Party
NGO	Non-governmental organisation
NISS	National Intelligence and Security Services
OCHA	Office for the Coordination of Humanitarian Affairs (of the United Nations)
ODA	Official development assistance
ODI	Overseas Development Institute
OECD/DAC	Organisation for Economic Co-operation and Development/Development Assistance Committee
OLS	Operation Lifeline Sudan
OAU	Organisation of African Unity
PPP	Public–private partnership
RRC	Relief and Rehabilitation Commission
RSF	Rapid Support Forces
RUTF	Ready-to-use therapeutic food
SC-UK	Save the Children – UK
SLA	Sudan Liberation Army
SPLA/M	Sudan People's Liberation Army/Movement
SSU	Sudan Socialist Union
UNAMID	UN-African Union Mission in Darfur
UNDP	United Nations Development Programme
UNHCR	United Nations High Commissioner for Refugees
WFP	World Food Programme
WoT	War on Terror
WTO	World Trade Organization

Acknowledgements

I would like to thank Mark Duffield and Jutta Weldes for their support, intellectual stimulation and patience in supervising the PhD on which this book is based. David Keen was the best external examiner I could have wished for, and I'd like to thank both Mark and David for their continued support in publishing a book based on my thesis.

There are many other people who helped with the research presented in this book. First of all, I want to thank Professor Atta Al-Battahani, of the Political Science Department at the University of Khartoum, for agreeing to be my sponsor in Sudan. I also thank Dr Shafie Al-Mekki and Dr Sahar M. El-Faki who, as Heads of Department, wrote letters to invite me to Sudan and to request travel permits to Darfur. I could not have done my research in Sudan without their support.

Special thanks also go to my research assistants: Dr Abdeljabar Abdellah Al-Fadul, Mariam Adam Musa and Abdelwahab A.M. Ahmed, who helped with interviews and provided valuable insights during discussions. Sincere thanks also to the staff of the Darfur Rehabilitation and Reconstruction Agency. I thank Youssif Al-Tayeb in particular for his interest and encouragement, for commenting on notes and drafts, and for his support with organising a workshop in Khartoum to discuss my findings. Many other Sudanese friends and former colleagues helped me with my research. I thank all of them.

I thank the World Food Programme (WFP) for helping with organising interviews, for allowing me to give presentations at their Khartoum office and for their feedback, and for providing assistance and accommodation in Al-Fashir. Thanks also to Practical Action for providing accommodation. In Khartoum, the Acropole Hotel provided a welcoming and friendly environment, with George, Makis, Thanasis and Paul always ready to help out with the practicalities of working in Sudan. I am grateful to the Bristol Alumni Foundation for providing a grant to give a presentation at WFP which helped pay for my flight to Khartoum. I thank WFP and the Save the Children (UK) archives for allowing access to their documents, and Andreas Psoroulas and Amy Bangs for finding documents and arranging permission on behalf of WFP and Save the Children (UK) respectively.

Helen Young, my friend and research partner since we first met in Sudan in 1988, provided encouragement, stimulation and practical advice on doing research in Sudan. Mary Atkinson directed me to the literature on food policy and commented on a draft of Chapter 2. Ed Clay and Dan Sparks helped with issues on food aid governance and quantitative data on food aid to Sudan. Thank you!

Finally, a huge thank you to my husband Rick and son Josh for their patience, practical support and love during the many years it has taken to complete this book. Rick also helped with proofreading and with solving all manner of computer problems. Thanks also to my mother, Bea Jaspars, who sadly passed away before this book was published, for financial support and faith in my decision to do a PhD at age fifty. I could not have done it without them.

Preface

This book builds on my own experience of working on issues of food aid for almost thirty years, much of which has been in Sudan. I first worked in Darfur from 1989 to 1990 as a nutritionist for Oxfam, with responsibility for establishing a nutritional surveillance programme in drought-prone areas. It was part of a Famine Early Warning System established to prevent a famine as severe as that in 1985 from happening again. Since then, I have continued to work professionally on issues of emergency nutrition, food aid and food security, including frequent visits to Darfur. I am therefore an insider in the world that is the subject of this book. In the thirty years that I have worked as an aid practitioner and researcher, emergencies have become more complex and protracted, disasters have become more frequent and the international humanitarian system has expanded. In 2016, the UN Secretary-General stated that the humanitarian system is broken and is unable to address today's crises. In this book, I examine in detail *how* and *why* the system failed in Sudan, a country where every humanitarian and food aid practice has been tested, in the hope that such an analysis will contribute to reform of the humanitarian system.

The profession of nutrition has changed beyond recognition since I gained my MSc in Human Nutrition in 1986. At that time, nutrition was considered a social as well as a medical science. The then Director of the Department of Human Nutrition at the London School of Hygiene and Tropical Medicine, Professor Philip Payne, had made a decision that if politics, and the distribution of resources, was a major determinant of nutrition, then this is what students should learn about. We were encouraged to think critically about the geopolitical objectives of food aid, and the effects of agricultural technologies, multinational food and agribusiness, trade and commodity agreements, on the food system, inequality and ultimately poor people. This approach to nutrition stands in stark contrast to the medicalised nutrition used in the emergencies of today, which is largely concerned with measurement, treatment and behaviour change. Food and agri-business at global and local levels have come to be seen as the solution – not the cause – of malnutrition and food insecurity.

My own experience and research has repeatedly revealed the social and political dynamics of nutrition and food security. Political vulnerability or marginalisation has frequently been a cause of malnutrition and food insecurity, and food aid has often become part of local power relations. Working with Somali refugees in Kenya, for example, I found that refugee groups with the highest prevalence of malnutrition were excluded from food distributions, and that the excluded clans were the same as those who had been politically marginalised in Somalia and the subject of attacks by stronger clans during the conflict. When I was reviewing targeting strategies in southern Sudan, shortly after the 1998 famine, I found the weakest clans were excluded from food distribution, as were displaced populations, and female-headed households – groups generally considered as amongst the most vulnerable (Jaspars and Shoham, 1999). In response, I tried to find ways of improving food distribution by developing a framework for analysing the accountability of local leadership and by applying humanitarian principles (Jaspars, 2000). In 2008, I took part in a study on food aid targeting in complex emergencies, in which we analysed transparency, accountability, fairness or impartiality, gender sensitivity of local institutions and committees, and how food distribution was influenced by the local political economy and vice versa. Not surprisingly, local institutions varied in their degree of participation and representation, and those with the lowest participation were more subject to diversion or manipulation of food aid (Jaspars and Maxwell, 2008). In Darfur, newly established food committees were linked in varying degrees to local politics through the involvement of tribal leaders and the newly elected leaders of displaced populations (Young and Maxwell, 2009). In my later research at the Overseas Development Institute (from 2008 to 2010), I found overlaps in membership and function between the relief committees and the leadership of displaced populations in camps and between relief committees and Popular Committees (Jaspars, 2010). Popular Committees had been introduced by Sudan's Islamist regime in the 1990s for political as well as administrative purposes. This is something I wanted to investigate further. To get a new perspective, in this book I take a different approach by looking at food aid practices as a way of governing. I examine not only how effectively institutions perform their intended functions, but also the actual effect of the strategies and tactics used.

My work has essentially followed the prevailing trends in food aid in emergencies – starting with nutrition and refugees, followed by drought response and famine early warning, food distribution in conflict and the application of humanitarian principles, livelihoods and protection in conflict situations, and most recently food security and local institutions in protracted crisis. What became

evident after twenty-five years, however, was that important technical innovations had been made but many practices and problems
experienced in implementation remained the same. The humanitarian community seems to be continually reinventing solutions: the
repeated failures of targeting yet continued emphasis on doing this
better is a case in point. Food security, livelihoods, protection and
resilience programming appear to present linear progress but often
involve the same practices – even if their meaning and interpretation has changed. At the same time, studies of food aid have focused
on particular points in time, covering a particular humanitarian
crisis or a famine, for example the refugee crises in the 1970s and
1980s, famines in the Horn of Africa in the mid-1980s, and complex
emergencies in much of sub-Saharan Africa in the 1990s. Studies
on food aid in the 2000s are few, despite the acknowledgement of
an increase in protracted crises and food aid remaining the main
component of humanitarian response. Sudan, Somalia, Ethiopia
and Kenya have all received food aid for many decades. Yet until
now the history and evolution of food aid policy and its effect in any
particular country has not been systematically analysed. In Sudan,
more than fifty years of food aid raises questions about how effectively it has saved lives and supported livelihoods and also about
the wider social and political effects, such as its role in supporting
an exclusionary development process and maintaining inequality
between Sudan's centre and periphery. I decided to take some time
out to do a PhD examining the history and politics of food aid in
Sudan, on which this book is based.

I
Introduction: food aid and power

The crisis in Sudan

In 2004, the United Nations Humanitarian Coordinator for Sudan called Darfur the world's worst humanitarian crisis (BBC, 2004). This was soon followed by the World Food Programme's (WFP) largest food aid operation globally. WFP's food aid operation in response to the Darfur crisis was not the first time that Sudan had received food aid but was the latest in a long line of regular food distributions. Sudan has received international food aid since 1958. It has experienced an emergency requiring external assistance every year since 1984 and is on the Food and Agriculture Organization (FAO) list of low-income, food-deficit countries (FAO, 2012a, 2012b). In 2013, acute malnutrition levels were above internationally agreed emergency thresholds for most of the country's population (Federal Ministry of Health, 2014). This makes Sudan one of the longest running recipients of food aid and its crisis one of the most severe and protracted.

The Darfur crisis has been ongoing for almost fifteen years. Violent conflict has caused destruction, death and displacement for large numbers of people and has restricted movement and thus access to land, markets and work. The years since 2013 have seen the highest number of newly displaced people in Darfur since 2004: over 1 million people were newly displaced between 2013 and 2015 (UN OCHA, 2015: 11). New conflicts started in Sudan's South Kordofan and Blue Nile states in 2011. The UN estimated a total of 5.8 million people to be in need of humanitarian assistance in Sudan in 2016, with the majority being in Darfur, South Kordofan and Blue Nile (ibid.). However, international agencies are unable to access many conflict-affected populations in these areas (UN OCHA, 2016: 16). They risk being attacked or kidnapped and a system of government permits often means that access is denied. The Sudan government closely monitors international agencies because it perceives them as political tools of the West and as threats to national security. International aid programmes have to be managed remotely, which means that national staff, local partners, local authorities, private contractors or community-based organisations (CBOs) implement programmes on the ground, but decision-making remains with international staff (Stoddard et al., 2006). Through these remotely managed programmes, international agencies measure food security status using newly developed quantitative and allegedly universally applicable indicators. As the crisis has become protracted, agencies have decreased the quantity of food aid and have initiated food vouchers and food-for-work and targeted nutrition programmes in attempts to encourage recovery and promote resilience. At the same time, the government has 'Sudanised' the aid industry by promoting national non-governmental organisations (NGOs), developing a national strategic grain reserve and distributing government food aid. This is not necessarily a positive move from the perspective of those affected by conflict and humanitarian crisis, as food distributions are in government-held areas and often limited to government employees and supporters. Most people's options are limited to marginal and precarious activities or, if they are lucky, they will find ways to leave Darfur or to benefit from the war or aid economy. They have been abandoned and forced to become resilient in a context of permanent emergency.

This book is about the abandonment of crisis-affected populations and about the indirect effects of food aid in developing the Sudanese state and its closely aligned private sector. The abandonment has several components. Successive Sudanese governments have concentrated their development efforts on Khartoum and surrounding areas, have used food aid as a way of obtaining political support and have responded to famine, disaster or displacement as security threats. Donors at first supported the Sudanese state, then bypassed it, and most recently have failed to successfully challenge the Sudan government's denial of access to crisis-affected people in Darfur. Instead, the UN has aligned itself with the government to maintain access to at least some conflict-affected populations, and international NGOs (INGOs) have largely kept quiet for fear of being expelled. The result is limited information which means that programming, such as the move from relief to recovery, is largely based on distant assumptions rather than on evidence of the ongoing threats that conflict-affected people face and their humanitarian consequences.

The abandonment is also a consequence of new food aid practices. Contemporary food aid practices reflect neoliberal strategies of making individuals responsible for their own nutrition and food security problems. Emergency nutrition and food security expertise currently focuses on quantitative measures of household food security, nutritional status, and on treatment and behaviour change. The private sector plays a role in the provision of food-for-voucher programmes, producing specialised nutrition products and new agricultural technologies. In Darfur, these practices form part of attempts to promote resilience amongst communities but have also facilitated the withdrawal of food aid from conflict-affected populations. Resilience approaches require the creation of responsible subjects who can adapt to an environment of permanent emergency, and they lower expectations of material development. Instead, the objective becomes survival in the face of constant danger (Cannon and Muller-Mahn, 2010; Haldrup and Rosen, 2013; Welsh, 2014). From a global perspective, strategies based on universal indicators, behaviour change, technical solutions and private sector engagement offer the possibility of containing the threat posed by permanent food emergencies using remote management technologies. For poor or conflict-affected populations, however, regularly high levels of acute malnutrition or food insecurity no longer result in a general food aid response and social, political and economic causes are not addressed.

Over the fifty years that Sudan has received food aid, it has rarely had its intended effect of improving production, saving lives or supporting livelihoods. It did, however, lead to a semblance of development in that it indirectly provided benefits for the Sudan government, private sector and aid professionals. Duffield (2002a) has used the term 'actually existing development' to describe the development that occurs indirectly as a result of, or in spite of, official development efforts. The 'actually existing development' resulting from food aid in Sudan also has several components. Fifty years of food aid have enabled the government to develop its own food aid apparatus modelled on the perceived political functions and practices of international food aid. It can use this to maintain or elicit political support, both nationally and internationally. It has also learnt how to control international food aid and the agencies that distribute it, in part by adopting tighter regulations and in part through denials of access. In addition, international food aid has unintentionally provided a valuable source of foreign exchange and has indirectly supported the national strategic reserve and grain traders and transporters in central Sudan. The food response to the Darfur crisis in 2004–05 was an exception in that it successfully prevented famine but it also provided a massive boost to Sudan's private sector. Politically, food aid enhanced the authority of often newly elected leaders for populations displaced in the early stages of the conflict and humanitarian operation. Later, the reduction of food aid in Darfur from 2008 onwards had different political and economic effects. While aid agencies reduced food aid in order to encourage recovery and promote resilience, this also supported government objectives of encouraging internally displaced persons (IDPs) to leave the camps. Finally, beneficiaries and Sudanese aid workers also learnt from fifty years of food aid. Long-term food aid in Darfur has created a cadre of experienced Sudanese aid professionals and beneficiaries who manage to navigate their way between the expectations of international agencies and the intricacies of local politics. Yet with the increase in remotely managed, medicalised and quantitative practices, their knowledge and experience is less powerful in influencing food aid programmes than those of the government and international aid agencies. Despite fifty years of food aid and today's positive ideology of resilience, most populations in Sudan's peripheries are left to follow their own livelihood strategies and adapt to permanent emergency.

The starting point of the book is the context of limited international access and reduced food aid amidst ongoing violence and high levels of acute malnutrition, and at the same time food aid's indirect effect of benefiting Sudan's government and private sector. It examines how this situation came about by analysing the evolution of international food aid practices over a period of fifty years, its interactions with local government and private sector, the actual effects of food aid in Darfur, and the perceptions of those who distribute and receive food aid. In this analysis, I consider food aid not simply as a source of nutrients or a gift but also as a technology of governance in that it has the power to change behaviour, attitudes and power relations. Such a historical analysis of food aid and its effects helps explain why the Sudan government views international food aid as so subversive, the inability of aid agencies to negotiate access to conflict-affected populations, the dominance of technical and medicalised approaches to food security and nutrition and the negative consequences for the well-being of most ordinary people in Darfur.

This book is not only about Sudan. It is also about global food aid practices, about nutrition, and about governance. Food aid in Sudan reflects both Sudan's history and the history and politics of global food aid policy and practice. Sudan's history, in terms of conflict, political ideologies and changes in the Sudanese state, is revealed in the changing quantities of food aid and how it has been provided. Food aid in Sudan reflects global food aid practices because from the late 1950s the country has received every type of food aid and from the 1980s it has been 'a laboratory for humanitarian ideas' (African Rights, 1997a: 2) in response to refugees, conflict and drought. At the same time, this experience in Sudan has informed food aid practice globally: it has frequently been a case study in international conferences and many research studies on famine, aid and the political economy of aid have been carried out in Sudan. In a recent virtual issue on famine by *Disasters Journal*, which provided the journal's seminal papers on famine published over thirty years, thirteen out of nineteen articles were either exclusively on Sudan or included information and analysis on Sudan (Pantuliano and Young, 2011). The book is also a story about the changing concepts and ideology in the discipline of emergency nutrition, and how this has influenced food aid and humanitarian assistance more generally. It discusses how and why for a brief period from the late 1980s to the late 1990s nutrition in emergencies came to be seen as a social science and nutritionists examined nutrition within its wider social, economic and political context. Since the early 2000s, however, emergency nutrition practices have been medicalised and de-politicised, which has had the effect of normalising violence and of hiding the political effects of food aid. Finally, the book is about governance, or rather about ways of governing. It examines the power effects of food aid not only by directly strengthening or undermining states or authorities, but also through a variety of techniques and practices such as surveillance, categorisation, comparison to norms, and the calculation of risk and judgements of what is acceptable. As the book will show, these practices have in turn influenced the Sudanese state first in the form of resistance to international food aid practices and later in adaptation. These days, food aid in Sudan exemplifies the protracted crisis and the failing international aid system found in many parts of the world. Analysing food aid policy and practice in Sudan is therefore relevant to food aid policy and practice globally.

What is food aid?

Food aid has been defined as 'a form of aid which is internationally sourced, has a significant grant element and can be either in the form of food or cash for the provision of food' (Barrett and Maxwell, 2005: 5). However, food aid is more than a grant or a source of nutrients: food distribution involves a range of activities, institutions and authorities. It is also an industry that employs thousands of people. The process of providing food aid includes procurement, logistics,

assessments, ration planning, targeting, distribution and monitoring (Jaspars and Young, 1995: 2). A range of policies, principles,
standards and guidelines have been developed to determine who
should receive food aid, how much, when, how and for what specific
purpose. This includes the professional study of emergency nutrition
and food security as subjects which determine what is to be known
about food needs and the right response to malnutrition or food
insecurity at particular points in time.

The nature of food aid has changed over time. From the late 1950s
to the early 1990s food aid was largely *programme food aid*, direct
government-to-government aid provided on concessional credit
terms. It was a means of disposing of US and European agricultural
surpluses and of promoting foreign policy and trade objectives, as
well as supporting state-centred development in recipient countries
(Singer et al., 1987; Shaw, 2001). *Project food aid* has been a form
of development food aid since the 1960s and is usually managed
by WFP or by NGOs. It is used as payment in labour-intensive
public works programmes and in school-feeding or clinic-based
programmes which provide food supplements to mothers and young
children (Shaw, 2001). Such programmes are now commonly part
of protracted emergency food aid operations as ways of targeting or
reducing food aid, while WFP development projects have decreased
over time (Shaw, 2011).

The main form of international food aid is now *emergency food
aid*, targeted and distributed free of charge to victims of natural or
man-made disasters (Clay and Stokke, 2000: 25). It has been, and
remains, the largest component of humanitarian assistance (Harvey
et al., 2010). In theory, therefore, emergency food aid is provided
according to humanitarian principles of humanity (address human
suffering wherever it is found), impartiality (provide assistance on the
basis of need), neutrality (not take sides in hostilities) and independence (autonomy from political, economic and military objectives)
(UN OCHA, 2012). Until the mid-1980s, emergency food aid was
intended to save lives and to meet nutritional needs, but it later
acquired objectives of livelihood support, conflict prevention, peace-
building and humanitarian protection (WFP, 2002; Were Omamo et
al., 2010). In WFP's latest strategic plan, food aid objectives include
building resilience by supporting nutrition, by the establishment of
safety nets and by working with the private sector (WFP, 2013a).
For the past fifty years more than half of global food aid shipments
have been US food aid (Harvey et al., 2010: 60), but the agencies
and institutions involved in food aid have expanded over time, and

now include a range of donors, UN agencies, recipient government authorities and international and local organisations and committees.

From the early 2000s, aid agencies changed from food aid to food assistance. No commonly agreed definitions of food assistance as yet exist, but it can include locally purchased food aid, food vouchers, direct cash transfers, food- or cash-for-work as well as in-kind food aid (food aid shipped from donor countries rather than purchased locally) (Harvey et al., 2010). While seen as a new and innovative approach, it bears some resemblance to the interventions by the British colonial government in Sudan, which included food- or cash-for-work to build airfields, roads and public buildings, free train tickets to enable migration for work and encouragement to grow drought-resistant crops, as well as internationally or locally procured food for famine relief (Singer et al., 1987: 18; African Rights, 1997a: 21–23). The Sudan government's current food aid projects, such as the establishment of a national strategic grain reserve, the distribution of free or subsidised food or a preferential exchange rate for wheat, could also be considered as food assistance. This book considers both international transfers of food or funds to buy food and Sudan government food interventions as food aid, and distinguishes between them by using the terms *international food aid* and *government food aid*.

Emergency nutrition and food aid: a social or medical science?

Emergency nutrition can be seen as a medical science dealing with nutritional requirements, individual diets and the treatment of malnutrition, and as a social science examining the social, political and economic influences and constraints on adequate nutrition at the population level. While the former has been the dominant approach in international nutrition, social nutrition provided an alternative in emergencies for a brief period in the 1980s and 1990s. Social nutrition is described by Pacey and Payne (1985: 10) in *Agricultural Development and Nutrition* as a subject 'that examines those social, environmental, economic and political factors that determine the degree to which people have access to food and can assimilate its nutrients'. Published ten years after the World Food Conference of 1974, this book expressed a concern that after a decade of strategies to increase agricultural production and improve nutrition, malnutrition existed in the same populations that had experienced rapid progress in production and exports. There was more food *and* there were more destitute and hungry people. Feeding programmes and nutrition education were often totally ineffective. Pacey and Payne

(1985: 18) proposed a new, social nutrition which recognised that malnutrition had 'multiple causes, many of which are closely linked to the conditions of inequality of resources, or poverty, and of social discrimination'. New ideas about food systems, the epidemiology of malnutrition and livelihoods would take nutrition forward (Pacey and Payne, 1985: 19). From the 1990s, UNICEF promoted a similar approach, based on research carried out in Tanzania, which found that malnutrition and mortality were caused not only by low food intake and disease at the individual level but also by the interaction of poor health environment, food insecurity and care at community level and by the availability and distribution of resources at national level (Pelletier and Jonnson, 1994). This led to the UNICEF framework on causes of malnutrition and the adoption of a public nutrition approach in emergencies in the 1990s (UNICEF, 1990; Young et al., 2012). As discussed in more detail in Chapter 2, this led to the wider analysis of nutrition and its underlying causes, and recommendations for a range of interventions to address malnutrition, including agricultural programmes, safety nets and market interventions, as well as general food distributions and treatment (Borrel and Salama, 1999; Appleton et al., 2000; Young et al., 2004). Social nutrition in emergencies was also concerned with implementation and examined the social and political constraints in getting food to those who needed it most. Studies in Kenya, Sudan and Ethiopia showed that aid agency targeting strategies regularly failed to reach the most vulnerable. In the best scenario, local leaders redistributed food aid equally or to those they considered most in need. In the worst scenario, the most vulnerable, such as the displaced or pastoralists, were excluded and the wealthiest or those with political connections received more (Borton and Shoham, 1989; Keen, 1991; Sharp, 1998; Jaspars and Shoham, 1999; Taylor and Seaman, 2004). By 2012, however, nutrition as medical science once again dominated. A large number of new food products to treat malnutrition has once again led to a narrow focus on malnutrition as a clinical condition, with attention focused on a medicalised mode of treatment of individuals rather than a broader public nutrition approach (Young et al., 2012). Chapter 2 examines how and why a limited set of nutrition interventions focused on treatment and behaviour change came to form the basis of current approaches to nutrition, and the implications for the role of food aid in addressing malnutrition and food insecurity. It also discusses how a medicalised approach fails to acknowledge the political origins of malnutrition, the political constraints in getting food to those most in need, and food aid's political effects.

Food aid, politics and conflict

Food aid can address food shortages and malnutrition but also has intended and unintended political effects. These political effects range from the geopolitical functions of food aid during the Cold War and – more recently – the War on Terror (WoT) to support countries friendly to the West, to the manipulation of food aid in internal conflict. Despite aims of doing the opposite, food aid tends to support the more powerful and exclude the weak amongst crisis-affected populations. In a study on humanitarian principles, food distribution was considered the most difficult humanitarian operation in which to implement a principled approach (Leader, 2000: 37). The effect of humanitarian aid in supporting governments and particular political or social groups is a recurring theme in aid literature.

Geopolitics influenced the allocation of programme food aid during the Cold War, favouring countries friendly with the West, as exemplified by 75% of global food aid allocations in 1970 going to India, South Korea, Indonesia, Israel, India, Pakistan and Vietnam (Barrett and Maxwell, 2005: 10). In Sudan, food aid increased in the 1970s when left-leaning regimes took power in Ethiopia and Libya. For this reason, US programme food aid continued to support the Sudan regime until 1991 despite economic mismanagement, civil war and the government's role in the creation of famine (Keen, 1994). Cold War politics also influenced the provision of food aid to refugees. In the 1970s and 1980s, for example, refugee assistance in Pakistan and Honduras explicitly supported movements resisting the communist regimes in Afghanistan and Nicaragua respectively. Humanitarian assistance sustained resistance movements because controlling food aid meant control over the refugee populations (Terry, 2002). In his book *Famine Crimes*, Alex De Waal (1997a: 136) describes how emergency relief in Eritrea and Sudan in the 1980s tended to support governments, militia and urban populations rather than the rural poor. Food aid provided a source of much-needed hard currency through the manipulation of exchange rates and was taxed or diverted at all political levels.

A proliferation of internal conflict in the 1990s, following the end of the Cold War, drew attention to the manipulation of food aid by warring parties and its incorporation into the political economy of recipient countries. Warring parties obtain food aid through theft, attacks during delivery or distribution, taxation of food aid and inflation of beneficiary numbers to attract more aid. In part of southern Sudan in 1998, for example, food aid was taxed by the Sudan People's Liberation Movement (SPLM), residents were prioritised over the displaced, and the most powerful clans received more (SPLM, SSRA and OLS, 1998). Food aid has been used to feed troops and denied to contested areas. Food aid can also reinforce existing political processes by strengthening the authority of those in power and excluding the politically weak (Macrae and Zwi, 1994). The political effects of aid in refugee camps increased as direct military assistance decreased and, in some cases, provided unintentional support for political or military leaders. Support for Rwandan army leaders and militia guilty of genocide through the provision of assistance in Zairean camps is a case in point (Terry, 2002). In Sudan, as in other countries in sub-Saharan Africa, the control of emergency food aid became a key part of the country's political economy. The political survival of dominant groups (such as commercial farmers and traders in the north) had come to depend on the transfer of assets such as land, livestock and labour through violence, state appropriation and market manipulation. The manipulation of food aid became part of this (Duffield, 1994a; Keen, 1994). Restricting food aid increases food prices along with profits and asset transfer as it forces populations to purchase grain on the market, sell their livestock and – in the extreme – leave their land. This is discussed further in Chapter 3.

These issues have not gone away. Recent studies on food aid and protection linkages in Darfur highlight food aid strengthening the authority of IDP leaders and the exclusion of vulnerable groups from distributions (Mahoney et al., 2005; Young and Maxwell, 2013). However, there are few academic studies covering the local politics of food aid in today's conflicts. Locally, this could be because of limited access. Globally, issues of food diversion and manipulation at the local level have been overshadowed by the geopolitics of the 'War on Terror'. Food aid is once again part of the strategy to support states and its withdrawal a way of preventing food aid supporting terrorist groups. In Afghanistan, for example, the provision of large quantities of food aid in 2001 at the same time as military action was part of the counter-insurgency operation (Barrett and Maxwell, 2005: 44). US withdrawal of food aid to Somalia in 2009 was a means of stopping indirect support to Al-Shabaab, an Al-Qaida affiliate (Maxwell, 2011). Sudan is an ambivalent case as on the one hand it is an enemy Islamist state but on the other it is a provider of intelligence information to the US and, more recently, a contributor to the Saudi-led coalition fighting Iran-backed Houthi rebels in Yemen (Williams and Bellamy, 2005; Sudan Tribune, 2017). The WoT has led to a resumption of state authority, and a failure to develop coordinated donor strategies in response to access denials and INGO expulsions. In some contexts, the UN has had to compromise on humanitarian principles in order to gain or maintain at least some access to crisis-affected populations (WFP, 2009a). In Sri Lanka in 2009, for example, the order for international agencies to evacuate the contested north, the restriction of relief into the region and government manipulation of relief were not challenged so that aid agencies could access and assist the displaced (Keen, 2014). According to Keen (2014) agencies saw keeping silent as a 'lesser evil' but in the end it did not lead to better access and instead encouraged the escalation of war and ethnic cleansing. More recently, despite pretentions of neutrality, UN failure to challenge the Syrian government's denials of access has led to government-held areas receiving the bulk of food aid. Food distribution by the government-approved Syrian Red Cross and NGOs has led to further bias (Martinez and Eng, 2016). These situations have striking similarities to that in Sudan, in terms of aid agency silence in the face of ongoing crisis, the failure to successfully challenge limited access to war-affected populations and unintended support for the Sudan government.

Analysing food aid, power and governance

Food aid as a way of governing

Food aid can be seen as a technology of governance because it has the power to change behaviour, power relations, and to manage populations. Inspired by Foucault, this book takes power as not only exercised by the state but also through a variety of tactics and techniques. Such techniques can include disciplinary practices to regulate individual day-to-day activity such as observation, measurement, comparison to norms (for example in schools or public works projects) and/or forms of self-government through influencing attitudes and desires (for example the dignity of being self-reliant). It also includes technologies at the level of optimising the population's health and welfare, through surveillance and the calculation of risk, which Foucault later terms biopolitics or the administration of life (Foucault, 1991, 2007; Dean, 2010: 29). Foucault developed the concept of 'governmentality' to distinguish the technologies or practices of governing from its institutions, and to analyse how power is actually exercised.

Using governmentality as an analytical tool involves looking not only at the expected external functions of institutions, but also at the internal functions of the practices, strategies and tactics actually used, and the regime of truth they create (Foucault, 2007: 116–118). In this book, I analyse food aid as regimes of practices. While the concept comes from Foucault's work, Schaffer recommends analysing regimes of practices to examine public policy: '[t]o examine policy is to examine practice, and the practices are about selected problems ... [which] emerge from existing theories, institutions, apparatuses ... At any one time ... certain knowledge, problems, data and treatments are taken for granted, removed from debate or challenge' (Schaffer, 1984: 175–176). Clay and Schaffer (1984: 3) suggest that most policy is based on assumptions that need to be questioned, for example that policy formulation is separate from politics, that it is based on systematic consideration of all available evidence and that it can be separated from implementation. These assumptions mean that policy failure can be blamed on lack of political will, lack of certain expertise or problems with implementation, or what they call 'escape hatches'. In reality, they say, policy formulation is rarely a linear process and may be more about the unobjectionable or unavoidable, administrative rulings or categorisations and the avoidance of responsibility. Public policy may ultimately be about maintaining stability or power even if it fails to meet its stated aims (Schaffer, 1984). Foucault's study of the practices of punishment developed this kind of analysis. In *Discipline and Punish: The Birth of the Prison*, Foucault (1977) argued that even though prisons did not succeed in reducing crime, the practices produced a class of delinquents who could be monitored and controlled. In Sudan, the adoption of resilience approaches can in part be explained because contemporary medicalised practices to promote resilience are not controversial for the government of Sudan and because they enable aid agencies to remain in the country. The book explores changes in regimes of food aid practices, their underlying theories and concepts, the knowledge and truth they create, and their actual as well as intended effects. As such, it helps explore alternatives based on the actual impact of policy practice and on alternative views, perceptions and experiences (Foucault, 1977: 177).

A number of studies have looked at how aid presents a way of governing through practices such as normalisation, participation, monitoring and surveillance, and categorisation, as well as through directly influencing states or authorities. Normalisation influences actions by determining what is acceptable and may, for example, create a desire for a particular type of development through comparison between developing countries' gross national product (Brigg,

2002). Development partnerships have similar effects in that they expect countries to show that they are 'committed, responsible and willing to govern themselves wisely' (Abrahamson, 2004: 1461). At the local level, participatory approaches can hide unequal power relations because ranking and categorisation maintain and reify social norms (Kothari, 2001). Others have concluded that the monitoring and surveillance necessary in many development programmes maintains unequal power relations (Brigg, 2002; Abrahamson, 2004). In Sudan, Duffield (2002a) argued that the categorisation of displaced southerners into different wealth groups furthered a government process of de-socialisation and oppression. More generally, aid practices since the late 1980s reflect neoliberal governmentalities in that they encourage the creation of 'responsible' individuals who, using their skills and agency, develop and become self-reliant (Duffield, 2007; Chandler, 2013). As a theory of political economy, neoliberalism 'proposes that human well-being can best be advanced by liberating individual entrepreneurial freedoms and skills within an institutional framework characterised by strong private property rights, free markets and free trade' (Harvey, 2005: 2). In Africa, neoliberalism was first applied as part of World Bank and International Monetary Fund (IMF) structural adjustment measures in the 1980s, which minimised state intervention in the economy in the belief that economic growth could be promoted more effectively through the liberalisation of trade and free markets (Leys, 1996). Sudan, and other countries in sub-Saharan Africa, lurched into economic crisis and famine instead. By the late 1980s, development was largely influenced by neoliberal strategies concerned with improving individual agency and choice-making capacity. These strategies have been criticised for removing politics and power from development, for increasing inequality and for focusing on transforming the individual rather than society (see, for example, Harvey, 2005; Duffield, 2007; Chandler, 2013). Resilience approaches have raised similar concerns: they promote the creation of autonomous subjects who can adapt to repeated shocks and uncertainty but the causes of poverty or crisis are no longer addressed. Instead, the aim is simply to enable poor or crisis-affected populations to adapt and survive (Cannon and Muller-Mahn, 2010; Welsh, 2014). The governmental effects of food-based resilience approaches are a key subject of this book.

Aid practices have governmental effects even if they fail to meet their intended aims. In Eritrea, for example, Edkins (2000) concluded that the function of failed food-for-work projects was to reform and control vulnerable populations through work, maintain

particular authorities, organisations and companies, and maintain
the power of international agencies. In Sudan, Duffield (2002a)
found that aid agency attempts to encourage self-reliance by
reducing food aid and linking it to agricultural production failed,
and instead forced displaced southerners into exploitative labour
relations. Also in Sudan, Keen (1994) examined the functions of
failed relief operations in response to the Bahr Al-Ghazal famine
of 1988. Famine caused starvation and death for some people but
had economic benefits for government officials, military officers,
merchants and commercial farmers through speculation on grain
prices, displacement and the creation of cheap labour. These benefits
increased when the distribution of relief was restricted, and therefore
what appeared to aid agencies as a failed relief operation constituted
a success for a powerful and interconnected elite.

Any form of power involves resistance. In *Discipline and Punish*,
Foucault (1977) found that the severity of public torture led people
to side with the criminal, especially if the crime was linked to
social conditions or food riots. People's protests helped transform
punishment from public torture to imprisonment and disciplinary
techniques, with objectives changing from providing a spectacle and
deterrent to controlling behaviour through reform and surveillance.
Despite this analysis of practices of punishment, Foucault's analysis
of power is often criticised for neglecting human agency. Disciplinary
power, for example, can be seen as absolutely subjecting individuals,
of creating 'docile bodies' which are unable to escape their domination. Yet Foucault also defines power as a mode of action on the action
of others, thus presupposing a role for human agency (Gordon, 1991;
Foucault, 2000). According to Gordon (1991), governmentality was a
response to the critiques of *Discipline and Punish*. Adjustment or resistance are evident in a number of studies on aid. Ferguson (1990), for
example, describes violent resistance and non-participation in some of
the World Bank development projects in Lesotho. Chatterjee (2004)
shows how committees created for particular interventions can themselves become the basis for resistance and political claims. In Sudan, I
examined the governmental effects of food aid through interaction of
international food aid with local state and non-state forms of governance, as well as the perceptions and responses of food aid recipients
(beneficiaries and government officials) and aid agencies.

Analysing historical change

The book's historical analysis adopts Foucault's genealogical
approach by identifying lines of fracture, transformation and

consolidation in regimes of practices. It takes the current context of permanent emergency, reductions in food aid, but benefits to government and the private sector as its starting point and traces its origins by analysing regimes of food aid practice over the last fifty years. It asks what makes certain practices acceptable or self-evident and what is perceived as truth at a particular moment in time. *Discipline and Punish* and its analysis of changing practices of punishment provides Foucault's best example of a genealogical approach. He later applied the same methods to practices of governing in his lectures on *Security, Territory, Population* and *The Birth of Biopolitics*, which included an analysis of changes in governing food shortage (Foucault, 2007, 2008).

In seventeenth century Europe, food was seen as a moral entitlement and scarcity was prevented by law. A juridical and disciplinary system was implemented which controlled prices, prohibited hoarding and imposed limits on export and land to be cultivated. These systems failed, however, because low food prices reduced profits for rural producers who grew less in response, thus actually increasing the risk of scarcity. In the eighteenth century, freedom of commerce and circulation of grain became one of the fundamental principles of economic government. Grain was allowed to flow freely and the price regulated through subsidies and taxes. However, the free movement of grain could not prevent a rise in food prices when production failures were severe. This led to a perception of scarcity as a natural phenomenon and governance came to involve working with the reality of production and price fluctuations and careful management of population risks. This in turn required knowledge of production, markets, prices, imports and exports and of how and why people (both producers and consumers) act in response to changes in food prices. The final objective was now the security of populations and it was considered acceptable for some individuals to experience scarcity (Foucault, 2007: 32–42). In the subsequent lecture, Foucault introduces the idea of normalisation at the level of population. At an individual level, people can be treated or vaccinated against disease. At the population level, the 'normal' morbidity or mortality for a particular disease can be determined along with the deviations from normal that are considered acceptable (Foucault, 2007: 56–66). These practices are similar to food aid regimes of practices in the 1980s and 1990s, as described in Chapter 2. In this book, I identify three regimes of food aid practices in the fifty years that Sudan has received food aid, which I have called the state support regime, the livelihoods regime and the resilience regime.

Chapter 2 analyses changes in international regimes of food aid practices, what influenced change, the concepts and truths associated with it, and the implications for the provision of food aid. In the 1980s, food aid practices moved from state-centred development approaches to livelihood approaches, in which international aid agencies took responsibility for managing the lives and livelihoods of populations. Aid agencies bypassed the state and provided emergency food aid directly to communities. International agencies proliferated and so did their techniques – assessments, targeting, distribution and monitoring – and new areas of professional expertise such as emergency nutrition and food security emerged. Like Foucault's governance of food shortages described above, these areas of expertise function through assessment of risk, surveillance and normalisation. Emergency nutrition operates at the level of the individual, in terms of causes such as inadequate food intake and disease, body measurements and cut-off points to indicate malnutrition, and the risk of morbidity and mortality associated with different types and degrees of malnutrition. It also operates at the level of populations, in terms of social, political and economic causes, measures of the prevalence of malnutrition and agreed prevalence thresholds that constitute an emergency. While this involves the use of statistics and knowledge about risks to health, it also involves value judgements about the levels of risk and adaptation that are considered normal and acceptable. These judgements have changed over time. Cut-offs and thresholds have stayed the same, but their interpretation has changed. In 1995, the World Health Organization (WHO) adopted a prevalence of wasting (acute malnutrition) of 15% as an indicator of crisis, but by the end of the 1990s much higher levels of acute malnutrition were considered normal in African populations. By 2012, during the resilience regime in Sudan, levels of acute malnutrition well above emergency thresholds elicited little or no emergency food aid response. Instead, malnutrition and food insecurity were now seen much more as being a result of behaviour, and treatment and education as the correct intervention. Famine early warning systems, established in the 1980s and 1990s, included the monitoring of information on rainfall, production, markets, prices, imports and how people responded to food shortages. The difference between this and Foucault's analysis of the governing of food shortages in eighteenth century Europe is that, rather than a government managing populations within its own territory, food aid practices involved a complex network of donors, UN agencies and NGOs to govern populations in countries other than their own. This led to resistance by the Sudan government, and ultimately control of international food aid and the agencies that provided it in the resilience regime.

Food aid in Sudan

The three regimes of food aid practices produced different responses in Sudan, with the result that the effect was often very different from that intended. Chapter 3 analyses the effect at national level. Sudan first received international food aid in 1958, shortly after it gained independence in 1956. The state support regime of practices covered much of the regime of Nimeiri, who took power in a military coup in 1969. Like other development aid at the time, food aid in the state support regime aimed to assist the state in the modernisation of agriculture, industrialisation and urbanisation in central Sudan. Although these strategies largely failed in their intended objectives of supporting production, they did have other functions such as government budget support and addressing the security risks associated with urbanisation and influxes of refugees. Sudan's peripheries, including Darfur, were largely excluded. From the late 1970s, Sudan's economy deteriorated and government was increasingly centred on the political and economic survival of a minority elite amidst a mounting foreign debt. Famine, and Nimeiri's failure to acknowledge it, led to his overthrow through a popular uprising in 1985 (African Rights, 1997b). It also led to an increase in emergency food aid and the start of the livelihoods food aid regime in Sudan.

The livelihoods regime was a period of struggle over the control over food aid and the populations to which it was given in Sudan. The regime includes the ideological phase of President Al-Bashir's Islamist regime, whose aim was to change society based on Islamist ideas and to use state power to achieve this (Gallab, 2008; Sidahmed, 2011). Western donors withdrew development aid, including programme food aid, because of the new regime's support for Iraq in the Gulf War and because of the resumption of civil war with the south. Humanitarian aid increased in response to the 1991 famine, although fiercely resisted by the Sudan government because it conflicted with its aims of self-sufficiency. Over time, the Sudan government learnt how to benefit from, and control, international food aid, particularly after INGOs started working with war-affected populations in southern Sudan. At the same time, food aid became an integral part of Sudan's political economy. It provided a source of foreign exchange and funds for local government, and its denial or restriction to populations in contested areas provided benefits for traders and transporters closely aligned to government, commercial farmers and soldiers. Food aid's political and economic benefits continued to evolve over the following decades.

By 1999 the radical phase of the Islamist regime was over and, while maintaining the rhetoric of Islamism, government was once again about political survival, particularly when some of Sudan's leading Islamists joined the rebellion in Darfur. The Darfur conflict escalated in 2003–04, leading to a massive international humanitarian operation. From 2006 onwards, the government controlled international food aid through denials of access to conflict-affected populations, and the establishment of Sudan's own food aid apparatus – following a period of economic growth resulting from increased oil revenue – could be used directly to further the government's political and economic goals. Chapter 3 argues that the current situation with regard to limited access for international agencies is a response to the food aid practices of international agencies in Sudan.

Chapter 4 examines the effects of changing food aid practices in North Darfur in rural populations and, more recently, in camps for IDPs. Darfur has a long history of drought, famine and conflict, and North Darfur was selected for study in this book because it has received international emergency food aid almost continuously since 1984. North Darfur is also where I have many years of experience myself. This chapter analyses information from project reports and evaluations as well as interviews with beneficiary representatives from two chronically food-insecure and conflict-affected rural areas, and from two displaced camps close to Al-Fashir town (the capital of North Darfur). These represented a range of livelihoods, ethnic groups and political affiliations. In North Darfur, food aid in the livelihoods regime rarely met intended objectives of saving lives and supporting livelihoods. In addition to delays by traders and transporters, government resistance and donor priorities of keeping food aid to a minimum also led to delays and inadequate distributions. Food aid in the livelihoods regime in Darfur did, however, produce a highly trained cadre of Sudanese aid professionals and influenced local government structures. The 2004–05 response to the Darfur crisis can be seen as the peak of the livelihoods regime, as it was the first time that food aid successfully helped reduce malnutrition and support livelihoods. However, large quantities of food aid also had the political effect of supporting the leadership of displaced populations, sometimes linked to the rebellion. The resilience regime in North Darfur started in 2008, when reduction in food aid – intended in part to promote resilience – facilitated policies of dismantling the camps as well as counter-insurgency tactics to restrict supplies to rebel-held areas. In examining available information on the lives and livelihoods of populations in Darfur, Chapter 4 concludes that in the thirty years that people have received food aid, the majority have suffered a process of continuing impoverishment and permanent crisis.

Chapter 5 brings together government, international aid agency, beneficiary, long-term Sudanese aid worker, trader and transporter views and perceptions of food aid in the resilience regime. These views and perceptions are based on many years of experience and in-depth knowledge of food aid. The Sudan government views all food aid as a political tool, while international agencies view food aid as a cause of dependency and no longer necessary to address malnutrition. Long-term Sudanese aid workers and beneficiaries also see food aid as political, but that it continues to be needed in response to constraints on access to food, ongoing conflict and displacement. In the resilience regime, international agency practices have created a regime of truth in which malnutrition is due to people's own behaviours and food security is minimal. This enables agencies to remain in a highly politicised environment but also enables the Sudan government's use of food aid as a political tool. This regime can be maintained because of limited access and remote management which increases both the physical and emotional distance between aid workers and the victims of crisis. It leads to stereotyping of food aid beneficiaries which facilitates a decrease in food aid; it also removes government responsibility for creating the crisis and international responsibility for the protection of civilians. The views and perceptions of aid beneficiaries and long-term Sudanese aid professionals are not part of the dominant regime of truth.

Chapter 6 summarises the key findings presented in this book and provides some thoughts on the way forward for changing food aid practices in protracted crises.

The challenges of fieldwork in Sudan

The research presented in this book is the result of a combination of a review of policy documents, evaluations and interviews in Sudan. Doing research in Sudan – and particularly Darfur – is an exercise in patience, persistence and ingenuity. At the time of my research, access to conflict-affected populations was restricted through government

permits, riots and an atmosphere of suspicion and mistrust. The first
hurdle in doing research in Sudan is getting a visa and insurance to
work there. This can take months and can be expensive. My insurance went up from £20 (Khartoum only) in June 2012 to £270 in
January 2013 and to £700 in September 2013. Getting a grant for
fieldwork in areas where the UK Foreign Office advises against travel
proved impossible, so I had to fund the research myself. Once in
Sudan, I needed a travel permit for Darfur, which often takes many
weeks to obtain and may not be granted at all. If you make it to
Darfur, further questioning follows by the National Intelligence and
Security Service (NISS). Interviews need to be organised via trusted
intermediaries because the government accuses Western agencies of
spying and almost everyone in Sudan is closely monitored by the
security apparatus. During my fieldwork, the government imposed
austerity measures, which resulted in riots and police crackdowns in
many towns. On my first visit, reductions in bread and fuel subsidies
immediately led to riots in Khartoum. This affected me personally
as I was present when students at the University demonstrated and
were tear-gassed by the police. In September 2013, riots in Khartoum were so severe that most agencies closed their offices and
advised staff to stay at home. Al-Fashir, where I was at the time,
only experienced one day of riots but the government shut down all
mobile phone networks for several days, so no contact was possible
with my sponsors in Khartoum or my supervisors in the UK. This
created an added level of stress and delays in my interview schedule.
Sudan is not the only country in which research is difficult because
of access limitations (see, for example, Stoddard et al., 2006), but it
provides a good example of the challenges and the possibilities for
overcoming them.

My long-term experience in Sudan helped enormously in doing
the fieldwork. Some of the people I had worked with in the 1980s
or later were still involved in aid, often in senior positions in international agencies. They had also formed a local NGO (the Darfur
Rehabilitation and Reconstruction Agency), which agreed to support
my research. The Politics Department of the University of Khartoum agreed to sponsor me, which meant that it supported my visa
application and requests for permission to travel to Darfur. My close
relationship with Sudanese professionals meant that the access and
trust I had were much greater than if I had come to Sudan for the
first time in 2012. This is particularly so as these days relationships
between Sudanese and foreigners are often plagued by suspicions
that they are government informers or Western spies, respectively.

Sudanese colleagues helped in setting up interviews with government officials, getting my travel permit to Darfur, and helped persuade the authorities that I was a genuine researcher and not a spy.

I visited Al-Fashir in January and September 2013. This involved getting travel permission from the Humanitarian Aid Commission (HAC) in Khartoum, and in particular the NISS and Military Intelligence representatives within the Commission. I visited the HAC offices several times, with representatives from the University, the DRA and a former HAC official, whom I had met in the DRA's office, which showed that I had connections and support from various local institutions – academic, NGO and government. I had to provide copies of my checklists and research programme in North Darfur. It took ten days to get the travel permit in January and six days in September 2013, which is quick compared with INGO experience. In January 2013 I received a permit to go to Al-Fashir for three weeks, including travel to rural communities and camps for IDPs. However, even though HAC in Khartoum had given the travel permit, the NISS in Darfur asked me to leave after three days, telling me that it was not the right time to do the research and that it was not safe. Most of my three days were spent being questioned at the NISS office about my research and past activity in Darfur. I used the little time that was left to discuss my research with friends and former colleagues and with the local DRA team and to make plans for the possibility of having to do remote research later in the year. I was able to recruit a translator/research assistant and identify key informants to interview via trusted intermediaries. My final visit was delayed from May to September because security in North Darfur had deteriorated. I recruited a second research assistant to interview traders and transporters in Darfur and had regular discussions by phone or by Skype so that interviews with beneficiaries, transporters and traders in North Darfur could be done without me if necessary. In September, I got a travel permit for seven days (having asked for two weeks) just for Al-Fashir town, and after three days of questioning by HAC and NISS in Al-Fashir I was allowed to do my research.

Throughout my work in Sudan I was struck by everyone's interest in the research, including government officials, aid workers and the private sector. Despite the frustrations, it was an honour and a pleasure to interview Sudanese people with such extensive historical knowledge of food aid interventions in their country. The information from these interviews, combined with an extensive review of published and grey literature, forms the basis of this book.

2
From managing states and supporting livelihoods to abandoning populations

Aid agencies and donors have tried to achieve many different things with food aid. Over time, the objectives of food aid have changed from state support, to saving lives, to livelihood support and promoting self-reliance and – more recently – resilience. At each point in time, food aid can be seen as a regime of practices, informed by specific concepts or ideologies, involving a range of authorities and organisations, and producing a regime of truth which appeared self-evident at the time. This chapter analyses how food aid regimes of practices have changed over time, as a result of global and local politics, famine and food crisis, past failures and alternative functions, as well as scientific progress. It argues that shifts in regimes of practices have led to a de-politicisation of aid practices and to an effective abandonment of crisis-affected populations to permanent emergency.

The 1950s saw the emergence of a state support regime, characterised by the use of food aid to strengthen recipient states and to benefit its donors in the context of the Cold War. The end of the Cold War, failures in state support and in responding to the African famines and refugee crises of the 1980s, and new research on famine and vulnerability transformed the state support regime into the livelihoods regime. A new emphasis on people's coping strategies in response to the threat of famine, on livelihoods and on entitlements shifted responsibility from states towards individuals. The nature and objectives of food aid correspondingly changed. Food aid from the mid-1980s to the early 2000s entailed mainly emergency food aid with objectives of saving lives and supporting livelihoods and, later, peace-building and self-reliance. INGOs created new assessment, targeting and distribution methods. By the end of the 1990s, however, these new methods had often failed, crises were becoming ever more protracted and food aid was viewed increasingly in terms of its potential to fuel conflict and create dependency. This contributed to a shift towards the present-day resilience regime.

The practices of the resilience regime promote individual responsibility and capacity to withstand shocks, particularly following the

'War on Terror' and the 2008 food crisis. The regime is also characterised by declining access to crisis-affected populations as risks to aid workers have increased and states have reasserted their sovereignty. New practices include the development of quantitative food security indicators, medicalised approaches to nutrition, encouraging behaviour change, agricultural technologies and a shift from food aid to cash transfers, all with increased private sector involvement. While attempting to promote resilience, these practices also effectively abandon crisis-affected populations. New practices produce little information about the social and political context and make individuals rather than states or international agencies responsible for their malnutrition and food insecurity. This creates a regime of truth in which high levels of malnutrition no longer need a large-scale food aid response and the social, political and economic causes of malnutrition are not addressed. In Sudan, this benefits the government, because its policies are not challenged, and aid agencies, because they can remain in a highly politicised environment. It does not benefit those affected by crisis, as material assistance can be withdrawn.

The chapter is divided into three sections according to the three regimes of practices. Each section first discusses the global influences on food aid practices, such as global political economy, food aid architecture and donor policies. This is followed by the identification of new concepts or theories and agency experience which have informed changes in practices. The new practices are then described and analysed in terms of what they intended to achieve, their success or failure, critiques and the implications for food distribution, food security and nutrition. While the food aid practices described and analysed are global, the chapter uses examples from Sudan.

Managing states: food aid to strengthen states and benefit donors

> Wise statesmanship and leadership can convert ... [food] surpluses into a great asset for checking communist aggression. Communism has no greater ally than hunger; democracy and freedom no greater ally than an abundance of food. (US Senator Hubert Humphrey, 1953, quoted in Barrett and Maxwell, 2005: 38)

> I don't regard the existence of ... agricultural surpluses as a problem. I regard it as an opportunity ... I think the farmers

can bring more credit, more lasting goodwill, more chance of peace than almost any other group of Americans in the next ten years, if we recognize that food is strength, food is peace and food is freedom and food is a helping hand to people around the world whose goodwill and friendship we want. (John F. Kennedy in a pre-election campaign speech, 1960, quoted in Singer et al., 1987: 22)

The state support regime of practices was characterised by the dominance of the US programme of food aid provided from donor to recipient countries between the 1950s and 1980s. Its aims were: reducing the communist threat, disposing of surplus agricultural products and promoting trade and development. Project food aid emerged in the late 1960s with the establishment of WFP but did not gather substantial donor support until after the 1974 global food crisis, when donors aimed to make food aid more development-oriented. Food aid was mostly state-centred, which changed in the 1980s when a wide range of organisations became involved with large-scale response to refugee and famine crises. This section gives an overview of the early years of international food aid.

Global influence: geopolitics, surplus disposal and development

The first well-documented food aid donation was US food aid to Venezuela following an earthquake in 1812. Other US food relief operations followed in Martinique and Sicily in the early 1900s. Britain provided food aid as famine relief in its colonies, including to Sudan, around the same time (Singer et al., 1987: 17–18). Food aid was used in large quantities in Europe after the First and Second World Wars. Half of US assistance in the Marshall Plan was food aid, given to assist with reconstruction but also to stave off the communist threat and because a strong Europe was important for US trade, jobs and income (Cathie, 1982; Singer et al., 1987). Once Europe recovered, food aid was aimed at the newly emerging developing countries, as part of the development agenda and because Soviet influence posed a threat beyond Europe. In 1954, the US Congress passed Public Law 480[1] to give surplus food to the developing world for economic development, but also to expand international trade, support American agriculture, make use of surplus agricultural commodities and facilitate the expansion of foreign trade in agricultural commodities (Riley, 2004: 14). The more prominent objectives in the 1950s and 1960s were foreign policy, surplus disposal and the promotion of overseas markets (Barrett and Maxwell, 2005).

During the Cold War, programme food aid was intimately linked with geopolitics. US food aid was first provided to Sudan in 1958 to counteract Soviet influence in Egypt. Egypt itself became a major recipient of US food aid following the Israel–Egypt peace accord in 1979. Food aid formed the basis of Egypt's urban bread subsidy for many years, a smaller version of which was implemented in Sudan (Cathie, 1982; Bickersteth, 1990). Emergency food aid was not immune from Cold War politics. As seen in Chapter 1, refugee aid often explicitly supported rebellions against communist regimes. During the sub-Saharan famines of the mid-1980s the US was keen to support Sudan but initially denied aid to socialist Ethiopia (Cutler, 1991). Western support for the Sudanese government was one of the reasons for the late response to the 1988 conflict-produced famine in Bahr Al-Ghazal (Keen, 1994). This is further discussed in Chapter 3.

Surplus disposal was a key objective of programme food aid well into the 1970s, during which it composed about a quarter of US agricultural exports and a third of global trade (Parotte, 1983; Uvin, 1992). US surplus food was a product of agricultural subsidies and price support measures instituted after the great depression of the 1920s and 1930s, leading to peak food aid volumes in 1964. Like the US, Europe was committed to massive financial and regulatory support of its agricultural sector, implemented through its Common Agricultural Policy of 1962, which also led to large agricultural surpluses (Cathie, 1982: 26; Barrett and Maxwell, 2005). When US farm policy changed in the late 1960s, setting aside productive land as the cost of storing surplus food stocks had become prohibitive, it led to lower levels of global food stocks (and food aid) and contributed to the global food crisis of 1974. Other causes were thought to include adverse weather, USSR grain imports, a US fiscal crisis, a rise in global oil prices and growing export demands from transitioning countries (Cathie, 1982: 122; Barrett and Maxwell, 2005: 27; Duncan, 2014: 91).

The 1974 food crisis and the subsequent World Food Conference led to the consolidation of the state support regime of practices, guided by a new concept of food security and development-oriented food aid, and with WFP and the Food Aid Convention (FAC) taking a prominent role. Participants at the Conference recommended that development-oriented food aid should support agricultural production and national grain reserves and should be targeted to the poorest countries (FAO, 1974). The Conference also resulted in a universal declaration to eradicate malnutrition by ensuring adequate food production, distribution and the development of a global food security system (World Food Conference, 1974). Ways of making food aid more development-oriented included an enhanced role for WFP, a more effective FAC and a Global Information and Early Warning System. WFP had been established in 1966 as a multilateral food aid programme aimed at using food surpluses for development (Cathie, 1982; Shaw, 2011), and the FAC had been established in 1967[2] by eleven countries[3] plus the EEC to share the burden of food aid provision. The Conference recommended a 10 million metric tonne (MT) FAC target to prevent downward fluctuations in shipments of food aid at times of global food crisis (Parotte, 1983; Clay, 2010). The later stages of the state support regime were a period of optimism for donors and UN agencies about the development potential of food aid. By the 1980s, while food aid retained its political and economic objectives, 80–90% went to low-income food-deficit countries (Uvin, 1992: 306).

Concepts and practices

Like development theory more generally, food aid's development role initially supported states to promote modern agriculture, industrialisation and the transfer of technical expertise. Food aid adopted the prevailing theory of the 1960s and 1970s which argued that economic growth could be achieved by the adoption of modern Western technologies and that this was best done through processes led by the state (Leys, 1996). The proceeds from the sale of programme food aid initially benefited the donor but became more development-oriented from 1966 onwards (Shaw, 2001). WFP's projects supported development through agricultural schemes, schools, clinics and resettlement projects (Shaw, 1970). Donors, governments and charitable organisations provided emergency food aid to refugees or returnees (for example in Pakistan, Thailand, Somalia and Sudan). Church networks and the Red Cross also provided disaster and famine relief in the Congo, India (Bihar), Nigeria (Biafra), Uganda (Karamoja), Ethiopia and Cambodia from the 1950s to the 1970s, sometimes with funds from INGOs. Some INGOs also started implementing relief programmes directly on a limited scale in the 1960s (Black, 1992; Barnett, 2011).

The new concept of food security, which emerged at the World Food Conference, was defined as 'the availability at all times of adequate world supplies of basic foodstuffs ... so as to avoid acute food shortages in the event of widespread crop failures or natural disasters, sustain a steady expansion of production and reduce fluctuations in production and prices' (FAO, 1974). World food security was considered to be the responsibility of the international community. However, the emphasis on production and natural disasters excluded the political and economic factors that led to the 1974 food crisis (Alcock, 2009; Duncan, 2014). As a result, proposed interventions to improve food security were largely technical, including new agricultural technologies and information systems as well as food aid. The declaration on the eradication of hunger was ambitious in emphasising the role of poverty and inequality as causes and the responsibility of all countries in the international community to address it (World Food Conference, 1974). For a brief period, a number of countries established multi-sectoral nutrition planning units with the aim of influencing a range of development policies. By the early 1980s, however, these had largely failed as they lacked political clout or funding, and the emphasis shifted back to child feeding and micronutrients (Gillespie and Harris, 2016).

Most food aid projects were implemented through the state. Programme food aid involved recipient governments' ministries of finance, as it was intended as a form of budget support. For project food aid, WFP acted in an advisory role to the recipient government. Emergency food aid was often provided by countries themselves, bilaterally or through the Red Cross or charitable agencies. Early UN guides on food and nutrition in disasters made it clear that the main actor was government (Masefield, 1967; Protein-Calorie Advisory Group of the United Nations, 1977). INGOs often worked independently of donor and recipient governments and might even provide grants to the UN. Oxfam, for example, provided a grant of £300,000 to WFP under the UN's Freedom from Hunger campaign in the 1960s (Black, 1992: 74). Oxfam and the WHO produced the first guidelines for nutrition in emergencies in the 1970s. The European Commission started using INGOs as implementing partners in 1978 (Singer et al., 1987: 33) and WFP made its first formal agreement with INGOs for food distribution in 1995 (Uvin, 1992).

The famines and refugee crises of the mid-1980s brought about a massive transformation in regimes of food aid practices. International NGOs took on a much greater role in both refugee assistance and in famine relief as political instability, economic decline and corruption meant that governments were unable or unwilling to respond (Duffield, 1992; African Rights, 1997b). Official development policies moved away from state support models towards market-oriented models, which involved privatising public assets, reducing the scale and scope of government and giving up state

interventions such as exchange rate controls, subsidies and redis-
tributive taxation (Stiglitz, 2002). The experiences of international
agencies in responding to the crises of the mid-1980s helped shape
the livelihoods regime of practices.

Managing lives: food aid to save lives and protect livelihoods

[Food aid] can contribute to the process of transforming insecure,
fragile conditions into durable, stable situations with activities
that: meet the food needs of the most vulnerable through targeted
assistance, rehabilitate cases of acute malnutrition in mothers
and children, rebuild self-reliance and restore positive coping
mechanisms, restore social cohesion and human capacity, develop
better access to food by strengthening local food distribution and
markets, restore productive capacity and physical infra-structure.
(WFP, 1998b: 7)

The livelihoods regime of practices was characterised by emergency food aid and the attempts of international agencies to manage
the lives and livelihoods of marginalised and crisis-affected populations. The objectives of emergency food aid expanded from saving
lives to supporting livelihoods and self-reliance, and new practices for assessment, targeting and distribution proliferated. When,
following the end of the Cold War, aid agencies starting working
in situations of ongoing conflict, food aid practices also came to
include ways of minimising its negative impacts on the conflict
itself. New methods and contexts led to the creation of three separate areas of expertise: food aid, nutrition and food security. By the
end of the 1990s, food aid had come to be seen as creating dependency and fuelling conflict, while food security and nutrition had
become de-politicised. Many populations faced protracted crises
with ongoing high levels of malnutrition. This section analyses the
practices of the livelihoods regime, what influenced change, and the
effectiveness of these new practices.

Global influence: famine, complex emergencies and humanitarian assistance

Sub-Saharan Africa became the main recipient of food aid in the
mid-1980s, as donors provided large amounts of emergency food aid
in response to famine. In the five years between 1979/80 and 1984/85,
cereal food aid to sub-Saharan Africa increased from 17.1% to 39.9%

of total cereal food aid. In 1984/85, the region received 75% of global emergency food aid allocations, with Ethiopia and Sudan receiving the largest amounts (Benson and Clay, 1986: 306). Globally, overall food aid volumes decreased from the mid-1990s largely due to a reduction in programme food aid. Programme food aid decreased because of changes in geopolitics, development policies, US farm and export promotion policies and evidence on the inefficiency of in-kind food aid as a development tool. Development aid shifted towards agricultural research, multi-sectoral rural development and livelihoods approaches (see below) (Clay and Stokke, 2001; Barrett and Maxwell, 2005). Within the EU, the introduction of the single market in 1995 reduced the influence of individual countries on procurement. At the same time, an evaluation of EU food aid questioned the efficiency of supply-driven European food aid in terms of its appropriateness, speed and cost-effectiveness (Clay et al., 1996). This ultimately led to the untying of EU aid; food aid no longer had to be purchased within the donor country. Volumes of emergency food aid have exceeded those of programme food aid since 1996 (Barrett and Maxwell, 2005: 14).[4]

As emergency food aid increased, so did the role of WFP and INGOs. In the 1980s, INGOs became key players in the distribution of food aid directly to rural communities in countries affected by famine in the 1980s. Donors saw many African governments as weak, corrupt or incapable of launching a major emergency response, and INGOs presented an alternative mechanism for distributing and monitoring emergency food aid (USAID, 1986). WFP provided logistical expertise for emergency food distribution, including in-country transport and storage (WFP, 1986). The rise in the role of INGOs continued with an increase in conflict-related emergencies, also called complex emergencies, following the end of the Cold War. Aid in complex emergencies was largely limited to humanitarian assistance (Duffield, 1994b), much of which was emergency food aid. Food aid constituted around half of all contributions to the UN's Consolidated (Emergency) Appeals[5] in the 1990s and 2000s (see, for example, Development Initiatives, 2003, 2009). WFP and INGOs attempted to provide aid to all war-affected people, including in areas held by rebel movements, with access negotiated by the UN in a number of countries, including Sudan (Duffield, 1994b).

Also in the 1990s, aid agencies working in countries that had received emergency food for more than a decade promoted policies to link relief and development. They suggested that development aid should aim to reduce vulnerability to famine and that relief should contribute to development (Buchanan-Smith and Maxwell, 1994). In complex emergencies, however, the dominance of humanitarian assistance meant that the approach was limited to the use of relief to build capacity and promote self-reliance. At the macro level, the World Bank identified Africa's development problems as a crisis of governance, rather than being caused by its own neoliberal economic strategies, and promoted good governance as essential to development (World Bank, 1989). The essence of good governance was to have capable, accountable, participatory and representative institutions (Weiss, 2000; World Bank, 2002; Chhotray and Stoker, 2009). These approaches influenced food aid policy and practice.

Critiques and earlier experiences of food aid

Academic and NGO critiques of food aid in the state support regime helped bring about change in food aid practices. In the 1970s and early 1980s, criticisms of food aid included its failure to reach the poorest and most crisis-affected people, as well as its trade and foreign policy objectives. Nutrition students, of which I was one, were taught that 'food aid is not for nutrition' because most was 'distributed in urban areas, little attempt was made at targeting the most vulnerable countries and it merely replaces the food that would have been imported anyway' (Harriss, 1986: 19). Susan George's book *How the Other Half Dies* was particularly influential. First published in 1976, her study critically examines the global food system and the use of food aid as a political tool and to promote consumption and export of US-grown food (George, 1976). Other authors similarly highlighted the political and economic functions of aid, whether development aid generally or food aid specifically (see, for example, Cathie, 1982; Hancock, 1989). Project food aid's developmental effects were also questioned. Cathie (1982: 80) argued that the benefits of food aid often went to the better-off, for example those with access to credit for poultry and dairy projects, and that food aid negatively affected market prices of local goods because labourers inevitably sell part of their ration. Oxfam's publication *Against the Grain: The Dilemma of Project Food Aid* (Jackson, 1982) similarly argued that project food aid can worsen inequality, for example through the provision of free labour to wealthy farmers and by excluding the landless. According to this analysis, therefore, development food aid maintained or exacerbated inequalities at both local and global levels.

The experience of international agencies in the famines and refugee crises of the 1980s raised further concerns about the effects of the political and surplus disposal motivations of international food aid. A number of conferences were convened because of the widespread failures in response to famine and refugee crises. Participants considered donor food aid policies as one of the main reasons why food rations were late and inadequate, resulting in high levels of malnutrition and mortality.

> Policies of donor agencies reflect national interests; they usually donate according to existing and potential political alliances. Aid – particularly food aid during famines – is viewed as a strategic resource that is often allocated according to geopolitical priorities. Therefore, an adequate response to disaster depends on the perceived interests of both the host government and powerful donor nations. (UN SCN, 1988: 3)

Participants at a later conference on the nutritional crisis among refugees also concluded that the political priorities of donor countries and their agricultural policies contributed to the crisis (Refugee Studies Programme, 1991). The failings of the international community to provide sufficient assistance were exacerbated by a policy to assist refugees in camps, which made it difficult for them to acquire their own food (Refugee Studies Programme, 1991; Keen, 1992). In rural populations, agencies found it difficult to target those most in need. Early in the aid operations in sub-Saharan Africa, government priorities of distributing to urban populations often dominated, while rural populations and famine migrants received little (WFP, 1986; Keen, 1991). Aid workers felt that new practices had to be developed which could minimise the political manipulation of aid and improve emergency response. Participants at the 1988 and 1991 conferences recommended further enhancing the role of multilateral food aid to increase its allocation according to need. Technical recommendations included developing norms for emergency food rations, establishing famine early warning systems and fostering greater participation of refugees and disaster victims in planning relief programmes (UN SCN, 1988; Refugee Studies Programme, 1991).

Changes in practices were also influenced by research, including in Sudan, which found that in the absence of adequate relief people relied on their own strategies. In Darfur, research by De Waal (1989a) showed that during the 1984/85 famine many rural people had depended on a range of coping strategies, such as changing their food intake, migrating for work or selling assets, to meet their immediate needs and to protect their livelihoods. Studies in refugee camps in Sudan also found that refugees who survived had used their own strategies when food rations were well below nutritional require-ments (Toole et al., 1988; Young, 1992). Studies elsewhere in Africa and Asia similarly observed that 'households faced with acute threats to their food security will plan a range of responses to minimise their impact' (Corbett, 1988: 1110). While varying according to context, these coping strategies generally followed three distinct stages, starting with reversible strategies such as a reduction in food intake, collection of wild foods and labour migration, followed by disposal of productive assets (such as livestock or land) and finally distress migration (Corbett, 1988). Davies (1996: 55) later defined coping strategies as 'short-term responses to an immediate decline in access to food', and distinguished them from adaptation, which entails permanent change. Findings on coping strategies brought about radical changes in understanding of famine and in every aspect of emergency response. Famine was now seen as a process. This led to recommendations for using socio-economic indicators in assessing famine and emergency situations, the establishment of famine early warning systems and a call for early responses to support liveli-hoods rather than wait for people to become destitute and migrate to famine camps (Eldridge et al., 1986; Shoham and Clay, 1989). Assessments and warning systems monitored coping strategies, rain-fall, food production and market prices. The result of these changes was a new focus on what people *do*, not only as a reflection of the severity of famine or crisis or as a result of their social, economic or political marginalisation, but as an object of study in itself.

New concepts and theories

The focus on people's coping strategies was reinforced by new development theories based on supporting livelihoods, new famine theories centred on people's entitlements and vulnerability and a new definition of food security, all of which highlighted the impor-tance of people's ability to access food. Chambers (1989: 1) defined a livelihoods approach as one that starts with the livelihood strate-gies of the rural poor, their assets, needs and interests. The approach was a response to the failures of state-centred development and new ideas that development would be more effective if it focused on the priorities of poor people themselves at community level. Such people-centred development was explored further by Amartya Sen (2000), who argued that strengthening individual capacities was the means to development. In emergencies, livelihoods approaches became more common in the late 1980s, after research highlighted

that the priority of famine-affected people was to protect their livelihoods (see, for example, Corbett, 1988; De Waal, 1989a).

Concepts of vulnerability, entitlements and food security also
entered development discourse. Published in 1981, Sen's entitlement theory of famine states that 'starvation is the characteristic of
some people not *having* enough food to eat. It is not the characteristic of there *being* not enough food to eat' (Sen, 1981: 1; emphasis in
original). The notion that famine is the result of people's inability to
access food is also encapsulated in Chambers' concept of vulnerability. Chambers (1989: 1) defined vulnerability as having two sides:
'an external side of risks, shocks, and stress to which an individual or
household is subject; and an internal side which is defencelessness,
meaning a lack of means to cope without damaging loss'.[6] In other
words, shocks and disasters will have different outcomes in different
societies and on different households within the same society. In
1986, the World Bank defined food security as 'access by all people
at all times to enough food for an active, healthy life', and highlighted purchasing power as the key element (World Bank, 1986:
1). This notion of food security was agreed at the 1996 World Food
Summit: 'Food security exists when all people, at all times, have
physical and economic access to sufficient, safe and nutritious food
to meet their dietary needs and food preferences for an active and
healthy life' (FAO, 1996). Food security was no longer the international community's responsibility but something to be achieved by
individuals and households, thus adopting the neoliberal logic of the
time (Duncan, 2014: 97).

Entitlement theory was later criticised for failing to take account
of people's active responses to famine threats, the role of disease
in causing famine deaths and the social and political nature of
famine. Entitlement theory excludes violence and illegal transfers,
which are instrumental in causing starvation and death in conflict
(Rangasami, 1985; De Waal, 1990; Edkins, 2000; Devereux, 2007).
Furthermore, in the complex emergencies of the 1990s vulnerability
was often related to ethnic or political rather than economic status.
War strategies destroyed the livelihood base of civilians perceived
to be supporting the enemy, making wealth in assets such as land
or livestock a source of vulnerability rather than a means to cope
with shocks. In chronic emergencies, political survival depended on
asset-stripping – through state appropriation, market manipulation
or violence – of particular socially or politically marginalised groups
(Duffield, 1994a; Lautze and Raven-Roberts, 2006). The focus on
economic access to food in the concept of food security in the live-

lihoods regime fails to include these social or political differences in access to food.

More generally, the shift from state-centred to people-centred approaches was reflected in a shift from state security to human security as a development goal. Following the end of the Cold War, security was interpreted less in terms of protecting territory from external aggression, and human security came to the forefront as being essential for human development. Human security is understood as security of employment, income, health and safety, amongst other things. The lack of human security, moreover, was linked to famine, conflict, terrorism and drug-trafficking, which transcend national boundaries and therefore pose a threat to global security (UNDP, 1994). According to Clay and Stokke (2000: 4), from the 1990s 'food aid was increasingly organised as part of the effort to ensure human security in terms of livelihoods, food, health, environment, personal and political security'. The following subsection analyses how these new concepts influenced food aid practices.

New practices

New food aid objectives 1: livelihood support

Food aid objectives changed in light of the new understanding of famine and coping strategies. By the late 1980s, emergency food aid was no longer seen as something that would simply help save lives, but also as a form of livelihoods support. Within Sudan, livelihood recovery became an important reason for giving food aid in Red Sea State (Walker, 1988), whereas in Darfur an objective was 'to assist households which had lost their capacity to be self-sufficient to cultivate larger areas' (Buckley, 1988: 100). It has become an important food aid objective for WFP (2003, 2008a). Save the Children (SC-UK) in Darfur provided food aid throughout much of the 1990s to prevent people migrating from their villages. From the late 1980s onwards, food aid became an explicit way of changing people's actions, or coping strategies, in order to support livelihoods.

New emergency nutrition and food security expertise

In the 1980s, a new type of international nutritionist monitored the nutritional status of emergency-affected populations, investigated the social, political and economic causes of malnutrition and developed strategies for addressing malnutrition at the population level. Throughout the 1990s, these international nutritionists worked together as an ad hoc 'nutrition in emergencies working group', developing methods, guidelines and norms for assessments, food

rations, treatment, targeting, distribution and monitoring. Method-
ologies were standardised and agreed on amongst experts; emergency
nutrition was professionalised. Of central importance was WHO's
adoption, in 1995, of a prevalence of 15% wasting[7] as an indicator of
crisis, which was later included in its guidelines and in those of other
agencies (WHO, 1995; WHO et al., 2000). The response at these
levels of malnutrition was often general food distributions, although
nutritionists lobbied for a broader response. Emergency nutritionists
also developed methods for food security assessment and monitoring and famine early warning systems (see, for example, Cutler,
1984; Kelly, 1992; Shoham and Clay, 1989; Seaman, 2000). Nutritional problems were understood to be linked to political causes:
'[h]uman nutrition cannot be confined to its health and physiology
related issues. Nutritionists should not forget that in famine or abject
poverty, what matters is access to food, which relates to political,
economic, social and environmental factors. In this context, nutrition is a social and human science' (UN SCN, 1994: 134).

Reflecting this broader approach to nutrition, the first nutritional surveys in Darfur in 1985 and 1986 collected information on
the crop and livestock situation, markets, population movements,
services and the effectiveness of food aid distributed, as well as on
the prevalence of acute malnutrition (Hardy, 1985; Taylor, 1985;
Williams, 1986). In the early 1990s, emergency nutritionists adopted
the UNICEF framework on the causes of malnutrition, which links
multiple causes, from food intake and disease at the individual level,
to food insecurity, social factors and health at household or community level, and to structural causes at population level, including
governance, social institutions and the distribution of resources
(UNICEF, 1990). This led to recommendations for a wide range of
responses to address malnutrition, from advocacy to change refugee
and drought-response policies, to agricultural, market and employment interventions, as well as food aid and treatment (Appleton
et al., 2000; Young et al., 2004). However, in developing these
advances, emergency nutritionists had often worked in isolation, and
by the end of the 1990s decision-makers saw emergency nutrition as
feeding people and treating malnutrition. In addition, as practices
increased, food aid, food security and nutrition became separate
areas of expertise, and territoriality between these three led to a lack
of clarity about the role of the emergency nutritionist in food security and the social aspects of food aid programming (Young, 1999a).

Using the new concepts of food security, entitlements, vulnerability and coping strategies, aid agencies developed new food security

practices from the mid-1980s onwards, including new assessment
methods and the targeting of food aid to vulnerable households
(Borton and Shoham, 1989; MSF-Holland, 1997; Oxfam, 2001).
Socio-economic surveys were considered better than nutritional
surveys for estimating food aid needs, because of malnutrition's
multiple causes and because nutritional surveys in the same populations sometimes produced different results (Borton and Shoham,
1989). In addition, SC-UK Darfur felt that socio-economic surveys
were necessary to make sure food aid did not undermine the local
economy or people's own survival strategies (Buckley, 1988: 100). The
Food Economy Approach (FEA), using Sen's entitlement theory as
its conceptual basis, became the dominant food security assessment
approach in the 1990s. It was applied in southern Sudan from 1994
and Darfur from 1996. The approach categorises areas into 'food
economy zones' and people into wealth groups and assesses changes
in food and income sources, after which it calculates the food deficit
for different groups. The method is promoted for being an improvement over methods focusing on food availability (Boudreau, 1998).
Chapters 3 and 4 discuss its application in Sudan and Darfur.

New targeting methods
Targeting food aid to those most in need became a key operational
objective for agencies working with famine-affected populations
from 1984 onwards. In Darfur, the US Agency for International
Development (USAID) specified to its implementing partner
SC-UK that food aid should be targeted to the poorest third of
the population but until late 1985 government priorities of feeding
urban populations dominated (see Chapter 4). SC-UK was only
able to reach vulnerable rural populations after establishing its own
transport, targeting and distribution mechanisms. In both Sudan
and Ethiopia, the two largest food aid recipient countries in the 1985
African famine, donors worked with INGOs 'for a variety of operational, accountability and political reasons' (Borton and Shoham,
1989: 77). The main reasons for targeting were 'limited resources,
the desire to concentrate on the worst affected areas [and] the desire
not to damage the local economy' (Borton and Shoham, 1989: 79).
NGOs targeted food aid at areas or population groups in which
malnutrition was unacceptably high or according to socio-economic
criteria (Buckley, 1988; Borton and Shoham, 1989). Targeting within
communities, however, was considered problematic, as it 'lays those
responsible for the selection open to tremendous social pressures
and may skew distributions to those able to wield greater pressure.

Furthermore, it raises difficult issues over differences in perception of need between agencies and the affected population' (Borton and Shoham, 1989: 87).

Despite these initial reservations, community-based targeting – in which community representatives themselves are asked to select the poorest – became one of the most common ways of distributing food. First applied in Kenya in the early 1990s, it was later adopted in Sudan and elsewhere in Africa. Community-based distribution adopted good governance principles of transparency, participation and accountability, qualities which were considered absent in local government institutions (Oxfam GB, c.1995; WFP, 2000). In practice, the role of community-based relief committees varied from overall responsibility for targeting and distribution to assisting in the logistics of food distribution (Jaspars and Shoham, 1999; Taylor and Seaman, 2004). The advent of the FEA in the mid-1990s and its calculation of the percentage of the population with the greatest food deficit gave an additional incentive for trying to target food aid at the poorest. As the next two subsections show, attempts at targeting were also intensified in the light of conflict and protracted emergencies but were rarely successful.

New food aid objectives 2: social transformation, peace-building and self-reliance

Just as the African famines of the mid-1980s marked a shift in food aid practices, so did the end of the Cold War and the internal conflicts it generated. Agencies increasingly distributed aid during ongoing conflict, which led to concerns that it could provide indirect support to the warring parties and thereby fuel conflict. The potentially negative impacts of distributing food aid in conflict were wide-ranging: support to warring parties through the taxation or diversion of food aid, reinforcing the authority of those who controlled a particular area, the use of WFP-hired private trucks for military operations, facilitating forced displacement or population control, and more. Emergency food aid became part of the political economy of war, and agencies and governments alike feared that it could fuel and prolong conflicts (Ockwell, 1999a; WFP, 2002). Agencies developed new practices to minimise these effects, including the 'do no harm' approach, which analyses how food (and other) aid could create or exacerbate tensions between different groups during conflict (Anderson, 1999). The potential for food aid to exacerbate tensions in conflict also led to a belief that it could contribute to conflict prevention and peace-building:

Beyond ensuring food security, food aid can be a means to keep
the social fabric in place by bringing people together in food
committees, food for work, and food for vocational training and
thus helping re-establish dialogue and common grounds amongst
potentially conflicting ethnic groups or parties. Food committees
or other initiatives that bring people together can also be a
catalyst for the formation of other groups, thus strengthening
civil society and the people's accountability. (WFP, 2000: 27)

By the end of the 1990s, emergency food aid had come a long
way from its purely life-saving objectives. The drought-initiated
famines in the 1980s added livelihood support as an objective, and
the conflicts of the 1990s added building peace or influencing social
relations. Food aid had become an overt political tool at both the
local and the international levels.

In the late 1990s, as aid operations became protracted, fears of
food aid dependency came to the forefront. Although these fears were
not new (they had been raised since the first food aid programmes in
the 1960s), they were now related particularly to long-term refugee
situations. Some refugee camps had existed for decades and refugees
were still not self-reliant (Ockwell, 1999b; UNHCR et al., 1999).
Dependency was brought up in most food aid and nutrition conferences in the 1990s. In response, the need to link emergency food
aid to development and to promote self-reliance was a priority. For
WFP, this meant greater targeting, linking food distribution with
agricultural production, and greater reliance on local government
and local communities to meet needs. WFP's policy on moving from
crisis to recovery claimed that food aid can contribute to complete
social transformation, as the quote at the start of this section illustrates (WFP, 1998a). Similar sentiments were voiced at a nutrition
conference in 1992, which highlighted the developmental role of
food aid in creating infrastructure through public works projects
(UN SCN, 1992).

As aid agencies raised concerns about dependency, participants
at emergency nutrition conferences also highlighted the problem
of ongoing high levels of malnutrition and mortality amongst long-
term refugees (UN SCN, 1992, 1994; UNHCR, 1995). According
to conference participants, rations remained inadequate due to
donors' political priorities, administrative and logistical constraints
to food distribution and the lack of resources in host countries.
Clearly, food aid was not achieving its intended objectives of
reducing malnutrition and mortality, let alone assisting people in

becoming self-reliant. Conference participants made recommendations that food rations should not be reduced until there was sound evidence of self-reliance, while acknowledging that this was difficult to measure (UNHCR et al., 1999: 23). The need to reduce dependency remained the dominant discourse, however, despite the lack of evidence that food aid itself was the reason people failed to become self-reliant. New objectives of promoting self-reliance renewed the emphasis on targeting and developmental uses of emergency food aid.

New practices: negotiated access and distributing food aid in conflict
A number of new practices resulted from working to negotiate access to conflict-affected populations and to minimise the negative effects of food aid. Restricted access can be a result of insecurity, an inability or unwillingness on the part of state or non-state actors to allow access or deliberate attempts to obstruct humanitarian assistance (Ockwell, 1999a). Donors and aid agencies devised various ways of delivering aid in such contexts. In Somalia, the US military intervened to protect humanitarian aid corridors in 1992, with spectacularly disastrous results. In Sudan, Ethiopia and Angola, the UN mandated cross-border or cross-line operations (Duffield, 1994b). Operation Lifeline Sudan (OLS) was the first and longest running operation to provide relief during a situation of ongoing war. Aid agencies had relative ease of access and movement in opposition-controlled areas of southern Sudan, as the Sudan government had effectively ceded sovereignty of large parts of the south to the UN (Karim et al., 1996). OLS in southern Sudan established ground rules which attempted to apply humanitarian principles in the distribution of aid and to guide the conduct of aid agencies and rebel movements (Levine, 1997). These rules included aspects of the 'do no harm' approach mentioned above, and were enthusiastically adopted by a number of food distribution agencies (see, for example, CARE, 2001; WFP, 2002). Similar attempts at using humanitarian principles and 'do no harm' approaches to minimise the manipulation of aid and to promote cooperation between aid agencies were attempted in Somalia and Liberia (Leader, 2000). OLS is discussed further in Chapter 3.

Critiques, failures and alternative functions
By the end of the 1990s, food aid was no longer perceived as a source of nutrition but was seen as a source of aid dependency and a contributor to conflict, while also having the potential for social transformation and peace-building. As emergency food aid

practices became more overtly political, food aid became the expertise of programme managers and political analysts. Nutrition and
food security, as areas of expertise which influence decision-making
about food aid, split and became more specialised and technical,
losing much of their social and political dimensions. A proliferation
of new practices followed.

Despite the advance, however, new practices sometimes failed
to detect famine and often failed to elicit a response. Famine early
warning systems established in the late 1980s failed to lead to early
and adequate response, including in Sudan in 1991 (Buchanan-Smith
and Davies, 1995a). Even in emergencies, donors preferred to
earmark humanitarian aid for specific disasters and did not provide
cash funds to enable WFP to respond rapidly to new disasters (Shaw,
2001). In southern Sudan, the FEA failed to pick up the early stages
of the 1998 Bahr Al-Ghazal famine, as it was based on the assumption
that 'Africans do not starve, they cope' (Deng, 2002: 35). In taking
Sen's entitlement theory as the basis for the approach and focusing on
the household, the FEA excluded violence and political vulnerability
as causes of famine. From 2002, the approach was no longer used
in South Sudan because, amongst other reasons, it did not consider
damaging coping strategies, was considered too food-focused and
was difficult to use without access and reliable population figures
(Maxwell et al., 2006). In Darfur, the FEA was no longer used by
SC-UK from 2004 because during the conflict it was difficult for the
agency's national staff and government partners to incorporate political vulnerability and the government's war strategies as causes of food
insecurity (Buchanan-Smith, 2006).

Nutritional surveys often failed to elicit a response, as perceptions
of what was normal and what constituted a crisis changed towards the
end of the livelihoods regime. Although WHO guidance maintains
an emergency threshold of 15% wasting, in practice the threshold for
response was raised during the 1990s. In the Sudan famine of 1991,
levels of 25–30% malnutrition were necessary to trigger an emergency response, compared with 15% in the 1984 famine (Kelly and
Buchanan-Smith, 1994). While this was most likely due to a political climate in which donors were reluctant to respond (the Islamist
coup in Sudan and its support for Iraq during the first Gulf War),
similarly high levels of malnutrition did not lead to a response for
war-displaced people in 1996 because they were considered normal
(Karim et al., 1996: 127). Sudan was not alone in this 'normalisation
of crisis'; similar trends were seen in Somalia, Uganda and Rwanda
and have been attributed to the consequences of developmental

relief strategies that simply reduced the amounts of food aid during situations of ongoing conflict or crisis (Bradbury, 1998).

Reviews and evaluations of targeting practices found that they were rarely successful in reaching the poorest or most food-insecure (see, for example, Sharp, 1998; Jaspars and Shoham, 1999; Taylor and Seaman, 2004). A review in 1999 of recurring food distribution challenges in a large number of emergency contexts concluded that despite improvements in assessments, 'field staff in different operations describe targeting as one of their most intractable problems' (Ockwell, 1999a: 30). Evaluations from food distributions in 1990s Darfur showed that they were usually unsuccessful in targeting the poorest (see Chapter 4). In southern Sudan during the 1998 famine, despite the earlier establishment of community-based relief committees, the poorest clans, displaced populations and female-headed households were regularly excluded from food distribution and the most powerful clans or families received most food aid (SPLM et al., 1998). As Edkins (2000) concludes about food-for-work projects in Eritrea, the main function of targeting emergency food aid could be to control vulnerable populations and to maintain the power of organisations and authorities through monitoring and surveillance.

Rather than becoming self-reliant, by the late 1990s aid recipients were experiencing long-term crisis associated with ongoing risks to lives and livelihoods. This is what Duffield (2007) has called the permanent emergency of self-reliance, where non-insured life outside of Western consumer societies is expected to be self-reliant through capacity-building initiatives and uncertain humanitarian safety nets. Rather than achieving self-reliance, the ongoing crisis signalled the beginnings of a global food aid regime in which the north is primarily concerned with containing or accommodating growing levels of violence within acceptable humanitarian boundaries (Charlton, 1997; Duffield, 2007). The focus of food aid on influencing people's actions also reflected a shift towards neoliberal strategies of moving responsibility away from the state and towards the individual. These new aims and ideologies were taken to a new level in the next regime of practices.

Abandoning populations: food aid, global instability and resilience

Fighting malnutrition is key to resilience-building because well-nourished individuals are healthier, can work harder, and have

greater physical reserves, which enable them to manage better
shocks as they arise. (FAO, 2012d: 21)

Although addressing general deprivation and inequity would
result in substantial reductions in undernutrition and should be
a global priority, major reductions in undernutrition can also be
made through programmatic health and nutrition interventions.
(Black et al., 2008: 1)

The third regime of practices has seen a shift from taking responsibility for the lives and livelihoods of crisis-affected populations to
abandoning them to become resilient to permanent emergency. In
the contemporary resilience regime, aid practices aim to enhance
people's ability to withstand or adapt to repeated and ongoing
shocks and instability resulting from state fragility, climate change
and uncertain global food supplies. The food aid practices of the
resilience regime are a response to this context of uncertainty and
crisis, as well as the failures of past practices. They are characterised by the neoliberalisation of food security and nutrition, including
an emphasis on individual responsibility and behaviour change,
increased private sector involvement and new quantitative measures
of household food security status. This section discusses how the
shift from the livelihoods to the resilience regime of practices also
reflects an abandonment of crisis-affected populations – by no
longer addressing the social and political causes of malnutrition or
examining the political effects of interventions, by shifting responsibility from the state or international community to the individual
and by moving away from food aid. In many conflicts, populations
have been further abandoned because recipient governments have
restricted access to war-affected populations, a move to which international agencies have been unable to mount a serious challenge.

Global influence: the War on Terror and the global food crisis of 2008

Fears of global instability as a result of terrorism, food crisis and
climate change influenced changes in food aid practices and led to
a number of global initiatives, many of which involved food and
agribusiness corporations. The WoT shifted Western attention from
complex emergencies to fragile states, defined by the Organisation
for Economic Co-operation and Development (OECD) as states
which 'lack political will and/or capacity to provide the basic functions needed for poverty reduction, development and to safeguard
the security and human rights of their populations' (OECD/DAC,

2008: 16). Fragile states were considered potential havens for terrorists. Development now aimed to strengthen the state's basic functions, including the use of food aid as part of long-term safety nets, and new whole-of-government approaches linked political and development strategies. In the resilience regime, the geopolitical aims of food aid came to the forefront again, and were used to support or to undermine states perceived to be either 'with us' or 'against us' (Maxwell, 2011). The rhetoric of the WoT, and donor and UN links between political, military and development assistance, compromised the neutrality of humanitarian assistance and facilitated its manipulation by recipient countries. This contributed to a resumption of state authority and increased denial of access to conflict-affected populations in a number of countries, including Sudan. Aid agencies found themselves facing difficult choices of accepting access limitations, compromising humanitarian principles or speaking out (WFP, 2009a). Sudan's status as an Islamist pariah state but also an intelligence provider to the US hindered a coordinated response to access restrictions in Darfur (Williams and Bellamy, 2005; Traub, 2010).

Global instability was also linked to unstable global food supplies and food prices, as shown by the food riots in numerous countries between 2008 and 2011 (Hossain et al., 2014). As in 1974, the causes of the 2008 global food crisis have been attributed to climate shocks and crop failure, increased oil prices, changing demand from emerging economies such as China and India and a global financial crisis (FAO, 2008). Furthermore, disasters and food crises were expected to become more frequent and to worsen due to threats from climate change and global financial instability. The 2008 food crisis also highlighted the inadequacies of the global food aid architecture. The high cost of food during the crisis made it difficult to purchase the quantities of food aid needed, and food aid purchased in the US could not reach people within the required timeframe (Clapp, 2012: 140). The 2008 food crisis, like the 1974 crisis, led to a number of initiatives to develop a more responsive global food aid architecture, and to improve nutrition and food security. These initiatives included (briefly) negotiations on the World Trade Organization (WTO) food aid regulations, a revision of the Food Aid Convention (FAC), a UN-led Comprehensive Framework for Action and a number of global public–private partnerships (PPPs).

WTO and FAC negotiations failed to develop a more needs-based and responsive food aid architecture. Food aid formed part of the discussions on agricultural subsidies at the WTO Doha development round, which started in 2001 but stalled in 2008. In these discussions, the EU argued that US tied food aid was trade-distorting and should be subject to stricter rules, thus potentially reducing the use of US in-kind food aid (Clay, 2006; Clapp, 2012). As the WTO negotiations stalled, a revision of the FAC (last renegotiated in 1999) was the next best option for the global regulation of food aid. Some FAC member states, and many aid agencies, called for a greater proportion of food aid commitments to be in the form of cash, for the inclusion of recipient countries as members and for public reporting of contributions (TAFAD, 2006). Member states eventually drafted a new Food Assistance Convention in 2012. However, minimum commitments were not set out and the Convention continues to allow in-kind food aid in the form of loans. The Food Assistance Convention consequently does not address concerns about instability of global food supplies or the trade-distorting effects of food aid (Clay, 2012; Clapp and Clark, 2012). The possibilities for change are further hindered because of the ongoing influence of US domestic interests on food aid policy: US food aid volumes are determined by the US Department for Agriculture, 75% of US food aid has to be carried by US-flagged carriers and many US NGOs sell food aid to pay for other development programmes (Barrett and Maxwell, 2005: 20). Private sector interests also figure: in 2004–2007, more than half of US food aid was purchased from four large transnational agri-food companies (Clapp, 2012: 73). By 2010, there were only a few small US government initiatives for the local purchase of food aid or cash transfers (Harvey et al., 2010: 63). What this means in practice is that global food aid supplies will remain uncertain for the foreseeable future and much of the response to humanitarian crises will remain in-kind food aid.

While donor and UN global food aid architecture could not ensure timely and appropriate food aid responses, private companies produced specialised food products for the treatment and prevention of malnutrition. The 2000s saw the rise of ready-to-use therapeutic foods (RUTF), produced by a number of companies and used since 2002 in feeding programmes to treat and prevent malnutrition. Like in-kind food aid, this trend also unleashed trade-related disputes as the main producer, Nutriset in France, initially refused to allow mass production in the US. Since then, companies such as PepsiCo and Unilever have started producing other humanitarian food aid products (Clapp, 2012: 164–166). By 2013, there were more than twenty suppliers of RUTF (UNICEF, 2013). The Sudan government has so far limited the import of these products, but in 2013 WFP hoped to start importing new Nutriset products and supported the production of specialised foods in-country (Informant 84, 2013). The 2014 case by WFP and UNICEF for investment in nutrition in Sudan refers to a number of micronutrient supplements and food products for the treatment and prevention of malnutrition (WFP and UNICEF, 2014).

Many initiatives following the 2008 food crisis have included PPPs to promote global food security and stability. These initiatives include the Scaling Up Nutrition (SUN) movement, formed in 2010, and the New Alliance for Food Security and Nutrition, formed in 2012. Both followed the UN's 2008 Comprehensive Framework for Action, which stressed the importance of investment in agriculture, nutrition, cash transfers and social protection to meet immediate needs and to increase resilience to future climate shocks and food crises. A key aim was to strengthen the link between farmers and markets and to remove constraints on the functioning of local and global food markets (FAO, 2008). The SUN movement aims to scale up a standard set of medical and behavioural nutrition interventions identified by the *Lancet* as 'high impact and cost-effective', and it consists of the UN, donors, international NGOs, business and scientists (Arnold and Beckmann, 2011). The Sudan government joined SUN in 2015 (UN OCHA, 2015). The aims of the New Alliance for Food Security and Nutrition (2014) include promoting agriculture-led growth and leveraging 'the potential of responsible private investment to support development', and it consists of the G8 countries, African governments and private sector actors. The SUN movement is a partner in the New Alliance (2014). US President Barack Obama launched the New Alliance because by 2012 only half the pledges made by G8 countries to address global food insecurity had been met (G8, 2009; Provost et al., 2014). The New Alliance has been the subject of numerous critiques from NGOs and human rights movements. Their studies have found that despite a stated aim of supporting smallholder farmers, the modern agricultural technologies (improved seeds, fertiliser) promoted by the New Alliance have mainly benefited large-scale commercial agriculture (see, for example, Africa Centre for Biosafety, 2013; ActionAid, 2014; Oxfam, 2014). Academic research has also questioned the effectiveness of addressing malnutrition through micronutrient supplementation or agricultural technologies and argues that in many instances the main objective appears to be expanding markets and making a profit (Patel et al., 2015; Vercillo et al., 2015). Other global initiatives include the Global Alliance for Improved Nutrition (mainly consisting of the food industry), which focuses on food fortification and agricultural technologies to enhance the nutrient composition of crops, and the Nutrition for Growth movement, launched by the UK government in 2013, in which governments and aid agencies set out their commitments to address malnutrition (UKAID et al., 2013).[8] These initiatives highlight the growth of private sector involvement in addressing food security and nutrition since the 2008 food crisis.

New concepts

The promotion of resilience has been central to post-2008 global food security and nutrition initiatives. Rooted in ecosystems theory, resilience has become the ideology underlying responses to climate change, critical infrastructure protection, natural disasters, pandemics and terrorism (Walker and Cooper, 2011). Resilience is usually defined as the ability to resist, recover from and adapt to shocks (Béné et al., 2012), and has been applied to countries, organisations, systems and people. Nutrition has emerged as the key to resilience because stronger, healthier populations are considered better able to endure emergencies and conflict (Scaling Up Nutrition Movement, 2014). Food security and coping strategies are also considered part of resilience (Béné et al., 2015; Upton et al., 2016), and food security interventions such as production, income generation, public works and early warning systems have been reinvented as resilience initiatives (Levine and Mosel, 2014).

In the resilience regime, the definition of food security has changed again. It retains the three components of availability, access and utilisation, and adds stability. New definitions also incorporate nutrition, individual capacity and knowledge. The 2009 World Summit on Food Security added that '[t]he nutritional dimension is integral to the concept of food security' (FAO, 2009: 1). The UN's Updated Framework for Action states that food and nutrition security, 'because of its focus on the attributes of individuals also embraces their energy, protein and nutrient needs for life, activity, pregnancy, growth and long-term capabilities' (FAO, 2010: 1), and the US Feed the Future initiative (through which the US contributes to the New Alliance) adds that '[p]eople must also have the knowledge and basic sanitary conditions to choose, prepare, and distribute food' (US Government, 2010: ii). Both nutrition and food security are mainly concerned with individual knowledge and capacity in the resilience regime. Social and political differences in access to food remain excluded.

The aid community saw resilience as necessary because of the effects of climate change, because it had the potential for linking relief and development in protracted crisis and because it increased funding for food security interventions (Béné et al., 2012; Levine and Mosel, 2014). On the other hand, it has been criticised for its tendency to focus on ecosystems rather than social systems, prioritising the ability to withstand shocks over well-being, and a lack of clarity about what resilience actually is or what a resilient system should look like (Béné et al., 2012; Levine et al., 2012). In contrast to the earlier concept of vulnerability, resilience approaches do not take account of power relations or the socio-economic conditions of the population concerned (Cannon and Muller-Mahn, 2010). Others have argued that focusing on adaptation removes the power of resistance and therefore inhibits political action (Evans and Reid, 2013). Resilience approaches can be seen as neoliberal governmentalities which aim to produce autonomous and entrepreneurial subjects who are able to live in a world of uncertainty and crisis (Welsh, 2014). Expectations of state services, good governance and ending of poverty or conflict can correspondingly be lowered (Haldrup and Rosen, 2013; Levine and Mosel, 2014). Duffield (2013, 2016) links the neoliberal governmentality of resilience approaches with the rise of digital humanitarianism, in which crisis-affected populations are supported with information to promote adaptation and self-organisation rather than with material assistance and protection. These changes in ideology and expectations are illustrated well by the food aid practices of the 2000s, discussed in the following sections.

New practices

Since the early 2000s, food aid practices have been characterised by a move from food aid to food assistance, and by a shift towards quantitative, medical or technical approaches to food security and nutrition.[9] New practices such as cash transfers, agricultural technologies and medicalised nutrition received a boost after the 2008 food crisis because they were recommended in the UN Comprehensive Framework for Action (FAO, 2008). Of critical importance to conflict-related protracted crises, where access is often limited, these new practices could also be applied remotely. As the following sections show, remote management and the practices of the resilience regime introduce both a physical and an emotional distance between international aid workers and disaster victims, which makes it easier to withdraw assistance and to make people responsible for addressing their own problems. Consolidation of power within the aid system makes critiques of these food-based resilience approaches unlikely.

New food aid objectives 3: protection and resilience

In the 2000s, food aid acquired new roles of protection and resilience promotion. In 2005, world leaders adopted the Responsibility to Protect at the UN World Summit and committed themselves to protect people from mass atrocities when states are 'manifestly failing' to do so (Traub, 2010). Darfur was its first test, and failure. Darfur was labelled the first 'protection crisis' because of the severity and nature of the violence, which included widespread destruction of villages, death, displacement and sexual violence (Pantuliano and O'Callaghan, 2006: 6–7). The West's reluctance to respond with military force and, later, the inability of the African Union (AU) and UN-African Union Mission in Darfur (UNAMID) to ensure the protection of large sections of the population left protection to humanitarian actors or to conflict-affected populations themselves. Emergency food aid acquired a protection role by reducing the need to venture into unsafe areas to find work or food, helping some people to stay in their villages. It also provided the only registration for displaced populations, thus recognising their status and need for assistance and protection (Mahoney et al., 2005; Young and Maxwell, 2009). The notion that 'food assistance should contribute to the safety, dignity and integrity of vulnerable people' was later adopted in WFP's global protection policy (WFP, 2012a: 7). The Sudan government, however, linked humanitarian protection monitoring to the indictment of President Bashir by the International Criminal Court in early 2009 and protection activities became almost impossible following the subsequent expulsion of thirteen NGOs. This is examined further in Chapters 4 and 5.

By the late 2000s, resilience became an overriding objective for many donors. They saw food assistance and nutrition interventions as a cost-effective way of promoting resilience. USAID representatives, for example, saw their Darfur strategy of shifting from general food distributions to food-for-assets, cash-for-assets, food-for-training and vouchers as a means of enabling people to recover and build resilience. Vouchers, for example, would do this by strengthening markets and improving dietary diversity (Informants 98, 2014). The EU also links resilience with food security, and includes cash transfers, agricultural support, grain reserves and safety nets in its approach to resilience (EU, 2012). USAID, the EU and DFID all have a nutrition strategy that emphasises its role in achieving resilience (DFID, 2009; EU, 2012; USAID, 2014). Not surprisingly, improving resilience has become a key strategy for UN agencies too. According to WFP's latest strategic plan, food assistance can contribute to resilience by supporting nutrition, by establishing safety nets and by working with the private sector (WFP, 2013a). For UNICEF, nutrition is both a means and a result of resilience (UNICEF, 2013). For the FAO, improving resilience requires a range of food security and livelihoods interventions, but nutrition is considered to be the key to resilience (FAO, 2012d). The Office of Humanitarian Affairs (OCHA) in Sudan, meanwhile, assures readers of its 2014 strategic response plan that 'the "resilience" objective is not to shift the burden of humanitarian response onto crisis victims' but that 'strengthening the resilience of households, groups and communities will enable them to enjoy greater autonomy and dignity and reduce the number of calls for short-term external assistance' (UN OCHA, 2014b: 18). In practice, resilience means that the direct provision of material assistance can be reduced. These issues are explored further in the following sections.

From food aid to food assistance
Food assistance can include a range of interventions, including local purchase of food aid, food-for-work and cash transfers, such as cash grants, cash-for-work, food vouchers as well as food aid (Harvey et al., 2010). The idea of providing cash in emergencies is not new. It was recommended, for example, in the early 1990s because refugees often sold food aid to meet other needs and because it had fewer logistical constraints than food aid (Wilson, 1992). In the 2000s, evidence of the cost and ineffectiveness of in-kind food aid mounted (see, for example, OECD, 2005) and INGOs piloted cash transfer programmes in a number of emergency contexts. The Indian Ocean Tsunami appeal provided INGOs with flexible funding to implement large-scale cash programmes, which was then also taken up by WFP (Harvey, 2007). In protracted crises, donors and UN agencies began to support cash transfers as part of longer-term safety nets (FAO, 2003; Alinovi et al., 2008). The UN Comprehensive Framework for Action in response to the 2008 food crisis further highlighted the importance of food assistance, rather than food aid, in addressing the emergency needs of vulnerable populations and as part of longer-term social protection systems to promote resilience (FAO, 2008, 2012d).

A growing body of evidence shows that cash transfers are an effective way of improving access to food and supporting livelihoods.

Cash is often cost-effective, quick compared to food aid, provides beneficiaries with choice, and beneficiaries generally spend it on essential goods and recovering their livelihoods (Harvey, 2007). In Darfur, an added objective of vouchers was to revive local markets, as local traders rather than WFP supply locally produced food to beneficiaries (WFP Sudan, 2011). Reducing the role of IDP leaders in aid provision was a key reason for WFP to shift to vouchers in Darfur, as it considered many of these leaders to be corrupt (Informant 56, 2013). Vouchers are also suitable for remote programming as they transfer the constraints in delivering food across war zones from aid agency to local trader. Cash transfers have been made via mobile phones, smartcards or remittance companies in a number of countries, for example Kenya, Lebanon and Somalia (Vincent and Cull, 2011; ODI, 2015). As such, cash transfers introduce new actors, such as local traders, banking agents and money-brokers, and technologies, including digital technologies such as biometric registration and mobile phone networks. Each of these will have their own interests and effects. A new risk associated with digital technologies is that the data gathered could be used for commercial and security purposes (Duffield, 2016). While the use of cash by beneficiaries and its impact on markets has been rigorously evaluated, the wider political and economic effects have not. Cash transfers may reduce the risk of theft or diversion in transit, but cash – like food aid – can also be taxed by warring parties or diverted by aid agencies or money transfer companies (Hedlund et al., 2012). Targeting remains difficult, whether for cash transfers or food aid.

Remote programming
Remote management requires new technologies and changes agencies' knowledge about conflict-affected populations. It became common in the late 1990s and 2000s as the number of agencies working in conflict situations increased and the WoT led to the political targeting of international aid workers. In Sudan, access to conflict-affected populations is restricted by government denial of access, as well as attacks on aid workers (see Chapter 3). Between 2006 and 2008 attacks and kidnappings of international agency staff in Darfur, Somalia and Afghanistan increased sharply, resulting in greater reliance on military escorts or withdrawal of staff and/ or programmes (Stoddard et al., 2009). Remote technologies rely on national staff, local organisations or authorities to implement programmes on the ground and/or on remote sensing, mobile phones and other digital technologies. In Darfur, WFP gathers much

of its food security data through the Ministry of Agriculture and local NGOs. Globally, WFP has been making advances in collecting quantitative food security data via mobile phone networks, which reduces the risk faced by aid workers. These technologies are also promoted as a cost-effective way of reaching remote populations and for rapid and frequent data collection (Morrow et al., 2016). By 2016, WFP had implemented this approach in twenty-three countries (WFP, 2016). For food distribution, WFP's implementing partners in Sudan established Food Relief Committees (FRC), which could distribute food when international agencies did not have access, and both WFP and Khartoum-based transport companies monitor their trucks in Darfur with GPS technology. As mentioned in the previous section, cash transfers are more easily provided remotely than food aid. While usually planned as a short-term measure, remote management often ends up being a long-term arrangement. When international aid workers spend time outside of the conflict area, they lose their familiarity with the situation on the ground, their working relationship with national staff changes and they become more reluctant to return (Stoddard et al., 2010). The practices of the resilience regime are ideally suited to remote management, but over time they fundamentally change aid workers' relationships with national aid workers and beneficiaries and their understanding of the problems faced by conflict-affected populations.

The medicalisation of nutrition
Improvements in the treatment of severe malnutrition led to a focus on case definition and treatment rather than examining its broader social, political and economic context. New medical and feeding protocols dramatically improved the survival of children with severe malnutrition. The biggest impact on emergency nutrition practice was the development of community-based management of acute malnutrition (CMAM), a method whereby severely malnourished children without medical complications could be treated at home with specialised foods, monitoring and health and nutrition educa-tion. Initiated in 2000, it was an established part of emergency nutrition practice by 2005. Emergency nutritionists developed new guidelines, new ways of measuring coverage and ways of scaling up the intervention to reach more people. Nutriset produced the first RUTF in 1997, which was piloted in Sudan during the Bahr Al-Ghazal famine in 1998 (Nutriset, 2015) and in North Darfur in 2001 (ENN, 2003). Emergency nutrition conferences in the 2000s focused exclusively on this topic. In contrast with the 1990s,

participants included not only NGO and UN nutritionists but also representatives from government ministries and donors, thus reflecting the interests of a range of stakeholders in this clinical view of nutrition (ENN, 2003, 2005, 2008, 2011). Ready-to-use foods for different types of feeding programmes have proliferated since the early 2000s (see, for example, WFP 2012b).

The second development in emergency nutrition practices followed a series of five articles in the *Lancet* in 2008. Members of the Maternal and Child Undernutrition Study Group[10] determined that a standard set of nutrition interventions at individual or household level could lead to substantial reductions in undernutrition, without addressing poverty and inequality. They focused on 'what works' in terms of medical or behavioural interventions (Black et al., 2008). Addressing malnutrition was considered important not only because it reduces child deaths but also because chronic malnutrition is a predictor of shortness in adults, lower cognitive development and low educational achievement, all of which can reduce employment opportunities and income (Victora et al., 2008). In other words, good nutrition is important for people's capacity to work and for economic growth. The risk factors identified included micronutrient deficiencies, sub-optimum breastfeeding and inadequate complementary feeding (child feeding when breastfeeding alone is no longer sufficient), and consequently the most effective interventions were food fortification, supplementation with vitamin A and zinc and breastfeeding counselling. Nutrition counselling, possibly in combination with food supplements or cash transfers, was recommended to reduce chronic malnutrition[11] (Bhutta et al., 2008). The authors later called these 'nutrition-specific interventions' (see for example Ruel and Alderman, 2013). Bryce et al. (2008) concluded that given the right combination of these interventions at national level, targeted at pregnant women and children up to twenty-four months, nutrition could be improved quickly. In the same *Lancet* series, Morris et al. (2008) justified these new approaches by claiming that past nutrition practices had failed. The international nutrition system was dysfunctional and fragmented, practices were underfunded, poorly targeted, too food aid-focused and did not build local capacity. The authors recommended, amongst other things, bringing in 'actors who are closer to the solution (such as politicians, ministries of finance, and the private sector)' (Morris et al., 2008: 618). This assumes, of course, that each of these actors has the same priorities as aid agencies. The findings of this study challenge this assumption.

The *Lancet* papers 'excluded several important interventions which impact nutrition, such as education, untargeted economic strategies or those for poverty alleviation, agricultural modifications, farming subsidies, structural adjustments, social and political changes, and land reform' (Bhutta et al., 2008: 418). A later *Lancet* series by the same group therefore added 'nutrition-sensitive' interventions to address underlying causes and accelerate nutritional improvements, but they only covered agriculture, safety nets, early child development and schooling (Ruel and Alderman, 2013). Actions to improve nutrition came together under the SUN movement and the New Alliance. Emergency nutrition, in the resilience regime, came to consist of a limited set of standardised micro-level technical and behavioural interventions with extensive private sector involvement. Nutritionists now see political commitment in terms of government commitment to scaling up the treatment of malnutrition, rather than addressing the underlying social and political causes (Gillespie et al., 2013).

A key point for the resilience regime is the massive and uncritical adoption of the new medicalised practices in emergency nutrition, despite the exclusion of emergencies in the *Lancet* studies (Bhutta et al., 2008: 418). Reference to the *Lancet* papers can be found in the nutrition strategies of key donors and aid agencies, for example USAID, DFID and WFP (DFID, 2009; WFP, 2012b; USAID, 2014). These developments did not result only from humanitarian or altruistic motivations. Donor, aid agency and academic papers often mention the cost-effectiveness of the new practices – a major consideration when many Western countries themselves are experiencing austerity measures (Gillespie et al., 2013). In addition, Victora et al. (2008) note that improved nutrition has the potential to lead to sustainable economic growth. In promoting nutrition interventions in Sudan, WFP and UNICEF present it as a cost-effective investment which could raise the country's GDP by 3% (WFP and UNICEF, 2014). Furthermore, in protracted crises nutrition promotes resilience by improving human capital (physical and mental well-being) and therefore the ability to withstand shocks and endure emergencies. Well-nourished people are stronger and healthier, can work harder, produce more and gain more income (DFID, 2009; FAO, 2012d; UNICEF, 2013; Scaling Up Nutrition Movement, 2014). Western governments also link nutrition interventions to their national security; addressing hunger is part of US and UK foreign policy and national security strategies as well as their development agendas (Essex, 2014; USAID, 2014). In recipient countries, the new medicalised nutrition interventions are an anti-political tool because malnutrition is no longer seen as a result of poverty, inequality or the way that wars are being fought. Nutritional or food security surveys will not challenge their development policies, war strategies or human rights record. Finally, as the private sector is considered key to addressing problems of malnutrition, another motivation must be profit. In the resilience food aid regime, malnutrition has become a business opportunity.

To conclude, in the resilience regime, nutrition itself rather than its underlying causes has become the aim of policy. It is seen as an investment rather than a precondition for a healthy life (Patel et al., 2015). Nutrition can be improved through a mixture of science, behaviour change and the involvement of the private sector. This resembles the nutrition of the state support regime, when nutrition interventions focused on micronutrients, feeding programmes and improving production, but which had little or no impact (Pacey and Payne, 1985). The difference is, however, that in the resilience regime neither food aid nor the state is seen as the solution, and the responsibility for improving nutrition rests mainly with the individual. The adoption of new quantitative indicators has had the same effect on food security.

Quantitative universal indicators
The adoption of universal indicators in food security assessments highlights a similar trend of removing the social, political and economic context. New assessment methods were introduced in response to the failure of those developed in the livelihoods regime and to better compare populations. The Food Economy Approach, the main food security assessment method in the livelihoods regime, had been criticised because of its failure to predict crisis and because it was viewed as too elaborate and therefore not suited to acute stages of an emergency (Shoham, 2005). In the early 2000s, a number of quantitative indicators of food security status were introduced, including dietary diversity (DD), the Food Consumption Score (FCS), the Coping Strategies Index (CSI) and more recently the cost of a minimum healthy diet. This section focuses on DD and the FCS – measures of the different kinds of foods consumed and the frequency of consumption – as two indicators used by WFP to determine the prevalence, and therefore severity, of food insecurity and to adjust food aid levels.

The shift towards universal quantitative indicators was justified by their proponents as 'part of a broad attempt to harmonize measurement tools and indicators for universal use in emergency settings' (Coates et al., 2007: 1). According to WFP, one of the main problems with measuring household food security was the absence of a single indicator that could define food-insecure households and compare food security 'across settings, population groups and time, and that could prioritise the allocation of limited resources' (Aiga and Dhur, 2006: 36). In Sudan, WFP justified quantitative methods as being more accurate and objective than qualitative methods, particularly in protracted crises (Informant 4, 2012). A quantitative measure of food security status, a cut-off point below which a person is considered food-insecure and a percentage threshold above which populations are considered to suffer unacceptable levels of food insecurity could in theory do this. When WFP took over responsibility for food security assessments in Darfur in 2004, the FCS was part of its assessment.

Despite being widely adopted in food security assessments, there is little evidence to support the use of these indicators in all emergency contexts. Existing studies show a strong association between DD or FCS and calorie intake (used as the 'gold standard' for measuring household food security) but did not include emergencies, the association did not apply to the poorest, and food aid weakened or negatively affected the association (Hoddinot and Yohannes, 2002a, 2002b; Wiesmann et al., 2008). The main study referenced in WFP's 2005 Emergency Food Security Assessment guidelines found that the relationship between DD and calorie intake was weak or not significant for those with the lowest calorie intake; below 'a subsistence constraint, households focus primarily on acquiring additional calories' (Hoddinott and Yohannes, 2002b: 32). This is consistent with Lipton's work on poverty, malnutrition and hunger, which showed that 'as outlay and income rise, ultra-poor ... households maintain food/outlay and cereal/calorie ratios, thus revealing their top priority for more calories' (Lipton, 1983: iii). Later studies highlight the need for validation in emergency settings, including an analysis of the effect of wild or famine food consumption, and express reservations about its use in populations heavily dependent on food aid (Coates et al., 2007; Wiesmann et al., 2008). Furthermore, a number of studies advise against the use of universal cut-offs and consider WFP's FCS indicator to under-estimate the percentage of food-insecure households compared with other indicators (Ruel, 2002; Wiesmann et al., 2008; Maxwell et al., 2014; Leroy et al., 2015). The meaning of DD and the FCS is likely to be context-specific and to vary between urban and rural settings, and between emergency and stable settings.

In most of its Darfur assessments, WFP combined the FCS, food aid access and expenditure to determine whether households were food-insecure. In other words, households were classified as food-insecure if they did not consume many different foods on a regular basis, or they consumed a reasonable variety of foods on a regular basis but much of this was food aid (0–50 or >50%) or they had acceptable consumption but a high dependence on food aid and spent very little on food. The assessments showed little change in the percentage of food-insecure people between 2005 and 2007, which is surprising given that conflict worsened in 2006, and 2007 was a drought year (see Chapter 4). The lack of change in the FCS could also be because people in Darfur are at the lower end of calorie intake – and thus change the *quantity* of cereals they eat rather than the diversity of their diet. WFP food security assessments have consistently failed to show a relationship between malnutrition and food insecurity, even as assessment methods and measures of acute malnutrition have changed over time. This is commonly explained as being due to health, hygiene and cultural practices, but it could also be that some households increase their range of strategies – and food sources – as their food access decreases.

Given the limited evidence to support the use of the FCS in emergencies, what could be the reason for its widespread adoption? As already mentioned, a single quantitative indicator of food insecurity is useful for comparing needs across populations and contexts in times when resources are scarce. However, a quantitative measure of household food insecurity status says little about its nature, its underlying causes or the risks associated with the strategies that conflict-affected people use to access food.[12] Like the nutrition approaches described above, it reflects a de-politicisation of food security assessments and the people it assesses. But this too can be seen as positive as it means that the findings are unobjectionable and uncontroversial. In the highly politicised context of Darfur, this is an important requirement for being able to disseminate assessment findings. From an operational perspective, too, it has certain advantages: the data is relatively easy to collect and does not require analysis on the part of those who collect it. As such, data to work out the FCS is now often collected remotely. Furthermore, as it delinks food security from nutrition and cause from effect, the response can be a relatively simple and standardised set of interventions. If it can be shown that food insecurity is not the cause of malnutrition, then levels of malnutrition above emergency thresholds do not require a general food distribution and behaviour change becomes an appropriate response. This too is good for remote programming.

The latest WFP food security assessments in Darfur (carried out in 2011 and 2012), called Comprehensive Food Security Assessments, focus on chronic and household-level causes of food insecurity and are conducted by State Ministries of Agriculture. Food security is related to levels of education, employment, livelihoods, head of household, residential status and food consumption (WFP, 2009a). The 2011 survey concludes that the most vulnerable households are those headed by women, or in which the head of household is not educated or is unemployed (WFP et al., 2011). The 2012 survey makes similar conclusions and took eighteen months to be released; it was clearly not intended to inform an emergency response (WFP, 2014a). The vulnerability of particular social or political groups to attacks, restriction of movement, coercion or exploitation, or their limited access to land, markets, social networks, or changes in the way these institutions work, are not considered. Following a similar trend, national nutritional surveys, now done by the Ministry of Health (MoH) with UNICEF technical support, relate nutrition to vaccination status, maternal health, hygiene and dietary practices. They determine food security by asking people how often they have gone to bed hungry in the past month, which apparently most had not. This means that malnutrition levels well above emergency thresholds have not been linked to food security. The 2014 report does, however, recommend scaling up CMAM and education about infant feeding, health and hygiene practices (Federal Ministry of Health, 2014).

Like standardised interventions, the use of quantitative food security and nutrition indicators in the resilience regime reflects a declining concern with causal relationships at the population level. While they are promoted for reasons of accuracy and comparison between populations, the shift towards these indicators can also be linked to the increased need for remote management of international aid programmes. The convergence of interests between governments, the UN, NGOs and the private sector in the resilience food aid regime, and the dominance of WFP, makes criticism within the emergency nutrition and food security world almost non-existent. This is explored in the next two subsections.

Concentration of power within the food aid business
The transformation from the livelihoods to the resilience food aid regime has also changed the organisations involved and the relationships between them. In the livelihoods regime INGOs dominated,

but in the resilience regime WFP and private sector dominate, which has implications for innovation and critique.

From the mid-1980s, international NGOs involved in emergency food aid programmes and humanitarian assistance have increased in number and have expanded their activities. Each of the major crises in Sudan, for example, was associated with an increase in the number of international NGOs and humanitarian workers. Most of the eighty-six INGOs working in Darfur in 1985 had come to respond to the famine that year (Buchanan-Smith, 1989). Operation Lifeline Sudan increased the number of INGOs working in rebel-held areas from six or seven in 1992 to nearly forty in 1996 (Karim et al., 1996). In the Darfur crisis, the number of organisations increased from twenty-three in 2003 to 258 in 2008, of which eighty-one were international (Humanitarian Aid Commission, 2009). Food distribution NGOs worked as WFP implementing partners – International Committee of the Red Cross (ICRC) is an exception – whereas in the 1980s and 1990s INGOs were often funded directly by USAID, the EU or DFID. USAID, the main food aid donor, felt that WFP was the only agency capable of the scale and speed of response needed for the Darfur operation and initially did not face the same access constraints as INGOs (Informant 95, 2014).

The rise of WFP and its changing role is one of the biggest transformations in international food aid of the 2000s. From being a minor actor on the development scene, it has become *The World's Largest Humanitarian Agency* (Shaw, 2011). In the 1960s and 1970s, WFP started as an advisor to recipient governments and in the 1980s its role in emergencies increased to deal with food aid logistics (Shaw, 1970; WFP, 1986; USAID, 1986). By the late 1990s, its main business was emergencies, and WFP adopted many of the policies and practices first initiated by INGOs (Shaw, 2011). In the 2000s, WFP was involved in all aspects of the food aid process; it had produced policies on food aid and livelihood protection, emergency needs assessment, humanitarian principles, humanitarian access, targeting, vouchers and cash transfers, and protection. In 2011, 70% of WFP's budget for Sudan was non-food costs, reflecting the cost of programme support, management and administration (ibid.: 95), as well as security and the cost of delays. WFP's domination of emergency food aid practices limits the scope for innovation and change and allows the quantitative approach to food security assessments, and the apolitical food security discourse, to go unchallenged. In Sudan, donors have no alternative provider of food aid services (Informant 55, 2013). Emergency nutrition and food security

specialists are unlikely to criticise the de-politicisation, medicalisation or privatisation of their professions because they see the new
food aid practices of the resilience regime as progress.

Critiques and alternative functions

The contemporary convergence of political, aid agency, academic
and private sector interests stands in sharp contrast to the late 1970s,
when NGO and academic critique of the economic and political
motivations of food aid contributed to changes in practice. While
aid agencies now promote private sector involvement to address
malnutrition and food insecurity, in the 1970s George argued that
the speculation of multinational grain traders, the expansion of
agribusiness and the increased inequality resulting from the introduction of modern agricultural technology contributed to the 1974
world food crisis (George, 1976). The resilience regime of truth is
that emergency levels of malnutrition no longer need a general food
aid response and can be addressed with specialised food products
and behaviour change. In reducing food aid, targeting has received
renewed emphasis but few studies have examined its effectiveness.
The few that have, show – as before – that the wealthiest or those
with political connections receive more (Caeyers and Dercon, 2012).
The limited information on whether food aid actually reaches beneficiaries, and the constraints in doing so, can be attributed to the
demise of social nutrition, limitations in access, or perhaps that the
main aim of targeting is now simply to reduce food aid. The role of
the private sector, the use of universal quantitative indicators, the
medicalisation of nutrition and the focus on individual behaviour
have not been challenged from within the emergency food security
or nutrition profession. Instead, the focus has been on the advantages of new approaches and the consensus is that these are an
improvement on previous practices.

The main criticisms of the resilience food aid regime come from
human rights organisations, social movements concerned with food
and a number of social scientists working on nutrition. The trend
of reducing food to nutrients, or treating nutrients as medicine,
has variously been called 'nutritionism', 'nutritionalising food' or
the rise of 'nutraceuticals' (Patel et al., 2015; Street, 2015; Sathyamala, 2016). Rather than focusing on problems of poverty and
inequality, or how government policies and the food industry may
cause nutritional problems, thinking about malnutrition has shifted
towards 'eating wrongly' (Sathyamala, 2016: 826). As the International Baby Food Action Network (IBFAN, 2012) has pointed out,

the responsibility of business to shareholders rather than to public health is well illustrated by the epidemic of dietary-induced diseases such as diabetes, heart disease and obesity caused or exacerbated by diets promoted by multinational food businesses. The use of RUTF beyond the treatment of severe malnutrition in emergencies has been criticised for removing the emphasis on issues such as rising food prices, reduced access to land, water and seeds, and the exploitation of labour (Gupta et al., 2013). SUN has similarly been criticised for promoting private sector-led technical solutions rather than addressing social determinants of malnutrition and for diverting government funds towards specialised food products (Schuftan and Holla, 2012). A letter in the *Lancet* questioned the recommendation in the nutrition articles that the private sector generate 'evidence about the positive and negative effects of private sector and market-led approaches to nutrition'. Two of the authors were on the board of a Nestlé advisory committee and the Global Alliance for Improved Nutrition (GAIN), the food industry alliance (Gupta et al., 2013). Specialised food products typify the resilience regime as they 'sell the possibility of survival amidst the struggle to sustain life in the present' (Street, 2015: 369).

The role of the private sector in the New Alliance for Food Security and Nutrition has also been challenged. Rather than improving food security and nutrition through increased food production, the New Alliance may increase the vulnerability of local populations. African countries which joined the New Alliance have been required to change their laws on land, seeds and trade to open them up for investment by multinational agribusiness companies. This risks accelerating a process of land-grabbing that has been under way in much of Africa since the 2008 food crisis. South Sudan and Sudan are amongst the top ten countries in Africa where such land grabs are taking place (Africa Centre for Biosafety, 2013; ActionAid, 2014).[13] Sudan is currently not a member of the New Alliance but nevertheless financial institutions and agribusinesses, for example from Egypt, are appropriating land in the country and see WFP as a potential customer (Dixon, 2014). Even if these arrangements do not result in land grabs, new agricultural technologies assist mainly large commercial farmers. Small farmers and herders may be displaced or unable to afford the improved seeds, fertiliser and pesticides (Harrison, 2013; McKeon, 2014; Patel et al., 2015; Vercillo et al., 2015). It is unlikely that emergency nutrition and food security specialists will detect such negative impacts by measuring dietary diversity, behaviour or other quantitative indicators.

In the resilience food aid regime, global food and agribusinesses dominate global food systems and influence not only how and what food is produced and people's diets, but also how malnutrition is treated and how food security is improved. Instability in the global food system may in fact be the result of a food supply chain in which power is in the hands of traders and retailers (Lang, 2010). Social movements argue that this system promotes unhealthy and unsustainable diets and dispossesses small-scale producers (Civil Society Forum, 2014). It turns addressing malnutrition and food insecurity into a business opportunity rather than a humanitarian imperative. For Western governments, it also provides a cost-effective means of containing the risks associated with global instability and food crisis.

Conclusions

Over the past fifty years, food aid regimes of practices have gone from support for the recipient country's existing development process to supporting the lives and livelihoods of crisis-affected populations with food aid, to finally expecting those same populations to become resilient through technical fixes and behaviour change in a context of permanent emergency. This has happened through transformation in regimes of practices, resulting from changes in the global political and economic context, global food crises and the failures and criticisms of past food aid programmes. From the 1980s onwards, food aid regimes of practices have incorporated neoliberal approaches which locate the causes of food security and malnutrition within the individual, and which see the private sector as key in providing the necessary resources, goods and services. This is in sharp contrast to the practices of the livelihoods regime of the early 1980s, when malnutrition was considered to be the result of unequal distribution of resources in society, poverty and social or economic marginalisation, and food or agribusiness was seen as a cause of, rather than the solution to, malnutrition.

In the state support regime, donors used food aid as a geopolitical tool and supported an existing state-led development process that was concentrated on the modernisation of agriculture and industrialisation. The sub-Saharan famines of the mid-1980s contributed to the transformation to the livelihoods regime, in which INGOs distributed emergency food aid and developed new assessment, targeting and distribution practices. Emergency nutrition and food security emerged as areas of expertise, based on new concepts of famine, vulnerability and coping strategies, and emergency food aid acquired objectives of livelihood support as well as saving lives. The end of the Cold War further changed practices as aid agencies started distributing food in the midst of civil conflicts, leading to fears that food aid could be diverted by warring parties. By the end of the 1990s, many populations had received food aid for a decade or more, but were still experiencing high levels of malnutrition and mortality. New food aid practices linked food aid to production and favoured further targeting to promote self-reliance and reduce dependency. It also became clear, however, that new practices such as famine early warning or targeting the most vulnerable were rarely successful. The late 1990s were associated with a normalisation of crisis: levels of malnutrition that previously triggered an emergency response were now considered normal.

The 2000s were dominated by attempts to promote the resilience of populations affected by repeated emergencies. This was driven by the 2008 food crisis, climate change and the fear that people living in fragile states would turn to terrorism and the global shadow economy. The profile of nutrition received a huge boost as a cost-effective way of strengthening people's ability to withstand shocks. It was accompanied by a move away from food aid because food aid had become an increasingly scarce and uncertain resource and because of the widely agreed inefficiency and inappropriateness, as well as ongoing political use, of in-kind food aid. A shift to food assistance entailed local purchase, cash transfers and food vouchers, but as nutrition and food security expertise advanced in the resilience regime it was also de-politicised. New nutrition interventions focus on successful treatment and behaviour change rather than malnutrition's underlying causes. New quantitative food security indicators allow comparison between populations, but remove their social and political context. Donors and aid agencies promote the involvement of international food and agribusiness to improve production and produce specialised foods for treatment. The combination of these practices has produced a regime of truth in which malnutrition and food insecurity can be solved by modern agricultural technologies, behaviour change and specialised food products. The social and political causes are no longer identified and large-scale food distribution is rarely considered to be needed. With aid agencies' increasingly limited access to crisis-affected populations, these new practices have the advantage that they can be done remotely. The de-politicised nutrition and food security of the resilience regime is also attractive to recipient governments because it is non-controversial. For the private sector it provides a business opportunity, and for Western governments it provides a cost-effective way of containing permanent emergency. The following chapter analyses what food aid donated by Western governments has *actually* done in Sudan.

3
Food aid in Sudan: government and private sector response

The effect of food aid in Sudan has often been very different from that intended. The Sudan government has frequently resisted food aid on ideological and political grounds but at the same time food aid has become part of the political economy of Sudan. Over time, the Sudan government has established its own food aid apparatus, including a national strategic grain reserve, national NGOs and government food aid, and has developed mechanisms for controlling international food aid. This chapter argues that the current situation of limited access for international agencies and the Sudanisation of food aid can be seen in part as a response to the food aid practices of international agencies in Sudan during the livelihoods regime.

Sudan has received food aid since the late 1950s and is one of the world's largest recipients. It has experienced frequent famine, conflict and disasters. Sudan's protracted emergency is evident in ongoing high levels of acute malnutrition and food insecurity, continued threats to livelihoods and emergency food aid operations every year since 1984. But not everyone experiences crisis in Sudan; wealth is concentrated in the centre, while the country's peripheries (Red Sea State, Kordofan, Darfur and previously South Sudan) are marginalised and suffer repeated crisis. Food aid has been part of this process by supporting development in the centre during the state support regime and by addressing the consequences of failed development in the peripheries in the livelihoods and resilience regimes of practices.

In Sudan, food aid regimes of practices are characterised by changes in government and political systems and their response to different international food aid practices. The state support regime started in 1958 when Sudan accepted its first US food aid. It includes President Nimeiri's regime, which began with a military coup in 1969 and ended with his overthrow, incited by famine, in 1985. During this period, food aid formed the basis of an urban bread subsidy, supported government development projects in central Sudan and helped address the economic and security threats posed by large numbers of refugees. INGO activities for refugees initiated the transformation into the livelihoods regime, which was consolidated with the 1985 international famine response. It ended in the late 1990s, which was also the end of the revolutionary phase of the current Islamist regime (headed by President Al-Bashir). The livelihoods regime saw an increase in emergency food aid distributed in Sudan's peripheries, and the manipulation of this food aid provided political and economic benefits to government and the private sector. It led to one of Sudan's most severe famines: the 1988 famine in Bahr Al-Ghazal. The increase in food aid and INGOs in the livelihoods regime, and the methods they used, raised concerns amongst government officials. They were soon seen as a threat because they undermined the Islamist regime's aim of self-sufficiency and were thought to support rebel movements and, during the Darfur crisis, to be cooperating with the International Criminal Court.

The resilience regime in Sudan is characterised by the government's response to the perceived threat posed by international food aid and the agencies that distribute it. Control over international agencies working in the north was gradually tightened during the 1990s and the 2000s. While the government granted international agencies access to work in Darfur in 2004, this decreased as the conflict continued. International access to war-affected populations in Blue Nile and South Kordofan, where conflict started in 2011, is almost non-existent. The government carried out its own food distributions in government-held areas. The large quantities of food aid provided in the Darfur crisis from 2005 to 2008 met emergency food needs, but at the same time strengthened the state and boosted its closely linked private sector.

The chapter starts with an overview of food security and governance changes in Sudan, briefly explaining the nature of the different political regimes, Sudan's unequal development and the vulnerability to food security and famine in some populations. The main part of the chapter analyses the effect of different food aid regimes of practices in Sudan, in particular the responses of government and its closely aligned private sector.

Sudan's protracted crisis: food, governance and inequality

Sudan's protracted crisis, and distribution of emergency food aid since 1984, is the result of an unequal development process and governance based on patronage, personal gain and crisis management, which has left many populations in the country's peripheries increasingly vulnerable (a detailed chronology of political events is given in Appendix 1). In 2010, FAO included Sudan on its list of countries in protracted crisis, based on the longevity of crisis, the proportion of humanitarian assistance out of total assistance and its economic and food security status (WFP and FAO, 2010: 12–13).[1] It was in the top 10% of food aid recipients for nineteen years between 1988 and 2010.[2] It is also on the OECD's list of fragile states (OECD/ DAC, 2010). As expected, acute food insecurity and malnutrition are alarmingly high for a large proportion of Sudan's population. According to WFP, 'localised nutritional surveys across Sudan reflect that the nutrition situation has not improved in any significant way in the last 25 years' (WFP Sudan, 2010: 9). A national health survey done in 2010 shows a prevalence of acute malnutrition above the emergency threshold for Sudan as a whole (Federal Ministry of Health and Central Bureau of Statistics, 2012). High levels of malnutrition were not found everywhere, however. Central Sudan, including Northern Province, Khartoum and Gezira (see Map 3.1), were not experiencing emergency levels of acute malnutrition.[3] Similar patterns were found in a survey done in 2013, but because a new methodology assessed rural and urban areas separately, this showed higher levels of acute malnutrition in rural areas, including pockets of emergency in those central states not experiencing emergency in the 2010 survey (Federal Ministry of Health, 2014).

Inequality is a major contributing factor to food insecurity in Sudan. This inequality is both social and geographic. Historically, development policies have focused on the introduction of modern commercial agriculture in central Sudan, Khartoum and its surroundings, and have neglected subsistence farmers in the peripheries. This dates back to colonial times, when Sudan was ruled as an Anglo-Egyptian condominium (from 1898 to 1956) established to maintain Britain's hold over the Suez Canal and to assert Egyptian claims on Sudan. The development of Sudan's economy was dominated by the needs of Britain's cotton industry. Cotton was produced on irrigated state farming schemes along the Nile, particularly in Gezira, just south of Khartoum. The colonial government preferentially provided tenancies on these schemes to traditional and religious leaders (in particular the Al-Mahdi and Al-Mirghani families, which have led the sectarian Mahdist and Khatmiya movements respectively) as part of its strategy to prevent resistance or reward loyalty. These same groups later invested in mechanised farming schemes in the east of Sudan, in trade and in real estate. By the time of independence in 1956, there was an interconnected political and economic elite composed of religious and traditional leaders,

Map 3.1: Sudan before 2011

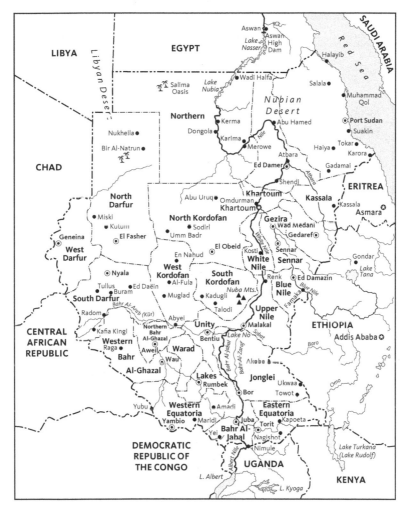

Source: Collins (2008: 186).

Map 3.2: The riverine heartland of Sudan

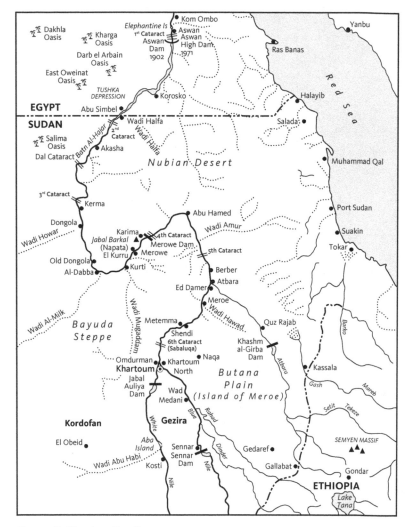

Source: Collins (2008: 96).

ministers and businessmen – mostly from Arab tribes in the riverine heartland of Sudan (see Map 3.2) – who dominated government (Niblock, 1987; Ali, 1989). Southern interests were not represented in the new government; the colonial government structure was simply transferred to northerners, which immediately led to civil war (Johnson, 2003).

The first years of independence were tumultuous times, with six changes in government in thirteen years, as the political and economic elite struggled to hold on to power through alliances with the two main political parties. The Umma party was aligned with the Mahdist movement, land-owning interests in central Sudan and traditional leaders in western Sudan, and the National Unionist Party with the Khatmiya movement, trade interests and traditional leaders in the north and east. In the process leading up to independence, the Umma party favoured ongoing cooperation with the British, and the Unionist party promoted unity of the Nile and was therefore pro-Egypt. After independence, the influence of Abdirahman Al-Mahdi and Ali Al-Mirghani forced the resignation of Sudan's first Prime Minister and the formation of the new coalition government. The Mahdists had close ties with the government of General Aboud, who took power in a military coup in 1958 (Niblock, 1987). Economically, the independent government continued to favour cotton production in the northern Nile Valley, which benefited the elite. By the late 1950s, however, Sudan's cotton was no longer competitive on the world market, resulting in a deteriorating economy and a decision to accept US aid in 1958 (Collins, 2008: 70). Aboud's government was overthrown by a popular uprising in 1964, following strikes by workers and tenants' unions over conditions on commercial farms along the Nile, displacement caused by the Aswan Dam on the border with Egypt and demonstrations against the war in the south. The new government was independent of the establishment but a coalition of the old political parties, now joined by the Islamic Charter Front, forced it to resign after four months (Niblock, 1987; Ali, 1989).

The overthrow of the government in 1964 provided the first, but brief and unsuccessful, opportunity for a new political system and a more inclusive form of development. A more sustained attempt at social transformation was made after Nimeiri's military coup of 1969. Initially socialist, Nimeiri's government modernised the state and its control over production. Banks and companies were nationalised and the state took control of import–export, financial institutions and industry. Native administration,[4] in which traditional leaders were responsible for justice, administration of land and natural resources,

and tax collection, was replaced in 1971 by a system of local councils and functional or popular organisations, for example unions and
village development committees (Niblock, 1987). These changes
caused conflict in many parts of the country, as one tribe could
now control the territory of another. The new rural elite consisted
of teachers, traders and government employees, although traditional
leaders continued as heads of their tribes and sought representation on the councils. Traditional leaders continued to administer
customary law, and native administration was reinstated in Darfur
in 1983, although its role changed with successive governments
(Abdul-Jalil et al., 2007; Tanner et al., 2012). The Sudan Socialist
Union (SSU) was the only political party. Nimeiri planned basic
units at village level to promote SSU policies and socialist thought, to
solve problems and mobilise efforts to increase production (Niblock,
1987). In theory these initiatives promoted greater participation in
government, but in practice they were also a tool for promoting political aims and removing the power base of the traditional political
parties (Woodward, 1990).

The socialist project was abandoned after a failed communist
coup in 1971. Diplomatic relations with the US, which had ceased
during the socialist phase, resumed and food aid to Sudan increased.
The early 1970s were a period of government optimism. The government's new priorities were to achieve national unity and to attract
foreign investment for development projects. It signed the Addis
Ababa peace agreement with the Southern Sudan Liberation movement in 1972 and large numbers of Sudanese refugees returned
from Ethiopia to southern Sudan. Development expenditure rose
dramatically on a number of ambitious plans, including agricultural projects in the east, oil exploration, the Jonglei Canal in South
Sudan and a range of industrial projects (African Rights, 1997b).
The rapid expansion of commercial agriculture was made easier by
the abolition of native administration, as the state could appropriate
land for large-scale commercial farming schemes (Johnson, 2003).
Economic policy was geared towards self-sufficiency, and for a brief
period in the 1970s the country achieved self-sufficiency in sorghum
(Barnett, 1988). Sudan aimed to become the bread-basket of the
Middle East. In contrast with neighbouring countries, it was able
to deal with the 1970s food crisis through a combination of government responses and the availability of agricultural work in central
Sudan (O'Brien, 1985; African Rights, 1997b). Refugees fleeing the
civil war in Ethiopia in the 1970s also formed an important part of
the agricultural labour force (Karadawi, 1999). Subsistence farmers

in Sudan's peripheries were largely excluded from national development as subsidised credit, a favourable exchange rate for inputs and floor price support by the Agricultural Bank of Sudan (ABS) was aimed at large-scale farmers in central Sudan (Maxwell et al., 1990: 54). As a consequence, many people from western Sudan came to work on the farming schemes in the centre (O'Brien, 1983).

By the end of the 1970s, few development projects had been completed on time or had reached production targets. According to Niblock (1987), reasons included deficient planning, corruption and rising oil prices. IMF loans, first provided in the early 1970s, could not be paid back, necessitating measures to privatise state assets and reduce the role of the public sector, removal of food subsidies and later the repeated rescheduling of loans. People migrated to the Gulf for work, the resulting remittances contributing little to government revenues but pushing up prices. As some businesses sold their assets, Islamic banks and merchants invested in farms and transport companies, and bought former state assets, facilitated by the inclusion of the Muslim Brothers in government from 1971. As Attorney General, Hassan Al-Turabi (leader of the Muslim Brothers) Islamised the legal system and demanded the operation of Islamic banks (African Rights 1997b: 11–14; Gallab, 2008: 91).

Sudan's peripheries suffered as government expenditure declined, basic goods were scarce and inflation was high (Niblock, 1987). Rural food security was undermined by the abolition of native administration, by the failure of Nimeiri's basic units as a tool for development and by conflict. With the new system of local government, traditional leaders no longer represented their communities to the authorities and under-financed local councils were unable to safeguard local food supplies (Norris, 1983; De Waal, 1997b). The system of basic units was only sparsely implemented and by 1977 only a few were active (Niblock, 1987; Woodward, 1990). The introduction of regional governments in 1981 caused conflicts within Darfur (between Fur and Arab tribes) and Kordofan (between Nuba and Arab) in the west and, together with the introduction of Islamic law in 1983, led to a resumption of civil war in the south. Nimeiri's alliance with the Muslim Brothers meant he no longer needed the support of the south to hold on to power, and the introduction of Islamic law provided a way of managing social unrest and economic decline in the north (Woodward, 1990; African Rights, 1997b).

In 1985, drought and economic crisis led to a severe famine in Darfur, Kordofan and Red Sea State.[5] The government's denial of the famine mobilised opposition and ultimately led to a popular uprising, which deposed Nimeiri in April 1985. International food aid, provided by international agencies, rose dramatically in the first of many international relief operations. Under the new government, the formal economy continued to deteriorate and a new economic regime emerged that was dependent on the manipulation of markets for profit and the use of state office for personal gain. These strategies often incorporated the diversion and manipulation of food aid (Duffield, 1990a). The government's war strategies, including the use of militia recruited from marginalised pastoral populations, were increasingly destructive and led to one of the most severe famines in Sudan in 1988.

A brief period of democratic rule (1985–1989) ended with the military coup by Colonel Al-Bashir. His regime constitutes the second attempt at radical transformation of society, driven to a large extent by Al-Turabi. President Al-Bashir's National Salvation government transformed all social, economic and administrative institutions into agents of Islamisation (De Waal, 2007b; Sidahmed, 2011). The establishment of an Islamist state was an alternative to the many years of failed development interventions from the West. The Islamist government was a civilisational project at the heart of which was the 'comprehensive call': i.e. bringing all Sudanese into the project through a process of coercion, religious indoctrination and political mobilisation (Gallab, 2008: 11). Jihad, the mobilisation to establish an Islamic society or to fight Islam's enemies, was a key component of the comprehensive call. Islamic aid agencies, police, army, paramilitary forces and tribal militias worked together to transform society (De Waal and Abdelsalam, 2004; Gallab, 2008). The new regime established Popular Committees[6] in towns and villages to take care of social services and community mobilisation. In theory these were elected by the people, but in practice they were often closely linked to the ruling National Congress Party (NCP), dominated by Islamists and tightly managed by the new regime. Political mobilisation and jihad were part of their role (Sidahmed, 2011; Hamid, n.d.).

When the Islamists took power, part of their project was once again to be self-sufficient in food production and to reduce dependence on Western food imports. The country-wide famine in 1991 and the international response were therefore a source of particular embarrassment. The National Economic Salvation Programme and the Comprehensive National Strategy in 1990 and 1992 included investment in agriculture (such as expansion of the area under sorghum and wheat in the irrigated sector), liberalisation of trade, privatisation of state-owned enterprises, removal of food subsidies and the establishment of a national strategic reserve (Elbashir and Ahmed, 2005). When state assets were sold, they often ended up in the hands of Islamists, with many 'private' companies owned by government officials or by those with close links to government (African Rights, 1997a; De Waal and Abdelsalam, 2004; Informant 83, 2013). The expansion of commercial agriculture in central and eastern Sudan accelerated.

The marginalisation of Sudan's peripheries remained manifest in a lack of political representation of westerners and southerners in government. The *Black Book*, distributed in 2000 and attributed to Darfuri intellectuals (including some prominent Islamists), highlighted the concentration of wealth and power in central Sudan. For example, while only 5.3% of Sudan's population is in the northern region, it held between 50% and 80% of ministerial posts between 1954 and 1999 (Yongo-Bure, 2009: 70). While central Sudan's elite has maintained economic power over the years, no group has been able to achieve political dominance over the state. Even Al-Bashir's continuous government since 1989 masks an ongoing struggle for power. This unstable centre of power created a form of governance which involved constantly changing allegiances between central elites and provincial and tribal leaders, depending on the need for votes and militia and the financial rewards. It also resulted in crisis management and low-cost approaches such as the use of militia to fight wars (such as the Janjaweed in Darfur), and governing through the security apparatus to maintain power (De Waal, 2007a). From 2000, the revolutionary phase of the Islamist regime was over, as it split along ethnic lines and was undermined by Arab racism and resisted by non-Arab Muslim populations in Sudan (e.g. in Darfur) (Gallab, 2008). These factors were crucial in the Darfur conflict from 2003 onwards and later in Blue Nile and South Kordofan, conflicts which led to major humanitarian crises in the 2000s.

The first decade of the 2000s was also accompanied by the longest and strongest period of economic growth since independence, largely as a result of the advent of oil revenue and the Comprehensive Peace Agreement with South Sudan in 2005. Growing Middle Eastern and Asian investment in telecommunications, commercial farming and in Khartoum real estate, as well as the energy sector, made Sudan one of Africa's fastest growing economies during these ten years. Wealth and services, as before, were concentrated in central Sudan (World Bank, 2009: 5; National Population Council General Secretariat et al., 2010: 22). Increases in government revenue were

spent on defence, national security, public order and safety rather
than on education, health or sanitation (Patey, 2010). After 2005,
the government renewed its efforts to achieve food self-sufficiency,
including a wheat self-sufficiency strategy from 2003 and an agricultural revival strategy from 2008 (Sudan Council of Ministers, 2008),
which became all the more important after the secession of South
Sudan in 2011 and the subsequent disputes over pipeline charges,
production stoppages and conflict in South Sudan and on Sudan's
southern border. As before, much of the emphasis is currently on
large-scale irrigated and mechanised farming in the centre.

To conclude, for over fifty years, wealth and services in Sudan
have been concentrated in the centre, leaving the peripheries vulnerable and suffering repeated emergencies since the 1980s. Successive
governments have aimed to achieve self-sufficiency but have ended
up in debt and corrupt, and undermining rural livelihoods by
prioritising modern agriculture in the centre, manipulating local
government for political ends and governing through alliances with
economic and political elites and through their security apparatuses.
Sudan has been at war with itself for most of the time since independence. The remainder of this chapter examines how the different
international food aid regimes of practices have interacted with these
processes at the national level.

The early years of food aid in Sudan: urban food subsidies, uneven development and refugees

Food aid was highly controversial when it was first introduced in
Sudan as it affected its relations with Egypt. Once it was accepted,
the state support regime of food aid practices supported an urban
bread subsidy and the modernisation of agriculture, and fed large
numbers of refugees. Sudan was first offered US food aid as part of
an American aid package in 1956, the year of Sudan's independence.
Aid, including surplus agricultural products, was offered as part of
the Eisenhower doctrine, under which a country could request US
economic and military assistance to defend itself against threats from
another state, in particular the Soviet Union. In the case of Sudan,
the offer came just after Egypt had purchased Soviet arms in 1955,
and the objective of US aid was '[t]o encourage Sudan to cooperate
with Egypt in cases where Egypt is friendly to US objectives and to
encourage Sudan to frustrate Egypt in all cases where the Egyptians
serve Soviet purposes' (US Government, 1955–57: 628).

The decision to accept US food aid was highly political, as it was intimately linked with national and regional politics. In the coalition government at the time, the majority Umma party wanted to accept aid, but cabinet members belonging to the minority People's Democratic Party argued against US aid as part of their pro-Egypt stance, because the aid was conditional on acceptance of an anti-communist agenda. In this context, the Sudan government was unwilling accept US aid in case it brought down the government (US Government, 1955–57). In discussions with the US Vice President, Sudan's Prime Minister had suggested it would be better to talk generally about problems of aggression rather than specifically about the communist menace, adding that Sudan did not feel menaced by Egypt (US Government, 1955–57: 634). One month later, in April 1957, during a second US mission, Sudan's Foreign Minister stated that the country's policy was positive neutrality and that it would not take sides in an East–West struggle as long as it did not pose a threat to Sudan's sovereignty. However, Sudan made an informal request for US assistance soon after the mission, most likely because of the deteriorating economic situation. A formal agreement for economic, technical and related assistance was signed in March 1958 (US Embassy in Khartoum and Sudan Ministry of Foreign Affairs, 1958). The agreement drew fierce opposition from the newly formed National Front, composed of the communist party and unions (tenants, farmers, students and southern federal), which demanded a change in government, cancellation of the US aid agreement and an immediate improvement of relations with Egypt (Niblock, 1987; Ali, 1989). Strikes and demonstrations followed, which led to the military coup by General Aboud, who confirmed acceptance of the US aid package soon after taking power. These events are remembered by many Sudanese as a key moment in their national history, as they highlight the start of the country's turbulent relationship with food aid.

Food aid in Sudan increased in the 1970s for several reasons (see Figure 3.1). First, the country's geopolitical importance increased as Nimeiri turned away from socialism while left-leaning regimes were established in neighbouring Ethiopia and Libya. Sudan became the chief anchor of US policy in the Horn of Africa (Ayers, 2010) and by the early 1980s it was the largest recipient of US foreign assistance in sub-Saharan Africa, much of it programme food aid in the form of wheat (African Rights, 1997: 16). Second, Sudanese refugees returned from Ethiopia following the 1972 Addis Ababa peace agreement (which ended the first war with the south) and

Figure 3.1: Total food aid to Sudan

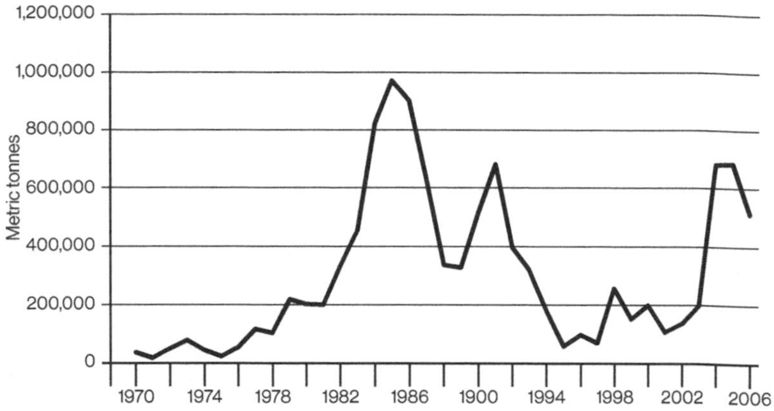

Source: Jaspars (2015: 148).

Note: The data for this graph were extracted from FAO's statistical database (FAO, 2012c) by combining food aid data for Sudan on total cereals and total non-cereals for all donors and all years for which data are available.

large numbers of Ethiopian refugees entered Sudan between 1977 and 1978 (Karadawi, 1999). Refugees and returnees both received emergency food aid. Third, WFP implemented its first development project in Sudan. During the 1970s and 1980s, Sudan received programme food aid, emergency food aid and project food aid.

Programme food aid was the basis of Sudan's most important food security intervention: an urban wheat subsidy (Maxwell et al., 1990). The expansion of modern commercial farming and a growing market economy led to rapid urbanisation from the 1960s onwards and urban populations needed a steady supply of affordable food. The Sudan government sold programme food aid at subsidised prices, in effect a wheat subsidy provided by the US. By the 1980s, much of Sudan's wheat consumption was food aid; the contribution of wheat aid to meet consumption requirements rose from 29% to 77% between 1978/79 and 1986/87 (Hussain, 1991). Other subsidies included fixed prices for locally produced wheat and a subsidy to bakers or flour mills to produce bread cheaply (Maxwell, 1989; Bickersteth, 1990). The government's need for these measures is illustrated by the inevitable demonstrations and riots that followed any cuts in subsidies. In 1985, for example, IMF demands to cut subsidies and the resulting riots helped bring down Nimeiri's government (DeWaal, 1997b: 95).The US continued wheat aid until 1990 to maintain some leverage over the Sudan government (Bicker-steth, 1990; Hussain, 1991).When the US cut programme food aid, the Sudan government had to apply production and consumption subsidies, as well as exchange rate and floor price mechanisms, to maintain stability in the face of serious food shortages (Patel, 1994).

Both programme and project food aid supported Sudan's existing development process. The funds generated by the sale of programme food aid were initially used to support the American diplomatic mission and the Sudanese government, and to extend credit to the Sudanese private sector (Ali, 1989: 149). From the mid-1960s, the funds were used for development projects such as the construction of dams and roads to support irrigated agricultural schemes along the Nile. Sudan's Finance Minister was under pressure to fund projects the US thought important and which would not compete with US exports (Informant 20, 2013). WFP project food aid similarly supported irrigated agriculture in central Sudan. Other projects supported by WFP food aid included the resettlement of refugees, school feeding and commercial government projects, such as forestry, gum arabic or dairy schemes. With the exception of school feeding and timber production in South Sudan, these development projects were in central Sudan and thus reinforced the country's unequal development.

Although the development projects supported by WFP food aid rarely succeeded in improving production or creating viable commercial ventures, they supported government budgets by paying part of labourers' salaries in food. The first WFP project, in 1963, assisted the resettlement of people whose land in Wadi Halfa was flooded by the construction of the Aswan High Dam in Egypt to an agricultural scheme at Khasm Al-Girba in eastern Sudan (WFP, 1969). Like the acceptance of programme food aid in 1958, this was a highly controversial project. The construction of the dam was part of the Nile Waters agreement between Egypt and Sudan, and the displacement of Nubians resulted in violent demonstrations which galvanised government opposition and contributed to its overthrow in 1964 (Collins, 2008: 75). WFP provided food aid to Nubians during transit and for the first year of resettlement.[7] Although the contribution of food aid was small in economic terms, it was politically significant.WFP concluded that it helped settlers establish their farms (Shaw, 1967;WFP, 1969), but others expressed doubts about the settlers' willingness to change their livelihoods and about their production capacity, as most young men had long ago left to work in towns. By the mid-1970s, the scheme's productivity had declined because the government could not maintain irrigation mechanisms or necessary inputs (Sorbo, 1985). Later attempts to settle nomadic populations on the same scheme faced similar difficulties.

WFP school feeding, timber, gum arabic and dairy projects some-times took more than a year to get going, distribution was irregular due to poor transport infrastructure, and food aid often did not reach intended beneficiaries or projects never started. WFP's evaluations concluded that the main effect of food aid was to reduce the cost of projects for government (WFP, 1970, 1972, 1975a, 1983, 1988a). Given insufficient and irregular distribution and often unfamiliar foods, the intended effects in improving nutrition and creating devel-opment assets were minimal. The few WFP-supported development projects outside of central Sudan faced so many logistical, labour and financial constraints that, rather than being linked to work on devel-opment projects, food aid was given free of charge – rather than in return for work – to returnees from Ethiopia, to demobilised soldiers and to self-help and agricultural projects (WFP, 1975a, 1976).

Emergency food aid played an important role in addressing the security threats posed by large numbers of refugees and returnees and in eventually transferring responsibility for welfare provision to international agencies. From the 1960s, Sudan both produced and received refugees; Sudanese from the south fled to Ethiopia and the Congo and refugees from Congo, Chad, Uganda, Eritrea and Ethiopia came to Sudan. The peace agreement with the south in 1972 led to the return of about half a million refugees from Ethiopia (Karadawi, 1999). Depending on regional politics, the Sudan govern-ment either welcomed refugees or saw them as a security threat. For example, allowing Ethiopian refugees to engage in political activities would have antagonised the Ethiopian government and increased the threat from Sudanese refugees in Ethiopia. Sudan's refugee policy of 1967 was based on Organisation of African Unity (OAU) principles of sovereignty, territorial integrity and non-intervention in the affairs of member states; OAU member states would not tolerate subversive activities against the country of origin (Karadawi, 1999). Actions to reduce refugee political activity included moving them away from borders and placing them in camps, which facilitated surveillance. Aid agencies, at the time, supported the concentration of refugees in camps or settlements to facilitate the provision of aid (Harrell-Bond, 1986; Wilson, 1992).

From the mid-1970s, local authorities saw refugees as a socio-economic burden and responsible for the rise in crime and unemployment in urban areas. When they first arrived in Sudan in the 1960s, refugees were an important source of labour for mechanised and irrigated farms, and UNHCR placed the first refugees in agricultural settlements (WFP, 1974). However, by the late 1970s, as numbers increased and many spontaneously settled in Khartoum and other towns, the police requested the restriction of their movements from settlements and their evacuation from urban areas (Karadawi, 1999: 104). By March 1979, there were 419,000 Ethiopian refugees in Sudan, most of them placed in camps in eastern Sudan. To attract external funding, Sudan's Refugee Commission organised and participated in meetings to put pressure on UNHCR and its donors to raise funds. This was successful, but UNHCR preferred to work with INGOs as it considered the Refugee Commission to be inefficient and corrupt. INGOs welcomed the opportunity for funding and to establish themselves in Sudan. The number of NGOs working with refugees increased from seven in 1978 to twenty-three in 1981, and to fifty-seven in 1984, and the proportion of INGOs working with refugees gradually increased (African Rights, 1997b: 36).

The increased role of INGOs in refugee assistance externalised the responsibility for welfare provision in Sudan. INGOs also provided assistance to returnees in the south, where they ended up replacing the state in all except its security functions, as the new regional government was inexperienced and underfunded. NGOs had better finances and attracted the most highly educated people. Whole districts or sections of government were handed over to NGOs, thus removing domestic accountability for humanitarian action and welfare provision (Tvedt, 1994; Karadawi, 1999). The increase in the role of INGOs led to the transformation into the livelihoods regime of practices. From the 1980s, food aid practices in Sudan evolved as a result of the dynamics between aid agencies and government, which were in part determined by changes in the type and quantities of food aid provided.

Changes in quantities and types of international food aid in Sudan

The 1980s and 1990s saw a dramatic change in food aid in Sudan. The international response to famine in 1984/85 led to a doubling of the quantity of food aid received, and quantities remained high at around 900,000 metric tonnes until 1986 (see Figure 3.1). One-third of food aid coming to the country was programme food aid for use by the Sudan government, but for the first time donors provided emergency food aid in larger quantities. Emergency food aid has been the main food aid received by Sudan ever since (Benson and Clay, 1986). Programme food aid stopped in 1990 (see Figure 3.2), which was earlier, and more sudden, than the drop in programme food aid globally.

Western donors were reluctant to provide direct assistance to the Sudan government following the military coup staged by Colonel Al-Bashir (and masterminded by the National Islamic Front), the lack of progress in resolving the war in South Sudan and the Sudan government's support for Iraq in the first Gulf War. When the US, the EU and the UK stopped their development aid to Sudan in 1991, humanitarian aid was the only international aid source to the country (Buchanan-Smith and Davies, 1995b). From the mid-1990s to the early 2000s humanitarian aid remained the dominant form of

Figure 3.2: Trends in different types of food aid in Sudan

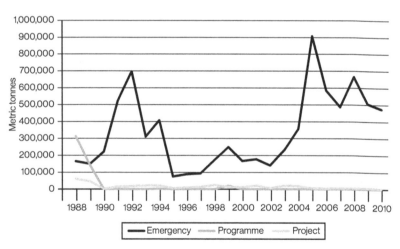

Source: Jaspars (2015: 150).

Notes: This graph only goes up to 2010 because in 2011 South Sudan became a separate country, so any statistics for Sudan from this date are not comparable to earlier years. In addition, part of the food assistance provided from 2011 was in the form of food vouchers which is not part of WFP's international food aid information database.

The data for Sudan by food aid type were extracted from WFP's international food aid information database (WFP, 2009b). The difference in the 2004/05 peak compared with Figure 3.1 is because FAO reports food aid on a split year (July–June) basis and WFP on a calendar year basis.

Figure 3.3: Trends in humanitarian and development assistance to Sudan

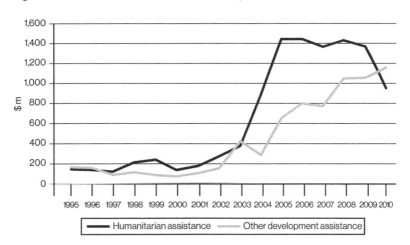

Source: data from OECD Creditor Reporting System, provided by Development Initiatives.

Note: This graph only goes up to 2010, as explained above for Figure 3.2.

aid to Sudan, but funding levels were low (see Figure 3.3). Much of this was food aid.[8] Both development and humanitarian assistance increased in 2005, development aid as the war in southern Sudan ended and humanitarian aid in response to conflict and humanitarian crisis in Darfur.

The shift to emergency food aid also reflected a change in its geographical distribution and implementation modality. From 1985 onwards, food aid was largely distributed in Sudan's peripheries, including emergency food aid and WFP's development programmes. Food aid shifted from supporting government development policy to addressing the negative consequences of excluding the peripheries from development. Until 2003, emergency food aid was distributed by INGOs directly funded by DFID, the EC and USAID in northern Sudan: Oxfam in Red Sea State, SC-UK in Darfur and CARE in Kordofan. In southern Sudan, most emergency food aid was managed by WFP through Operation Lifeline Sudan (OLS). The number of INGOs in Sudan increased with every major emergency, first the 1985 famine, then OLS and finally Darfur. From 2004, WFP was in charge of food distribution in Darfur, the Darfur crisis quickly becoming its largest operation globally.

Trends in emergency food aid from 1990 closely follow political
developments and crises in Sudan. Emergency food aid peaked in
1992, when OLS became fully active in providing aid to conflict-affected people in South Sudan. The next peak was in 1998, which
reflects the response to the second Bahr Al-Ghazal famine in South
Sudan; and in 2005 food aid reached its peak in response to the
Darfur crisis. The troughs are also revealing – 1988, the time of the
first Bahr Al-Ghazal famine, shows little humanitarian response.
During the Cold War period, donors were reluctant to challenge the
Sudanese government's conduct in the war with the south and its
strategy of restricting food aid to particular groups or areas (Keen,
1994). The drop in 1994 can be explained by donor, government
and aid agency perceptions that the emergency in Sudan was over,
leading to a shift to developmental relief. A similar trend can be
seen for the Darfur crisis. Food aid in response to this crisis peaked
in 2005 and has decreased progressively since then, partly because
of funding constraints, partly because of security and logistical
constraints and partly because of assumptions that conflict-affected
people had found other ways of accessing food (see Chapter 4). The
remainder of this chapter analyses the effect of the livelihoods and
resilience food aid regimes in Sudan, and the role of government
resistance and of the political and economic benefit of food aid in the
transformation from one regime of practices to another.

The famines of the 1980s and the manipulation of food aid

Government officials regard 1984 as a 'benchmark' year for food
aid in Sudan, as it brought more food aid and more international
NGOs to the country (Informants 17 and 20, 2012). During the livelihoods regime in the 1980s, control over food distribution changed
and emergency food aid was incorporated into Sudan's political
economy. Government maintained control of food aid during the
1984/85 famine. Despite donor requirements to target the most
vulnerable, food aid was slow to reach rural areas as government
prioritised the towns and its own employees (USAID, 1986; WFP,
1986; Keen, 1991). By 1986, however, international agencies had
taken control and established their own distribution systems, which
was resented but later copied by the Sudanese administration. For
the remainder of the decade, and beyond, the government tried to
regain control. At the same time, emergency food aid acquired alternative functions of benefiting the government and private sector.

A small unit had existed within the Sudanese Ministry of Finance to deal with programme food aid from the 1960s, and in 1983 this became a formal department called the Food Aid National Administration. This unit was responsible for consolidating information on donor contributions, preparing allocation plans and arranging port clearance and transport (Informant 20, 2012). Soon, however, with the influx of INGOs that wanted to implement their own programmes, the need for coordinating operational programmes and the detailed agreements required to deliver aid to war-torn areas meant that a new government structure was necessary; the Relief and Rehabilitation Commission (RRC) was created in 1986. The RRC was responsible for coordinating and controlling international agencies as the government was very concerned about the 'invasion' of foreign INGOS, in particular those working in South Sudan (Informant 22, 2012). Foreign advisors worked with the RRC to establish a famine early warning system, as lack of information was thought to be one reason for a late response and failed targeting. Although relations between the RRC, INGOs and donors were good, Sudanese government officials resented the lack of Sudanese staff in the aid programmes, as expressed by the first Relief Commissioner:

> the donor wants that money, or that donation or that food, that medicine to go to certain targets so they had all the rights to watch or to attend to supervise to participate in watching it. But you don't go to the other extreme where they want to do it themselves! Absolutely at first, there was no Sudanese association at all. It was all done by experts from outside, from top to bottom. (Informant 22, 2012)

Or as a Sudanese aid worker explained:

> For some time ... I struggled a lot to balance the influence of the local government and my organisation. But luckily aid organisations, using their food aid mechanisms, the resources they have, and everything they brought in they managed to influence the government, and then they just chucked the government aside. (Informant 27, 2013)

International SC-UK aid workers in Darfur also noted friction with government officials over their 1986 distribution policy (Buckley, 1988: 102). In response, one of the main objectives of the RRC was to reduce food aid and shift to rehabilitation such as agricultural

support, and to increase the number of Sudanese involved in aid operations. In 1988, the Sudan government passed a law to regulate the
activities of international agencies (Informant 22, 2012). The government also promoted the creation of local NGOs and the twinning of
international and local NGOs 'so that the INGOs could leave' once
local NGOs had learnt from them (Informant 17, 2012).

At the same time, food aid became an important part of the political economy of Sudan. As government budgets shrank, food aid was
diverted to feed soldiers or to subsidise local government. At central
government level, benefits could be gained through manipulating
exchange rates (Duffield, 1994a). Food aid could also provide lucrative contracts for transporters and traders – often closely linked to
government. Furthermore, as the formal economy weakened, traders
began to manipulate markets for greater profit, while the state appropriated land for agricultural schemes and fought the war in the south
through a combination of militia tactics and restriction of aid. In this
context, restricting or delaying food aid supplies could yield benefits
through raising grain and transport prices and thus creating greater
profits for merchants and farmers, usually from central Sudan. In
1988, the Western Relief Operation (WRO) suffered significant delays
in local food procurement and food aid transport to Kordofan and
Darfur. The WRO delivered only a fraction of the planned food aid.
Food aid was purchased from the Agricultural Bank of Sudan (ABS),
but the bank initially exported food stocks for higher prices than it
could achieve from the relief operation. It left poor-quality stocks for
the relief operation and increased the price when asked to provide
higher-quality food. Transport of WRO relief to Darfur was organised
via a private contractor, who only took food to easily accessible places
because price fluctuations had made the agreed contract unprofitable
(Buchanan-Smith, 1990; Duffield, 1990a). According to Duffield
(1994a), this reflected the growth in aggressive commercialism in
Sudan and showed that aid agencies should not assume that government or commercial elites would prioritise getting aid to needy and
distant populations. This pattern of delays and under-distribution
was repeated in many subsequent emergency operations. Delays in
local procurement and transport led to more lucrative contracts and
greater profits for merchants and farmers from central Sudan, both
important political constituencies for the Khartoum regime (CIJ,
2006: 88). The consequences of this for crisis-affected populations in
Darfur will be explored further in Chapter 4.

The restriction of relief was most extreme to populations
believed to support rebel movements in the south. In 1988, the

denial of relief to Bahr Al-Ghazal in southern Sudan was part of the government's counter-insurgency tactics and contributed to the severity of famine amongst the local Dinka. Bahr Al-Ghazal and South Kordofan in northern Sudan (to which people had fled) received only limited allocations of grain in the WRO and even less was delivered. Desperate populations sold their livestock and left to work as labourers in the north, leaving their land to be appropriated by northern pastoralists for grazing and by government for oil exploration. The interests of traders, landowners and the military converged in the restriction of relief. Police and military escorts carried their own commercial goods to sell at high prices in the south, took local products to sell in the north and took money from people who had no choice but to take their transport north. Delaying relief convoys meant that traders and soldiers could sell commercial sorghum at higher prices and purchase cattle at low prices. Commercial farmers benefited as those displaced to the north became a source of cheap labour (Keen, 1994). The famine resulted in a transfer of assets from southerners to political and economic elites in northern Sudan (Duffield, 1994a). The famine eventually led to Operation Lifeline Sudan in 1989. It also set a pattern for the alternative functions or 'actually existing development' indirectly resulting from food aid or its manipulation.

Islamism, self-sufficiency and war

The Sudan government maintained its ambivalent relationship with international food aid from 1989 onwards and tried to resist, adapt and benefit from it. The revolutionary phase of the Islamist regime (1989–99) coincided with the livelihoods regime of practices and was characterised by a struggle for control over food and the populations to which it was given. The regime started with government resistance to international food aid during the early 1990s but by the middle of the decade the government had learnt to manipulate food aid for its own economic and political purposes. Government and aid agency aims sometimes converged, for example in achieving self-sufficiency and in linking relief and development, which minimised food aid. Restricting relief to certain population groups remained part of the Sudan government's counter-insurgency tactics and helped with the expansion of mechanised farming schemes. The economic benefits to government and traders were increased by promoting local purchase. In southern Sudan, food aid provided assistance to

rebel movements such as the Sudan People's Liberation Movement
(SPLM), and the government's reaction to the provision of international food aid to war-affected populations in southern Sudan was a
key factor in influencing the transformation from the livelihoods to
the resilience regime of food aid practices in Sudan.

Self-sufficiency and food aid

During its ideological phase in the 1990s, the Islamist regime was
vehemently opposed to receiving international food aid. The government promoted food self-sufficiency and considered dependency on
Western food aid to conflict with this aim. The focus was instead
on improving agricultural production, in particular wheat. The 1991
famine created severe tension between the government and aid agencies, including donors, the UN and NGOs. Newly established early
warning systems and food security assessments were showing large
food deficits and the possibility of famine, but the Sudan government called this a 'food gap' (Informants 12 and 13, 2012). By calling
it a food gap rather than famine, the government tried to maintain
the illusion of self-sufficiency and avoid an international response.
As one aid worker recalls:

> Ali Shamar [Assistant Governor and responsible for NGOs in
> North Darfur] was saying it is a food gap. And Andrew Natsios
> [USAID] said, no, you people are hungry, you people have
> famine, and we are coming here to help you. And then after
> that there was a fight between Natsios and Abu Aof [Relief
> Commissioner]. ... I think the government deliberately [didn't]
> want to say it [was] a famine. Q: Why? A: Because they raise this
> slogan, we eat what we grow and we wear what we manufacture.
> That is the slogan. And they felt that by acknowledging it is a
> famine they are defeating their slogan. (Informant 26, 2012)

Sudan's Relief Commissioner at the time was convinced of the
inaccuracy of INGO data:

> The 1990/91 famine was a terrible year for Darfur and
> Kordofan. INGOs went there. For some time, there was a real
> understanding. Then the difficulties started. INGOs started
> to be information agencies: ' ... 7 million people will die ... .'
> [The] government asked for a plan, to work through government
> systems. The plan was wonderful, but NGOs exaggerated the
> situation. (Informant 17, 2012)

Sudan's politics meant that donors wanted to retain control over any food aid, insisting on a government declaration of emergency, recognition of the neutrality of aid (and support for INGOs) and favourable exchange rates. For six months, donors talked of impending famine, while the government claimed it was a manageable food gap. Eventually an FAO assessment, which estimated a food deficit of 1.1 million MT but did not use the word 'famine', was accepted by central government (Buchanan-Smith and Davies, 1995b).

Throughout the 1990s, information on food security was tightly controlled. Any mention of famine, malnutrition or mortality was highly controversial and assessments had to be cleared at state ministerial level to ensure that information did not contradict the policy (Informants 9 and 26, 2012). During the Salvation regime in the 1990s questionnaires had to be approved by the RRC, and the release of reports authorised by the state minister (Informant 9, 2012). It could take several months for reports to be released and no emergency appeals could be launched until that time (DFID, 1997: 16). The new food security assessment methods established as part of the livelihoods regime suited the political motivations of the government. As one aid worker explained about the Food Economy Approach (FEA): 'When we adopted this approach, it was highly appreciated by the government, because it was in line with the government intention to reduce food aid' (Informant 12, 2012). During the 1990s, interactions between the livelihoods regime of practices and the Sudan government ensured that international food aid practices did not contradict, and even supported, Sudan's policy of self-sufficiency.

A key aspect of Sudan's drive towards self-sufficiency was the further expansion of mechanised agriculture, which converged with aid agency objectives in the livelihoods regime to link relief with development. Sudan's development policy linked displacement, resettlement on agricultural schemes and the expansion of large-scale farms. Much agricultural expansion in the 1990s occurred by seizing land from which populations were forcibly displaced during conflict, for example in South Kordofan's Nuba Mountains and the area around Wau in Bahr Al-Ghazal. In these areas, displaced populations were settled in 'peace villages' where they received limited amounts of government relief and worked as farm labourers on what had previously been their own land (Karim et al., 1996; African Rights, 1997a). Concentrating people in peace villages also enabled surveillance and indoctrination to transform the Nuba's cultural and political identity as part of the Islamist plan (African Rights,

1997a: 179). Sudan's parastatal Peace and Development Administration, whose aim was to consolidate government control over land
through expansion of mechanised farming, was in charge of the
peace villages. Although the Nuba Mountains and the peace villages
in which the government settled displaced Nuba were excluded from
OLS, some UN agencies provided assistance, including the UNDP's
Area Rehabilitation Scheme, which included WFP food-for-work
activities (WFP, 1988b; Karim et al., 1996: 262). In South Darfur,
displaced Dinka populations were paired with local agricultural
settlements and had food rations cut once they were judged able
to produce food. Rather than improving self-reliance, this strategy
meant that displaced people from the south became integrated into
the local economy as a cheap agricultural labour force (Macrae et
al., 1997). According to Karim et al. (1996), in the 1990s Sudan's
'actually existing development' process was linked to its war aims
and relied on forced displacement and resettlement, and on exploitative labour relations.

Despite the government's ideological stance against it, food aid
was also a key source of foreign currency for Sudan's Central Bank.
For most of the 1990s, contracts could only be in Sudanese currency
and foreign currency was held by the Bank of Sudan. According to
Khartoum-based transporters, the government was able to take huge
amounts of money from the aid agencies in this way; one estimated
that 70% of the money brought in went to the Central Bank. The
government also benefited because from the start of Al-Bashir's
regime many transport companies were linked with, or owned by,
government ministers or their relatives, while others found it increasingly difficult to operate. In 1991, for example, SC-UK gave contracts
for transporting food aid to parastatals and unwittingly to a company
owned by a serving Islamist MP. The operation faced serious delays
and failed to deliver to remote areas, and deliveries sometimes only
took place after the promise of increased payments (SC-UK Darfur,
1991). From the mid-1990s, local purchase of food aid formed
another source of hard currency for the Sudan government, as agencies mostly had to purchase using unfavourable official exchange
rates. Some traders could have dollar contracts, which gave them an
advantage as they could import materials and equipment essential
for their business (the only reason for which dollar withdrawal from
the bank was allowed). Different rules applied for different traders.
Sudan's biggest grain trader had dollar contracts from 1998, whereas
another grain trader, whom I interviewed, could only have dollar
contracts from 2012 (Informants 40, 46 and 54, 2013).

The Sudan government's encouragement of local food aid purchase indicates a change in government strategy, from rejecting food aid on ideological grounds to manipulating it for its own political and economic ends. Government arguments against international food aid became couched in the language of aid agencies: for example, that imported food aid would undermine local production and create dependency, whereas local purchase would support local farmers and create work for displaced populations. One aid worker explains:

> when the government found they are looking ugly, they are
> looking unprofessional, in their fight they write that they
> [international agencies] are doing harm to the producers. At the
> beginning they are just saying no – there is a food gap and we
> can address that issue. When they found that this argument is not
> going to work very well, they changed the debate from this to say
> that actually you are harming the producers and they start to use
> the internationally recognised language. (Informant 26, 2012)

With pressure from the Sudan government and from aid agencies, DFID and the EC approved local purchase of food aid as a response to the 1996/97 food crisis. The government suggested that grain be purchased from stocks held by the Agricultural Bank of Sudan or from parastatals, but donors refused on the grounds that the government should already be distributing its own stocks (DFID, 1997). It took six months to agree on open tenders, by which time the price of sorghum was extremely high (SC-UK, 1997). According to one informant, the grain from the ABS was in fact sold to the private (but government-linked) company which got the contract. Local purchase for another Darfur relief operation, in 2001, raised similar issues:

> Late recognition of the problem will lead donors to purchase
> locally (no time to organise shipments from overseas) which in
> turn ensures that the large mechanised *dura* [sorghum] producers
> of eastern Sudan and the Khartoum-based merchants find a
> ready market for their grain, and at high prices. Transporters, a
> key constituency of the regime – and often so closely linked to
> the grain merchants as to be nearly indistinguishable – secure
> handsome trucking contracts when relief operations are organised
> on an emergency basis (moreover, during the hunger gap and
> then the rains, transporters are likely to find goods to haul back

from the west, namely Darfur and Kordofan livestock sold at
a discount). Finally, when the humanitarian situation becomes
so dire, and the rains make land transport so difficult, that
'something has to be done', donors and aid agencies will resort to
airlifts, using local air transport companies. (Tanner, 2002: 28)

The 2001 relief operation for Darfur was indeed delayed so much
that a government-linked company[9] was contracted to transport part
of the food aid by air. In each food aid operation since the mid-1980s,
the alternative function of food aid in the livelihoods regime has
been to support grain trading and transport companies close to the
regime. These economic motivations came to prevail over the ideological resistance to international food aid towards the end of the
1990s. In the south, in contrast, the economic support that food aid
gave to the rebel movements was viewed as undermining the government, which is discussed in the following section.

Operation Lifeline Sudan: suspicions of food aid as rebel support

OLS, the operation to provide food aid to war-affected populations
in Sudan in the 1990s and early 2000s, presents a unique period in
the history of aid in the country. It is remembered by the international community as a heroic programme, in which the UN for the
first time negotiated access to all war-affected populations during
a situation of ongoing internal conflict, and in which it was able to
provide assistance based on humanitarian principles of neutrality,
impartiality and transparency. Government officials, in contrast,
view the early 1990s as the time when international food aid became
highly politicised, and OLS as a programme that supported southern
Sudan's rebel movements and which may have ultimately led to the
secession of the south.

OLS originated in the international community's failed response
to the 1988 famine in Bahr Al-Ghazal. Although it was officially
initiated in 1989, President Al-Bashir's regime, which started shortly
after the establishment of OLS, renewed obstruction of relief to
the south. However, growing international pressure and a greater
willingness by Western donors to circumvent sovereignty following
the end of the Cold War meant that by 1992 OLS included food
distributions almost equal in size to the response to the 1985 famine
(Keen, 1994: 204; Karim et al., 1996: 15).

Government officials interviewed for this research repeated
views on OLS similar to those expressed to the OLS review team
in 1996.[10] First, they argued that the Sudan government was unique

in allowing food aid to go to rebel areas, therefore establishing its humanitarian credentials. As a former Relief Commissioner stated: 'I believe for the first time in aid, we got the concept of food going to both antagonists. Usually each party deprives the other of aid, but here the Sudan government agrees that food aid should go to the rebels' (Informant 22, 2012). Second, they considered that food aid and the NGOs distributing it supported the rebel movements. The high numbers of NGOs coming to Sudan to work in the south was a cause for grave concern to the government (Informants 19 and 22, 2012), as expressed by both the 1986 RRC commissioner and the Director-General of the Humanitarian Aid Commission in 2014:

[NGOs were] continuously increasing and that is why I say, this government started to get worried. There was a stampede of foreign agencies. These agencies, they were really worried about them. Q: But worried exactly about what? ... A: Their airplanes were carrying rebels, and [they were] suspected of carrying weapons and [of] financing the rebels [from] part from the aid that was allowed to go through. (Informant 22, 2012)

In 1989 a major change happened [with OLS] whereby the food can go to all. ... [But] food can be really used as – maybe not intended – prolonging the life of the war. Yes, in papers ... it was neutrally distributed, it was just for the civilian ... but the gunholders are part of the family. They are part of the people. In areas ... [the rebels] control, agencies distribute, ... they can confiscate the food from the civilians. (Informants 96, 2014)

From the early 1990s, the Sudan government considered US food aid to be a weapon intended to undermine it and to support the southern movements (Informants 17 and 20, 2012). As discussed in Chapter 2, the diversion of aid by rebel movements was also a key concern of international aid agencies, but despite the attempts of aid agencies to minimise the negative impacts of food aid, the government maintained that INGOs supported the southern rebel movements. A former RRC commissioner further questioned the neutrality of INGOs because he could see that staff moved between embassies (donors) and INGOs (Informant 17, 2012). A similar accusation was made by the OLS review about Sudanese NGOs: that NGO staff would later take up government positions (Karim et al., 1996: 98). One former Relief Commissioner was explicit about the use of local NGOs as political tools (Informant 17, 2012).

The third point repeatedly made in 1996 and in 2012/13 was that OLS focused only on relief whereas what was needed was development. One Relief Commissioner concluded in his own review of OLS:

> The international community through OLS wanted to impose itself by using human rights but in fact they assist through giving food and very small interventions for rehabilitation, without giving any attention to food security. And OLS did not solve the problem of food deficiency for thirteen years, for those who are affected by war. There is no food security in the area. (Khalifa, 2006)

Not surprisingly, the shift to developmental relief was perceived very positively by the HAC Commissioner from 1998 to 2003, although he also complained that the response remained largely food aid (Informant 41, 2013). As seen in Chapter 2, in the context of limited development funding, developmental approaches to food security usually meant greater food aid targeting and linking food aid to production.

Government suspicion of international agencies led to very different operating environments for agencies working under OLS in opposition-controlled areas in southern Sudan and those working in the north and in government-controlled areas of the south. In opposition-controlled areas, agencies had relative ease of access and movement as the government had ceded part of its sovereignty to the UN, which took responsibility for regulating aid and international agencies. In the north, however, the government tightly controlled INGOs (Karim et al., 1996). Given the Sudan government's mistrust of international aid agencies, why did it allow relative freedom of access in the rebel-held south? According to the OLS review, donors were able to exert pressure through negotiation and persuasion because the Sudan government could see that the alternative might be military operations like the ones in Iraq and Somalia. However, the negotiated access strategy still allowed the government to deny access, which it did increasingly from 1995. Some of the areas worst affected by conflict, such as Bahr Al-Ghazal, did not receive relief until 1992 and only erratically after that (Karim et al., 1996: 79). The denial of relief flights in early 1998 was a major causal factor of the famine in South Sudan in 1998 (Human Rights Watch, 1998). Another reason might be that in fact many of the aid resources under OLS went to the north. From 1989 to 1993, estimated needs for the north were much higher than for the south (Karim et al., 1996: 132).

The Sudanese treasury would have gained substantially from the aid operation. According to Duffield (1994a), the government made half its military budget from OLS in 1989.

The price of relative freedom of movement for international agencies in the south was government control over aid going to war-affected populations in the north and to government-held areas in the south. The government was able to exclude the Nuba Mountains (in South Kordofan) from OLS, despite it being war-affected and despite large-scale displacement from the area. The government determined war-affected areas by inclusion, or exclusion, in joint government and aid agency assessments, which in turn determined the assistance provided. A relief policy in 1991 made relief the property of RRC-led local relief committees, thus asserting government control over distribution (Relief and Rehabilitation Commission, 1991). INGOs were controlled through a country agreement, which committed them to a move from relief to development, to limit the number of international staff and to twin with government and Sudanese NGOs. International staff had to obtain permits to travel anywhere in Sudan, with permission to access displaced camps being particularly difficult to obtain (Karim et al., 1996: 97). From 1996, government control over food aid and aid agencies in the north was increased with the transformation of RRC into HAC. HAC incorporated the Commission for Voluntary Agencies (COVA) and RRC. COVA had been responsible for the registration of NGOs and was set up in 1994 following the establishment of Country Agreements. While HAC is responsible for the regulation of all humanitarian aid in Sudan, food aid is unique in that there is no other government body which deals with food aid (other sectors are coordinated by the relevant ministries). In contrast with RRC, HAC has only Sudanese staff. Some of its staff represent Sudan's security apparatus, thus reflecting the greater emphasis placed on international agencies, and food aid, as matters of national security.

During the 1980s and 1990s, the livelihoods regime in Sudan was characterised first by international agencies undermining government food distribution mechanisms and by the government response to control international food aid and the agencies that provided it. It was also characterised by the increasing importance of the economic and political benefits of emergency food for the government and its closely associated private sector. The provision of food aid to war-affected populations in the rebel-held areas of the south was crucial in influencing the transformation to the resilience regime, in which the government severely restricted access by international agencies and established its own food aid apparatus. This is discussed in the following section.

Control over international agencies and the Sudanisation of food aid

From the early 2000s, following a brief period of easy access to war-affected populations in Darfur, the movements of international NGOs were closely controlled and many were expelled. In contrast with the 1990s, the donor community was unable to successfully challenge the denial of access. The Sudan government completed its control over food aid by establishing its own food aid apparatus for distribution to populations affected by conflict and disasters from 2011 onwards, thus keeping the international community out. As stated by the Director-General of HAC: '[the government has learnt] from experience in southern Sudan and Darfur. The government in South Kordofan and Blue Nile, right from day one developed strategies to ensure that food aid is provided and led by the government' (Informants 96, 2014). The resilience regime in Sudan is characterised by restricted access, by international agencies' remote management and by the government's control over international food aid and the establishment of its own food aid apparatus. Access to war-affected populations was progressively denied, followed by a review of the elements of Sudan's own food aid apparatus, and how the economic benefits for traders and transporters changed during the 2000s.

Denial of access in Darfur, Kordofan and Blue Nile

Humanitarian access to conflict-affected populations was problematic throughout the Darfur crisis of the 2000s. It was not until May 2004 that humanitarian agencies were able to access Darfur, a full year after the start of the conflict. Rather than intervene militarily to stop the conflict, Western governments demanded that the Sudan government facilitate the delivery of aid and disarm the Janjaweed (government-aligned militia). They imposed an arms embargo and offered support for the AU protection force (Williams and Bellamy, 2005). From July 2004, the Sudan government agreed to a fast-track procedure for international NGO travel permits to Darfur (Humanitarian Aid Commission, 2009). A brief period of relative ease of humanitarian access followed; the number of staff working for INGOs increased massively from 228 in April 2004 to 13,500 in August 2005 (WFP, 2006). WFP achieved unprecedented access in its food distribution, but access in terms of information was uneven, as indicated by the drawn-out battles between WFP and HAC over assessments. The HAC Commissioner insisted on the FEA but WFP wanted to use its new quantitative food security assessment methodology. In the end, WFP agreed to organise FEA training in places other than Darfur, and HAC agreed to WFP assessments in Darfur. HAC, however, was reluctant to sign up to the results (Informant 1, 2012), which delayed the release of assessment findings and therefore WFP's response. From 2006, international agency access to areas held by rebels who did not sign the successive peace agreements became progressively more difficult (see Chapter 4). Attacks on aid workers also increased from 2006. By October 2008, the UN estimated that it could only reach 65% of the affected population, most of whom were in towns and IDP camps. International agencies had been unable to access rural areas for some time and had established mechanisms for remotely managing their programmes (Pantuliano et al., 2009: 8). From 2010, state ministries and local NGOs collected the data for many of WFP's assessments.

In March 2009, the International Criminal Court (ICC) indicted President Al-Bashir for genocide, crimes against humanity and war crimes, and issued a warrant for his arrest. This immediately led the government to revoke the registration certificates of thirteen INGOs and three local NGOs, accusing them of involvement in activities that violated their humanitarian mandates and threatened national security, for instance by cooperating with the ICC, false reporting and advocating with the international community and the UN Security Council for more pressure on Sudan (Humanitarian Aid Commission, 2009: 4). Many of the expelled agencies were involved in protection, food aid and livelihoods activities. For those that remained, access got worse – including for the UN. WFP, for example, was not able to gain access to people displaced by government aerial bombing in the rebel stronghold of Jebel Marra in 2010. From 2011, access to rebel-held areas was almost non-existent. Access in Darfur is further discussed in Chapter 4. International agency access to war-affected populations in South Kordofan and Blue Nile has been almost impossible. Neither WFP nor ICRC has been able to negotiate access to populations on both sides of the conflict and in May 2012 WFP finally accepted that it would work only in government-held areas with the Sudan Red Crescent as partner (Informant 16, 2012; Informant 5, 2013). ICRC decided to keep its operations small (Informant 58, 2013). Despite an agreement to allow access to rebel-held areas, the government has been reluctant to include the

Sudan People's Liberation Movement-North in negotiations because this would confer legitimacy on the movement. In practice, the government continues to place obstacles in the way of access for the implementation of relief programmes (Alertnet, 2012; Informant 72, 2013). The Sudan government expelled more agencies and agency staff in 2012, 2013 and 2014. In 2012, seven agencies were expelled from east Sudan, and in July 2013 twenty UNHCR staff working in Darfur did not have their residence permits renewed (Sudan Tribune, 2012, 2013). The limited response from the international community was due to the fear that challenging the government would lead to further restrictions. In January 2014, the government suspended the activities of the International Red Cross (ICRC Resource Centre, 2014) and in November of the same year two senior UNDP officials (the UN Resident Coordinator and UNDP Country Director) were asked to leave Sudan (Reuters, 2014).

The government's ability to deny access, and UN and donor acceptance of this denial, has parallels with the 1980s, the context of Cold War politics and the 1988 Bahr Al-Ghazal famine, of which Keen wrote:

> While problems of access were significant …, the most
> fundamental cause of the lack of relief distributions was the
> low priority attached to relieving famine by various levels of
> the Sudanese administration. Blaming problems of 'access'
> was a classic escape route, by means of which government and
> international donor officials were able to avoid blame from
> potentially critical elements of Sudanese and international
> opinion; at the same time, blaming 'access' problems appears to
> have narrowed the room for manoeuvre towards improving these
> relief outcomes. (Keen, 1994: 139)

In the 1990s, donors, the UN or INGOs would have challenged the government's denial of access. Instead, from 2009 onwards, WFP and other UN agencies aligned themselves with the government to maintain at least some access, aiming to 'empower the government and its people' to find solutions to food insecurity (WFP Sudan, 2013: 2), and INGOs largely continue to remain silent or leave.[11] According to the Darfur chief peace negotiator for the rebel movements, the recent decrease in food aid to Darfur and halting of food aid to rebel-held areas has been brought up many times during the peace process but with little response (Informant 101, 2015). There appear to be a number of reasons for the lack of a coherent donor response to the Sudan government's policy of access denial. First, the WoT has split donors and Sudan is seen both as an enemy Islamist state and as a provider of intelligence information. Second, during the early years of the Darfur conflict donors felt that tackling the government over its conduct in Darfur would jeopardise the peace agreement with southern Sudan. Third, Chinese economic interests in Sudan have led to the watering down of Security Council resolutions (Williams and Bellamy, 2005; Traub, 2010). In 2013 and 2014, in interviews for this study, donor representatives commented that they could not negotiate with an indicted war criminal and that lack of access leads to a Catch-22 situation where the lack of information (because of access denials) makes it difficult to argue for access based on the severity of the crisis (Informant 72, 2013; Informant 95 and Informants 98, 2014). This is especially the case when travel permits are denied to donor humanitarian staff on the basis that there is no emergency (Informant 28, 2013). In 2017, however, the US made lifting of sanctions conditional on improved humanitarian access and progress towards peace, highlighting that political pressure is possible but had not been a priority in the ten preceding years. What has changed in recent years is a greater involvement by Sudan in regional efforts in the fight against terrorism, particularly in Yemen. In parallel, the EU has made an agreement with the Sudan government to stem migration to Europe (PAX, 2016). In eight years, the indictment by the ICC has not led to the arrest of President Al-Bashir or the other government officials indicted for war crimes, crimes against humanity and genocide. President Al-Bashir has been able to visit neighbouring countries such as Chad, Kenya, Djibouti, Malawi and the Democratic Republic of the Congo without fear of arrest. In December 2014, the ICC prosecutor shelved the investigation into war crimes in Darfur due to lack of action by the UN Security Council in pushing for arrests (World Bulletin, 2014). The recent US and EU initiatives have further normalised the ongoing violence and human rights abuses in Sudan.

To conclude, compared with its brief period of autonomy during the negotiated access phase of the 1990s, the resilience regime of practices sees the UN once again conforming to the authority of the Sudanese state. The Sudan government's actions to restrict access were part of its response to the livelihoods regime of practices, in which international food aid was thought to support rebel movements in South Sudan. The other characteristic of the resilience regime was the establishment of Sudan's own food aid apparatus. This is discussed in the next section.

National NGOs, the strategic grain reserve and government food aid

While the ability of the government to restrict humanitarian access with impunity resembles the situation in the 1980s, in the intervening years it has developed its own food aid infrastructure and ability to respond by establishing a national strategic grain reserve, national NGOs and its own emergency food distribution apparatus. At local level, Sudan's food aid apparatus includes a network of Popular Committees that distribute food at town and village levels. This section discusses the Sudan government's food aid practices at national level and Chapter 4 will analyse local-level practices in Darfur.

According to government officials, the Sudanisation of aid began as early as 1988, following the 'invasion' of international NGOs during the 1985 famine, with the aim of handing over the distribution of relief to local NGOs (Informants 17 and 22, 2012). This was formalised in the first half of 1990, when the Sudan government issued a policy paper on the future of INGOs in the country, which introduced the concept of twinning them with local NGOS. At the time it was not clear whether twinning meant INGOs merely being funders or also implementers, but donors stipulated that INGOs had to retain control of international food aid (Williams, 1992). In the 1991 relief operation, Oxfam paired with the Islamic African Relief Agency and SC-UK was already working closely with Darfur's State Food Security Committee. Despite the discontinuation of twinning, Sudanese NGOs continued to grow and by the mid-1990s some had budgets and staff levels equal to or greater than those of INGOs (Karim et al., 1996). After the expulsion of thirteen INGOs from Darfur in 2009, President Al-Bashir announced that aid would be Sudanised. National NGOs took over much of the work of the expelled INGOs. In North Darfur, for example, the food distribution previously carried out by Action Contre La Faim (as WFP's implementing partner) was taken over by the Sudan Red Crescent and Africa Humanitarian Action (an African NGO). German Agro Action entered into new arrangements with local NGOs. Key elements of Sudanisation appear to be the requirements that INGOs should employ mainly Sudanese staff and work with local partners. When interviewed in 2014, the Director-General of HAC explained that he saw Sudanisation as Sudanese taking the initiative for intervention and responsibility for end delivery, while international staff could monitor (Informants 96, 2014). To a large extent, this was already happening in Darfur during the resilience regime, except that international staff were not always able to monitor (see Chapter 4).

The establishment of the national strategic grain reserve has been an essential component of the Sudanisation of food aid. A local strategic grain reserve was first attempted in the late 1980s in response to the Western-dominated relief operation in 1985; this was managed by the Agricultural Bank of Sudan and had the aim of acting as a buffer against crop failures and stabilising the market. It was a direct response to dependence on Western food aid. Until 2001, however, action on the national strategic reserve consisted of a number of ad hoc initiatives involving the ABS and the Ministry of Finance (MoF). The ABS was responsible for a national reserve until 1992 when the Salvation government abandoned it as part of its economic liberalisation strategy. Severe food shortages in 1996/97, however, led to the resumption of an ABS-managed reserve, perhaps to provide a source for locally purchased food aid by international agencies (Elbashir and Ahmed, 2005; Asfaw and Ibrahim, 2008; Ahmed et al., 2012). It was not until 2001 that oil revenue provided the government with sufficient funds to establish the national Strategic Reserve Authority within the MoF, which was changed to the semi-autonomous Strategic Reserve Corporation the same year. By 2012, however, the reserve returned to the ABS as spoilage of food and seeds, and accusations of corruption, led to the dissolution of the corporation. The quantity of cereal held in the reserve in 2011 and 2012 was just over 350,000 MT (Buchanan-Smith et al., 2014). The objectives of the reserve still include price stabilisation and acting as a purchase and sale agent, but in the 2000s it was also used to provide humanitarian assistance (Asfaw and Ibrahim, 2008; Informants 21, 2012). It has been used in Darfur, South Kordofan and Blue Nile to provide free or subsidised food aid to emergency-affected populations. The reserve has also been used to provide subsidised feed for poultry farms close to Khartoum, Gezira and Kassala to maintain low meat prices for large urban populations (Informant 50, 2013). Low bread prices in Khartoum and other urban areas are now maintained through preferential exchange rates, whereby the Ministry of Commerce issues licences to commercial importers to import wheat at these rates. In 2013, wheat exchange rates were very favourable at 2.9 Sudanese pounds (SDG) to the dollar, compared with SDG 6.8 on the parallel market (Informant 46, 2013).

The national strategic reserve has not fulfilled its official function of buying grain when it is cheap and selling when it is expensive, which is in theory how it should achieve price stabilisation. In practice, the reserve usually does the opposite. It does not buy immediately after the harvest, which allows brokers and middlemen to buy grain cheaply from farmers and sell it at high prices to the reserve. Furthermore, its preferred method of deferred purchase gives advantages to banks and large traders (Ahmed et al., 2012; Informant 25, 2012). When Ahmed et al. (2012: 3) interviewed staff from the Strategic Reserve Corporation, the ABS and the MoF, and cereal farmers, they reported that the main constraints of the reserve were lack of administrative autonomy, poor financial resources, lack of clear purchasing and reserve policies, insufficient storage and unfair distribution because of social and political influences. All respondents said that the practices of the reserve harmed producers, forcing them to sell at low prices and to go into debt. The political use of the reserve also came out during some of my interviews: senior government officials can allocate food aid to particular areas or populations at any time (Informants 19 and 25, 2012; Informant 50, 2013). In South Kordofan and Blue Nile, government food aid is provided soon after the army captures an area, and beneficiaries include government staff (including the army) as well as other war-affected populations. The Sudan government's food aid strategies are remarkably similar to those established by the British colonial government between the 1920s and 1940s, when it provided free food aid for the military and civil servants, subsidised food for urban residents and sometimes made small distributions in rural areas (often intended as loans) in response to food shortages or famine (De Waal, 1989b). In addition, the Sudan government has learnt from US food aid policy and donates food from the reserve to neighbouring and strategically important countries, including Chad, Ethiopia and Somalia (Informant 50, 2013), as determined by presidential decree.

With the strategic reserve, Sudan had its own food aid and the government strove to make sure that distribution was done by Sudanese government structures or local NGOs. According to the current HAC Director-General, food aid was also provided from one state to another – for example, from Gedaref in eastern Sudan to Darfur. Other northern states have made donations for government food distributions in South Kordofan and Blue Nile (Informants 96, 2014). As mentioned earlier, HAC wants Sudanese institutions to be responsible for initiating and delivering aid. A key policy is to avoid camps, which according to government officials have contributed to long-term displacement and aid dependency, as well as the presence of large numbers of INGOs (Informant 24, 2012; Informants 96, 2014). Government food distributions are only done in government-held areas. HAC's Director-General explained that the rebel areas in South Kordofan and Blue Nile are surplus production areas where many wild foods are available, that people could move into government-held areas to receive food aid or that family members could collect food aid and send it across lines. The government has also been distributing food in response to natural disasters. In 2013, it distributed food aid in response to floods, using donations and funds from Qatar, Egypt and other Arab states as well as the UN. In this operation, HAC carried out the relief distribution, which – like international agencies – was monitored by Sudan's national security services, thus highlighting who is in control.

By 2010 international aid agencies had very little access to war-affected populations in Sudan. The Sudan government had established close control over international food aid and the agencies that provided it, and kept international agencies out of new war zones by distributing its own food aid. Sudan's own food aid apparatus provided food to soldiers, government staff and war-affected populations in government-held areas. Like international food aid, the national strategic reserve brought profits for brokers and large cereal traders in central Sudan, which, as the next section shows, was partly supported by WFP.

Benefits for traders and transporters

The large quantities of international food aid provided during the Darfur crisis had huge benefits for traders and transporters. The nature of this was different from earlier food distributions in Sudan as delays due to trader and transporter actions were less frequent; few were prepared to risk losing large contracts with WFP by delaying deliveries or dropping food in easily accessible places to make a quick profit. In the 2000s, delays in food deliveries to Darfur were more likely to be caused by numerous checkpoints, insecurity and the need for security escorts and security clearance, as well as poor infrastructure, particularly during the rainy season. WFP had contracts with about 100 transporters in 2012, thus indirectly making a substantial contribution to the local economy (WFP, 2013a: 192). As one transporter commented: 'Darfur was a historical development of the transport fleet in Sudan' (Informant 36, 2013).

WFP provided direct support to three main Khartoum-based transport companies because, in 2004, it found itself competing for transport with the oil industry and could not get sufficient logistical capacity for the size of the operation (WFP, 2006). As a solution, WFP invited expressions of interest from existing transport companies to increase their capacity, offering to provide collateral for bank

loans. In this way, WFP built up three already large transport companies: Kiir, Rieba (part of the Nefeidi group) and Abarci. Each was
able to increase its fleet of trucks; Rieba bought 120 trucks specifically for Darfur and Abarci increased its truck fleet almost ten-fold
(Informant 36, 2013; Informant 49, 2013a).[12] WFP contracts enabled
traders and transporters to expand inside and outside of Sudan. The
largest grain trader established an international company which has
contracts with WFP Rome to supply white sorghum, and now exports
food to Somalia, South Sudan and West Africa. The majority of
Sudan's strategic reserve was bought by WFP Rome in 2012 via this
company. Abarci also transports food aid to Chad, Ethiopia, Kenya
and the Democratic Republic of the Congo (Informant 49, 2013a).

When WFP purchased food aid locally, it did so mainly from
one or two large traders with access to the government's Strategic
Reserve because they were the most reliable suppliers (Informant
31, 2013). WFP could not deal with farmers directly but had to go
through traders in Sudan. It could not purchase from the Reserve
either, because this required upfront payment for the total amount
purchased, which WFP procedures did not allow. The government
in turn encouraged traders to purchase from the Reserve. According
to one trader:

> They [the government] have a policy; if there is a tender [from
> WFP], if you go for it and there is stock in the reserve, it is
> better not to enter the market, as this will increase the prices.
> The policy is that it is better to buy from the reserve. They
> always have reasonable prices so you can make a bigger profit.
> (Informant 46, 2013)

As the Reserve actually benefits brokers, large traders and banks
(see previous section), WFP purchases have reinforced this trend.

To encourage the local purchase of food aid by WFP and ICRC in
Sudan, the government loosened the restrictions on dollar contracts.
Agencies could sign contracts with traders in dollars, making Sudan
traders more competitive on the international market and thus
making it more likely that WFP and other aid agencies would buy in
Sudan. For most traders, however, it was difficult to keep large stocks
in case of future demand, or offer to use the exchange rate most
favourable to WFP, because of the unpredictability of government
policy, thus keeping the cost of food aid high (Informants 40, 46 and
54, 2013). Although food aid volumes for Darfur reduced from 2006
onwards, the large traders and transporters have by now established

international companies and are not reliant on the Darfur crisis for their business.

Conclusions

The efforts of international aid agencies and donors have supported the state-led exclusionary development process and addressed its consequences with emergency food distributions in Sudan's peripheries. International food aid practices from the mid-1980s – the livelihoods regime – led to government actions to take back control over food aid and the agencies that provided it. It achieved this in the 2000s, when Sudan government control over international agencies and its own food aid apparatus characterised the resilience regime of practices. All food aid, including emergency food aid, indirectly supported the government and private sector in central Sudan. The state has adopted some of the practices of international aid agencies and has developed its own food aid apparatus modelled on that of international food aid. It appears, therefore, that food aid has contributed to Sudan's protracted food emergency as well as trying to address it.

Throughout its history, food aid has been politically controversial in Sudan, but also necessary for economic and security reasons. The first programme and project food aid were controversial because they affected Sudan's relations with Egypt and widened divisions between political parties in Sudan. Divisions over food aid contributed to riots, demonstrations and the overthrow of governments, including a military coup in 1958 and a popular uprising in 1974 during the state support regime. Programme food aid at the same time provided economic support, formed the basis of an urban bread subsidy and released funds through the sale of food aid to support the infrastructure necessary for irrigated farming along the Nile. Project food aid similarly supported development in central Sudan, although some distributions took place in the south. Emergency food aid helped contain the security threats posed by large numbers of refugees but also had the effect of letting a number of international agencies take over part of the welfare functions of the state and starting the shift towards the livelihoods regime in Sudan.

From the perspective of the Sudan government, the three regimes of practices were characterised by state-support, a struggle for control of food aid and the agencies which provided it, and government control. The livelihoods regime in the late 1980s and early

1990s was a period of intense struggle between international food aid agencies and the Sudan government. The government managed to keep control throughout most of the 1984/85 international famine response (most food aid stayed in urban areas), but INGOs took control in 1986, causing resentment and concern in central government. In the early 1990s, the government resisted emergency food aid because it conflicted with the self-sufficiency aims of the Islamist regime, causing a stand-off between the government and aid agencies during the 1991 famine. Government resistance was heightened with Operation Lifeline Sudan and the support that food aid gave to rebel movements. This resistance was a key factor in causing the transformation to the resilience regime of practices, where international agencies had little access to war-affected populations. Throughout the 1980s and 1990s, the manipulation of food aid was an important part of the political economy of Sudan by bringing in hard currency and lucrative contracts for traders and transporters, and subsidising local government through diversions. Over the course of the livelihoods regime, these economic benefits came to outweigh the political objections, particularly if the government could effectively control the agencies providing international food aid.

During the resilience regime, while aid agencies became more remote, the Sudan government used its knowledge of international food aid operations to Sudanise the food aid industry and take control of food aid. This included the development of its own 'non-governmental' infrastructure as well as a strategic grain reserve, and limiting the actions of, and access by, international NGOs and UN agencies. It has systematically adopted the language and strategies of Western agencies for its own purposes, for example the idea of moving from relief to development and local purchase to support local farmers. Furthermore, food aid has enabled the government to contain the protracted emergency in its peripheries whilst at the same time experiencing a period of economic growth in the centre. The following chapter looks at the effect that international and government food aid strategies have actually had on people in North Darfur, one of the areas of Sudan that has received food aid almost continuously since the mid-1980s.

4
The effects of food aid practices in North Darfur

North Darfur is geographically remote and politically and economically marginalised from Sudan's centre. Its population has suffered
repeated drought, famine and – most recently – violent conflict
resulting in large-scale destruction, displacement and reduced
access to land, work and markets for particular political or ethnic
groups. Since the 1980s, North Darfur has received emergency
food aid almost continuously but usually far less than the estimated
needs. As for Sudan generally, food aid has been the main form of
international aid. As a consequence, most people in Darfur have
experienced impoverishment and an increasingly severe permanent
emergency over the past thirty years. The last national nutritional
survey (done in 2013) showed North Darfur to have the highest
prevalence of acute malnutrition in the country.[1] It is one of the
most food-insecure places in Sudan.

Darfur received almost no international food aid during the state
support regime. For much of the livelihoods regime, in the 1980s and
1990s, food deliveries were insufficient, delayed and not targeted at
those most in need. It rarely had the intended effect of supporting
livelihoods. At the same time, Darfuri aid workers became experts
in assessment, targeting and food distribution. They, rather than
local government, came to represent crisis-affected and impoverished communities and lobbied government and donors to provide
assistance. Local government distributed some food and made a
number of attempts to establish state-level grain reserves. Government priorities have, however, been to feed government employees
and urban populations.

The first years of the humanitarian response to the Darfur conflict,
from 2004 to 2006, can be seen as the peak of the livelihoods regime.
For the first time, food aid met its intended objectives of improving
nutrition and supporting livelihoods. Food aid maintained cereal
markets in Darfur, provided an income for traders and transporters,
and increased the personal safety of conflict-affected populations
as they did not have to look for food or work in areas that might
expose them to attack. However, food aid also fed into the dynamics
of the conflict. Most food aid initially went to the camps, where it

supported a new leadership which sometimes promoted the political agenda of the rebellion. Arab nomadic populations, some of whom fought on the government side, were excluded. When aid agencies later reduced food aid, this converged with government priorities to empty the camps and defeat the rebellion.

From 2008 onwards, food aid practices were those of the resilience regime and became progressively more remote. Humanitarian access (including for food convoys) decreased as a result of risks to aid workers, government restrictions and a range of formal and informal taxes and fees to move food. Aid agencies switched to food vouchers, food-for-recovery and specialised feeding programmes, and reduced overall levels of assistance. This supported government strategies of denying aid to rebel-held areas and facilitated the use of government food aid to gain political support. Only large traders have continued to benefit from food aid. By 2013, the government was largely in control of who received food aid, when and where. Conflict-affected people had to rely on a limited and militarised range of coping strategies or leave Darfur.

This chapter starts with an overview of the history of drought, famine and conflict in Darfur. The bulk of the chapter then analyses the effect of food aid practices in North Darfur during the livelihoods and resilience regimes, and whether people were 'coping' in terms of protecting their livelihoods or becoming resilient. It uses information from interviews conducted in Darfur and Khartoum, as well as aid agency project reports and evaluations. I carried out interviews in Al-Fashir, the capital of North Darfur. Some interviews are not cited as informants could potentially be identified through cross-referencing. In 2013, Al-Fashir was home to three camps for displaced populations – Zamzam, Abou Shook and As Salaam – each with displaced populations from different parts of Darfur (see Map 4.1). I interviewed groups from each. Some of the displaced people I interviewed came from Jebel Si, an area mostly in rebel hands. The chapter also uses information from interviews with people from Malha and Kuma in north-east Darfur. In Kuma, the Arab nomadic pastoral population was drawn into the conflict on the government side. The population of Malha are also pastoralists (but not Arab). The town is in government hands but part of the surrounding area is held by the Sudan Liberation Army (SLA).

Map 4.1: North Darfur, including areas with IDP concentrations

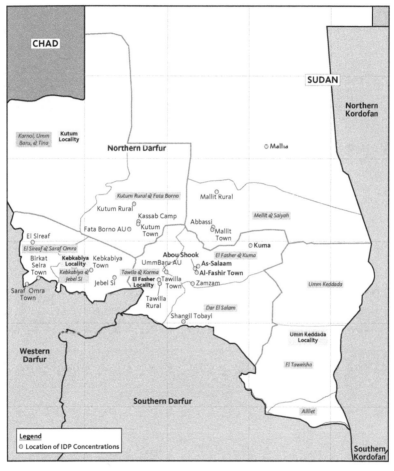

Source: Jaspars (2010).

Map 4.2: Tribal areas in Darfur

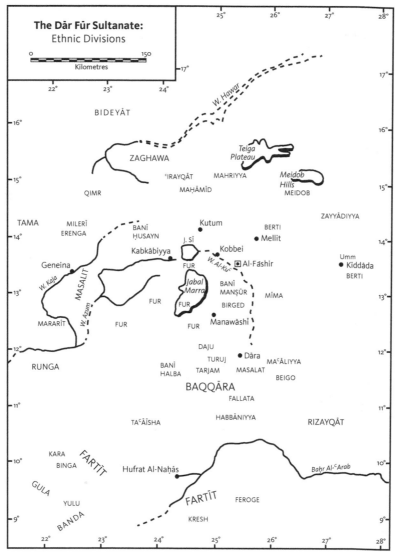

The Dâr Fûr Sultanate:
Ethnic Divisions

0 ——————— 150
Kilometres

BIDEYÂT

ZAGHAWA

Teiga
Plateau

ᶜIRAYQÂT   MAHRIYYA

QIMR   MAḤÂMÎD

Meidob
Hills
MEIDOB

ZAYYÂDIYYA

TAMA   MILERÎ
ERENGA

BANÎ
ḤUSAYN   Kutum   BERTI

J. SÎ   ● Mellit

Kabkâbiyya   Kobbei   Umm
● Kiddâda
Geneina   FUR   W. Al-Kuᶜ ▣ Al-Fâshir   BERTI

Jabal
Marra
FUR

MASALIT

W. Koja

W. Azum

BANÎ
MANṢÛR
FUR   MÎMA
FUR   BIRGED

MARARÎT   FUR   FUR   Manawàshî

DAJU
TURUJ   ● Dàra
BANÎ   MAᶜÂLIYYA
HALBA   TARJAM   MASALAT
RUNGA   BEIGO

BAQQÂRA

FALLATA

TAᶜÂÎSHA   HABBÂNIYYA   RIZAYQÂT

KARA
BINGA   Hufrat Al-Naḥâs

FARTÎT

GULA   Baḥr Al-ᶜArab

YULU   FARTÎT   FEROGE

BANDA   KRESH

Source: O'Fahey (2008).

Map 4.3: Darfur Region, showing North, West and South Darfur states

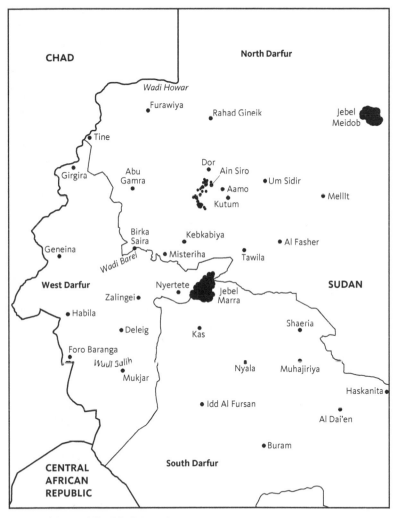

Source: Flint and De Waal (2008).

An overview of drought, famine and conflict in North Darfur

Darfur is located in the western part of Sudan and borders Chad in the west, Libya in the north and the Central African Republic and South Sudan in the south. Its huge size (similar to France) stretches from the Sahara desert in the far north to tropical savannah-lands in the south. The centre of Darfur is dominated by the Jebel Marra massif, which creates a zone of temperate climate suitable for a range of food crops. Livelihoods differ accordingly, with camel nomads in the far north, settled farmers and agro-pastoralists in the fertile centre and western part of Darfur and cattle nomads in the south. A number of tribes live in Darfur, with livelihoods and ethnicity closely linked; people can be assimilated into a new tribe as they migrate or change livelihood. Claims to Arab descent are an important part of the culture of the camel-herding Northern Rizeigat (Abbala Arabs)[2] and the southern cattle-herding Rizeigat (Baggara Arabs) (De Waal, 1989a; O'Fahey and Tubiana, 2007). Other camel nomads include the Zaghawa on the northern border with Chad and the Meidob and Zayyadia in the north-east – living in the Malha and Kuma areas respectively (Young et al., 2009). Settled farming tribes include the Fur in the centre of Darfur, the Masalit in the west and the Berti in the east (see Map 4.2). The Fur ruled Darfur in the years before the British conquest in 1916. 'Darfur' means 'the homeland of the Fur'.

The Fur Sultanate emerged around 1750 and at one stage ruled a territory extending as far as the Nile in the east and over much of what is now known as Chad in the west. Fur Sultans ruled over the territory of many other tribes, with tribal leaders responsible for defence and solidarity. They adopted Islam as the state religion. The Sultanate included the *hakura*, a system of land tenure, in which the Sultan granted administrative *hakura* to tribal leaders in exchange for minimal taxation; land was collectively owned and could be used by other tribes with the permission of the leader in exchange for customary dues. The land granted to tribal leaders was also known as *Dar*, meaning homeland; it effectively confirmed a particular group's communal ownership of land (Abdul-Jalil, 2006).[3] Under successive governments, colonial and independent, tribal leaders continued to be responsible for customary law, but their functions within local government changed and were progressively politicised. The British conquered Darfur in 1916,[4] annexed it to Sudan and established a system of native administration (or indirect rule) in which tribal leaders were responsible for administrative, judicial and police matters within their territories, specifically the allocation of land and the settlement of land disputes (Abdul-Jalil et al., 2007). The colonial government 'tidied up' the traditional governance system, which involved creating new tribal ranks (Omda or Nazir and Sheikh),[5] and linking tribal chieftaincies with Dars (Flint and De Waal, 2008: 11). Of central importance to the crisis in the 2000s was that the Northern Rizeigat were not allocated a Dar, as they were a smaller tribe who, being nomadic, did not need to own land at that time, and no Nazir was elected (Abdul-Jalil, 2006). The failure to resolve the political status of the Northern Rizeigat, and their subsequent economic and social marginalisation within Darfur, led to divisions and resentment, which the Sudan government and regional powers later used to foment division and conflict.

Darfur has a long history of famine. According to De Waal (1989a), a great famine occurred in the 1750s, largely as a result of the unequal social system and frequent wars fought by the Sultanate. From the 1800s to the early 1900s, conflict associated with conquests and rebellions caused major social upheaval and famine, with severe 'famines that killed' in 1888–92 and 1913–14 – the latter resulting from drought (De Waal, 1989a: 65). The worst famines were avoided during the period of colonial government because of relative stability, relief measures and, to some extent, the availability of agricultural work in central Sudan. In the first decades of Sudan's independence, Darfuris again avoided severe famines because family members could find work (now also on groundnut farms in southern Darfur), and the government provided assistance in response to food shortages (O'Brien, 1985; De Waal, 1989a, 1989b). Darfur experienced its first major famine since independence in 1984/85 as a result of drought, the country's failing economy and the collapse of local government. Further droughts and famines have occurred on a regular basis since: in 1987, 1990–91, 1993–94, 1996–97 and 2000–01, which was followed by a severe conflict-related humanitarian crisis from 2003 onwards.

The causes of conflict in Darfur include long-term marginalisation and neglect of Darfur by Sudan's governments, the marginalisation of Arab nomadic groups within Darfur and national and regional strategies of Arabisation, as well as drought and competition over resources. Colonial and independent governments prioritised development in Sudan's centre. At independence, Darfur had the least developed medical services in the country and only one intermediate school (Young et al., 2005). Subsequent governments also failed to provide health and education services in proportion to Darfur's population (Yongo-Bure, 2009). The capital of Darfur, Al-Fashir, is more than 1,200 km from Sudan's capital Khartoum and the two were not linked by tarmac road until 2014. Within Darfur, Arab nomadic groups were under-represented in local government because they did not control a Dar and received fewer services than others in Darfur (Young and Maxwell, 2013). From the 1980s onwards, Arab groups in Darfur demanded greater representation, which was boosted by regional and national strategies of Arabisation. During the 1970s, Libya's Colonel Gaddafi armed Arab nomads in Sudan and Muslims in Chad in his quest to Arabise the region and to oppose the Chadian government (Prunier, 2008). Libyan militia and the Chadian opposition set up bases in Darfur, using Darfuri Arabs as intermediaries. The Fur meanwhile, sought support from the Chadian government. With Fur and Arab both heavily armed, tensions over land and grazing between farmers and nomads in the droughts and famines of the 1970s and 1980s grew increasingly violent and led to the Arab–Fur war in central Darfur from 1987 to 1989 (Flint and De Waal, 2008; Prunier, 2008). From the mid-1990s, the Islamist regime favoured Arabs in government positions and started arming Arab militia. Chadian Arab nomads (often belonging to the same tribes as Darfuri nomads) were encouraged to settle in Darfur. In 1994, Darfur was split into three states (see Map 4.3), making the Fur a minority in each, and in West Darfur the government created new positions of *emir*, allocating five emirates in Dar Masalit to Arab leaders. This immediately led to conflict, in which the government armed Arab militia[6] to crush the Masalit uprising from 1995 to 1998. Zaghawa and Arab nomads also clashed over grazing and access to water sources, with violent conflict between 1999 and 2001 (Flint and De Waal, 2008).

An attack by the Sudan Liberation Army (SLA) on Golo in Jebel Marra in 2003 is usually taken as the start of the rebellion, but by this stage the SLA had already been attacking government outposts for some time and Jebel Marra was under heavy government attack (Flint and De Waal, 2008: 81). The Fur had pulled together a resistance movement in 1996, building on self-defence groups that had sprung up throughout Darfur in the 1980s and 1990s. They linked up with the Zaghawa in 2001 to form the Darfur Liberation Front (later SLA). Some of Sudan's key Islamists joined the rebellion in 1999, following Al-Bashir's ousting of Turabi (who had a large support base in Darfur) and formed the Justice and Equality Movement (JEM), the other key rebel movement at the start of the Darfur conflict. To quell the rebellion, the Sudanese government increased its strategy of arming a militia of Arab nomads, now known as the Janjaweed.

From 2003 onwards, the conflict escalated dramatically. As the SLA attacked government garrisons (including the army's air base in Al-Fashir in April 2003), and sometimes Arab groups, government forces and Janjaweed responded by destroying villages, looting, killing and ultimately displacing huge numbers of people. The scale and severity of government violence was such that the UN's Sudan Coordinator called it 'an organised attempt to do away with a group of people' (BBC, 2004). The level of sexual violence, including rape, was unprecedented. Darfur was the first emergency to be labelled a 'protection crisis', reflecting the recognition by the international community of its responsibility to protect civilians caught up in conflict[7] (Pantuliano and O'Callaghan, 2006). By early 2005, a large part of Darfur was destroyed, 2 million people had been displaced and 200,000 people had fled to Chad (Flint and De Waal, 2008: 145). Around 130,000 people were estimated to have died between September 2003 and January 2005 (Guha-Sapir and Degomme, 2005). A UN Commission of Inquiry on Darfur declared in January 2005 that the Sudan government and Janjaweed were responsible for serious violations of human rights and humanitarian law, and two months later the UN Security Council referred Darfur to the International Criminal Court (ICC).

During the twelve years of conflict, parts of Darfur experienced brief periods of relative stability, but people's access to land and markets remained limited and many living in the camps depended on precarious livelihood options such as brick-making and casual labour. Banditry, looting and informal taxes and fees imposed by government, militia and rebels increased over time. Movement outside of government-held towns or displaced people's camps, to farm, work or collect firewood, risked attack or rape. In parts of Darfur, Arab groups coerced farming communities to pay for 'protection' to access their land and markets. SLA-controlled areas were cut off from government health, education and agricultural services, traders needed permits to supply food, and access to markets and work in government towns were restricted. The conflict fundamentally altered trade in Darfur, as farmers had been displaced, movement restricted and livestock looted or sold in distress (Young et al., 2005; Buchanan-Smith and Jaspars, 2007). These factors considerably worsened the impact of drought in 2004, 2007, 2009 and 2013.

Peace agreements were made and failed. A ceasefire agreement in 2004 led to the deployment of an African Union Mission (AMIS), but violations were too numerous to monitor. In 2006, the Darfur Peace Agreement (DPA) was signed by the government and just one of the rebel movements, SLA-Minnawi. In 2005, the SLA had split along ethnic lines with the SLA-Minnawi retaining the Zaghawa support base and SLA-Abdel Wahid the Fur (Flint and De Waal, 2008). As part of the peace agreement, a UN peace-keeping role belatedly came into effect in 2007, when AMIS was replaced by UNAMID. UNAMID, however, had little more success in peace-keeping, protecting civilians or providing a secure environment for the delivery of relief (Jaspars and O'Callaghan, 2008; Kahn, 2008). In the meantime, the nature of the conflict changed. Splits in the SLA, the JEM and Arab militia led to an increase in localised conflict. Arab militia splintered over 'peace agreements' in which Khartoum had agreed to disarm the militia. Also, their livelihoods were in crisis; their migration routes were blocked and rural markets collapsed (Flint, 2009). New tribes were drawn into the conflict, banditry and looting increased, Chadian rebel groups and refugees came to Darfur, and IDP camps became increasingly politicised. Attacks on aid workers increased, making nearly half a million conflict-affected people inaccessible (International Crisis Group, 2007).

In 2011, the government and the Liberation and Justice Movement (LJM) signed the Doha Document for Peace in Darfur (DDPD). The LJM was formed as an umbrella for minority factions for the peace negotiations. The DDPD led to the formation of the Darfur Regional Authority (DRA) and the Darfur Recovery and Reconstruction Plan. The Sudan government and UNAMID declared that the war was essentially over. The major rebel movements had not signed up to the DDPD, but their position was weakened because they lost support from Chad and Libya after the normalisation of relations between Chad and Sudan and regime change in Libya (Tubiana, 2011). At the same time, a new surge of violence caused large-scale displacement in East, South and North Darfur. Government-armed new non-Arab proxies in Eastern Darfur and SLA-Minnawi withdrew from the DPA in 2010 (Human Rights Watch, 2011; Gramizzi and Tubiana, 2012).

The years after 2013 saw further escalation of conflict, including over resources between herders and farmers and between IDPs and Arab militia, and an increase in attacks by government paramilitary forces. In the face of crop failure, militia and herder attacks on farmers and displaced populations increased (Radio Dabanga, 2013a, 2013b, 2013c, 2013e). In the gold-mining area of Jebel Amer in North Darfur, battles took place in early 2013 between Arab militia and government forces, displacing many of the inhabitants. In late 2013, the government launched the Rapid Support Forces

(RSF), a new elite and highly trained paramilitary group that incorporated some of the Janjaweed militia,[8] who attacked, destroyed and looted villages in North and South Darfur throughout 2014 (Radio Dabanga, 2014a).[9] The total number of newly displaced people in 2013, at 460,000, was more than double that in the previous two years (UN Security Council, 2014). Over 1 million people were newly displaced between 2013 and 2015, many as a consequence of RSF actions (UN OCHA, 2014a, 2015). Many of my Darfuri key informants considered that 2014 was as bad as it was in the early years of the conflict in terms of attacks, destruction and displacement. Violence, destruction and displacement continued in 2015 and 2016, now also including aerial bombardments of Jebel Marra in central Darfur. By early 2017, 3.3 million people were still considered in need of assistance in Darfur (UN OCHA, 2017).

Food aid in response to drought and famine (the 1980s and 1990s)

Darfur has a long history of food aid in response to drought and famine. Until the mid-1980s it was largely government food aid. International food aid has dominated famine responses from 1985, after which international food distribution in Darfur was almost continuous. Despite ongoing food aid in Darfur during the livelihoods regime, it failed to have the intended aim of supporting livelihoods. It did, however, influence government food aid responses, whether by establishing local strategic reserves or local purchases or by establishing committees to manage food aid at village level. It also created a group of Darfuri aid professionals. This section starts with a brief overview of early government food aid, and then examines the effects of international and government food aid operations in the 1980s and 1990s. It ends with a look at the food security of Darfur's populations over this period.

Before the INGO invasion

In Darfur, food aid before the 1985 famine was dominated by government food aid, including subsidised food through Nimeiri's village-based consumer committees, traditional and local government strategic reserves and famine relief from central government. Activities in the few active Sudan Socialist Union (SSU) basic units focused on improving local services, in particular the establishment of consumer committees. Two focus groups remembered the distribution of subsidised food and other goods, such as oil, sugar, tea and soap, through the consumer committees as a form of state-led social protection (Groups 4 and 7, 2013). Other informants remembered traditional strategic reserves. One such reserve, organised by sheikhs and omdas, fed the army and prisoners, as well as those short of food during droughts and famines (Informant 27, 2013). Another reserve, organised by provincial and district commissioners, consisted of underground silos, which would be restocked in years of surplus and grain distributed in deficit years (Informant 23, 2012).

Darfur received little or no international food aid during the state support regime. As Chapter 3 illustrated, both programme and project food aid was used to support development in central Sudan. Only school feeding was planned for Darfur and this only reached provincial capitals (WFP, 1975b). Most famine relief in the 1970s was provided by the government. Darfuris remember the government sorghum, which was unfamiliar to them, as 'abu za'ouna' (meaning 'save us'). As famine loomed in 1983, following rain and crop failures in 1982 and 1983, regional government distributed 3,650 MT of food. Darfur's governor made appeals to the central government for assistance, and resigned when no response was forthcoming. In early 1984, WFP provided 12,000 MT of emergency food aid to the Darfur regional government,[10] but rather than being distributed to drought-affected populations, WFP monitors found that it had been diverted to government employees and to merchants, and used for private gain (Pearson, 1986: 8). Central government also sent supplies in early and mid-1984 (in total almost 20,000 MT). The government distributed food aid according to its own 'relief ideology', which was to meet its obligation to employees and urban residents first. Much of the village allocation was sold in towns to pay for transport (De Waal, 1989a: 205–206). The activities of voluntary agencies at that time were limited to small distributions by local Red Crescent committees in rural areas (Groups 2 and 6, 2013). Central government did not declare a national emergency until December 1984 (De Waal, 1989a: 202–205).

International food aid operations – did they meet their objectives?

International relief operations in response to drought were launched in Darfur from late 1984 to 1986 and again in 1988, 1991–94, 1996–97 and 2001–02, with various forms of food-for-work in between or at the same time. The general pattern was that drought- and famine-affected people received only little food aid. At first, government delays in declaring famine, agency inexperience and transporter priorities were major factors, but by the 1990s donors were reluctant to provide aid to the Islamist regime, and aid agencies reduced their estimates of need.

The first large-scale international emergency food aid response failed to reach rural famine-affected people when they needed it most. WFP was sceptical of FAO needs assessments and reluctant to get involved after the diversion of its consignment in 1984. It was also preoccupied with the refugee crisis in eastern Sudan. As WFP prevaricated, USAID stepped in and procured 82,000 MT of sorghum.[11] Unlike WFP, USAID did not rely on government transport but could contract a private company (Arkel-Talab) to transport food aid and had funds in-country from the sale of programme food aid. After WFP and Oxfam declined to take responsibility for food distribution to villages, SC-UK became USAID's implementing partner, despite its limited experience of large logistics operations (Pearson, 1986; SC-UK, c. 1986). USAID wanted food aid targeted at the neediest quarter of Darfur's population, and later raised this to the neediest third (De Waal, 1989a: 208). The first USAID food aid reached Darfur in December 1984, but at the height of the famine (mid-1985) the distributions were small and SC-UK was unable to ensure that food aid went to the most drought-affected areas or people. Towns received more than villages, rich more than poor, and displaced populations and nomads were often excluded (Keen, 1991). The average received by rural populations between March and May 1985 was 14 grams/person/day, instead of a planned 430 grams (Taylor, 1985). This improved later in 1985 and in 1986, but large variations in food receipts persisted (Hardy, 1985; Williams, 1986). The prevalence of malnutrition decreased from 14.1% in March/May 1985 to 7.5% in March/April 1986, but this was unlikely to be due to food aid as the distribution was uneven and limited (Williams, 1986). The 1985 harvest was the best in years.

Aid agencies failed to reach the most vulnerable rural populations because this conflicted with government and private sector priorities. While SC-UK was responsible for food delivery from Area Councils[12] to villages, local government remained responsible for allocations to Area Councils and for distribution at village level. For much of 1985 government priorities dominated and its committees favoured government employees (including police, army and prisons) and merchants, and continued to sell food aid to pay for transport and to raise revenue. Migrants and nomads were excluded to discourage population movement and because they had not been registered for earlier government-subsidised food. SC-UK was unable to counter these allocations because it did not have information on who and where the neediest were, and relied on commercial transporters for food deliveries. For much of 1985, staff and transport for the operation were limited (SC-UK, c. 1986). Earlier that year, the railways used by Arkel-Talab had failed to prioritise relief deliveries to Darfur, and transporters within Darfur had prioritised easy-to-reach destinations, or had delivered after the rains when transport was cheaper (Keen, 1991).[13] In some cases, traders who had been asked to transport food simply sold it instead of delivering it to rural areas (Informant 25, 2012; Informants 27 and 29, 2013). The result was that most food aid stayed in urban areas and that rural populations had to rely on their own strategies to survive and protect their livelihoods. As discussed in Chapter 2, De Waal (1989a) found that those who survived the famine and protected their livelihoods did so because of their own coping strategies. The poor performance of the international food aid operation also enabled Libya to establish a larger foothold in Darfur, thus feeding into regional politics and Libya's Arabisation strategy at the time. Providing food aid was part of this strategy. In August 1985, the first of many Libyan humanitarian and military convoys arrived in Darfur (Prunier, 2008: 55).

By 1986, SC-UK had established its own food aid system in Darfur, including its own fleet of trucks, food monitors and research and assessment teams. Donors had made SC-UK responsible for storage and distribution down to the village level (Buckley, 1988). With SC-UK controlling all aspects of food distribution, it could counter the government's ideology of prioritising its employees and urban populations. Despite a much better harvest in 1985, SC-UK determined that targeted food aid would be necessary because some people remained vulnerable, and it established an information system to help make targeting decisions (Eldridge et al., 1986). The aim of targeting food aid to rural areas was to encourage villagers to remain or return to their village to grow food, as well as meeting immediate needs. According to SC-UK's accounts, the 1986 operation was timely and distributed large quantities of food aid to those most in need (SC-UK, c. 1986). However, government officials who had been involved at area and village council levels in 1985 were now side-lined and often disagreed with, or did not understand, the 1986 distribution policy (Buckley, 1988). As a result, building local capacity became a key objective in future operations.

When Darfur experienced another drought in 1987, the Western Relief Operation used local institutions to provide relief, but food aid was once again late and failed to reach the neediest. This time, regional government was responsible for administration and distribution. The MoF would use counterpart funds from the sale of programme food aid to purchase grain from the ABS, the RRC organised its transport (using private companies) and the government's sugar cooperatives would distribute at village level.[14] None of these initiatives succeeded. Delays in the release of funds from the MoF and the ABS's prioritisation of export over famine relief meant that food was purchased late (see Chapter 3). Transport from central Sudan was further delayed because of insecurity, fuel shortages, increasing competition with government for trucks (for the army and for sugar deliveries) and cash-flow problems for the middlemen who subcontracted to transport companies. Only 14,400 MT of the 51,000 MT planned for Darfur was distributed. At village level, the government's sugar cooperatives distributed food to everyone registered rather than targeting the most vulnerable. An EC evaluation concluded that the WRO had failed to make any impact on relieving food insecurity in the region (Buchanan-Smith, 1989, 1990). The evaluation recommended the establishment of regional food stocks for future response to food shortages. The EC responded by supporting the establishment of a local strategic reserve in Al-Fashir, the first state-level reserve for North Darfur.

When the harvest failed again in 1989 and in 1990, regional government and NGO recommendations for food aid were highly controversial as they contradicted the government's policy of self-sufficiency. Donors, in turn, were reluctant to provide aid after the Islamist regime came to power, and insisted that food aid be distributed by INGOs and only to populations at immediate risk of dying. In 1989, the Agricultural Planning Unit (APU),[15] which had been established after the 1985 famine and which monitored food security, recommended distribution of 20,000 MT of food aid, but only the limited quantities in the strategic reserve were distributed. With further poor rains in 1990, the APU warned that the region would face famine unless food aid was provided (Buchanan-Smith and Davies, 1995b). The head of the APU was fired. After months of refusal, the government requested external assistance in late December 1990. The objective of the operation was to prevent distress migration, morbidity and mortality, and to assist in developing a relief system that could target vulnerable groups at village level (SC-UK, 1991). Donor insistence that food aid be allocated to INGOs caused further delays because of a stand-off between donors and government about transport arrangements. By July 1991, only 30% of estimated food needs had arrived in Port Sudan and internal transport from central Sudan faced similar constraints to the Western Relief Operation (SC-UK, 1991; Osman, 1993). Within Darfur, two parastatal transport companies monopolised food transport, which delivered late and demanded high prices. The newly established Popular Committees distributed food to everyone (SC-UK, 1993; Osman, 1993). By December 1991, only one-fifth of requirements had been met. Little monitoring took place – INGOs considered collecting information on famine deaths politically unacceptable – but just on the basis of the limited quantities of food aid delivered, the operation failed (Buchanan-Smith and Davies, 1995b: 107). Donors and aid workers eventually concluded that food needs for 1991 had been over-estimated and that the affected population had once again survived by using their own coping strategies (e.g. Patel, 1994; Informants 12 and 13, 2012), despite evidence of high levels of acute malnutrition in parts of Darfur (Kelly and Buchanan-Smith, 1994).

From 1991, food distribution was almost continuous in North Darfur and included emergency food distribution, food-for-work and government distributions (see Table 4.1), all with similar constraints to earlier food aid operations. The relief programme that started in 1991 continued until 1993, as North Darfur continued to face food deficits. When the harvest failed again in 1993, SC-UK recommended more emergency food aid for 1994 (SC-UK, 1993). Only 40% of estimated needs in 1994 were distributed, and once again late, largely because of low donor commitments.[16] SC-UK attempted a change in transport system to overcome the monopoly of the two parastatals in Darfur by organising transport direct from El Obeid (in Kordofan), but drivers refused to go direct to Darfuri villages and SC-UK was forced to pay more when rains had closed most roads. Some food aid arrived during harvesting when it was no longer needed (Diraige, 1994). For 1994, donors committed only half the estimated needs and when no severe famine had occurred by the end of the year they argued again that needs had been over-estimated (Bush, 1996). Similar conclusions were reached in evaluations of the 1997 and 2001 relief operations, when distributions were again late and much further below estimated needs. A DFID evaluation of the 1997 operation concluded that the amounts of food aid received were unlikely to have had a significant impact (DFID, 1997: 24). An SC-UK evaluation of the 2001 operation concluded that relief did little to ease the strain on coping mechanisms, or halt the resulting erosion of livelihoods, depletion of assets and distress migration, which had been the operation's objectives (Tanner, 2002).

Table 4.1: Continuous food distribution in Malha and Kuma

Year	Reason/type of food distribution	Committees responsible for distribution
1970s	Emergency (Kuma)	
1970s–now	School feeding Subsidised food	Schools Nimeiri's consumer committees
1980–84	Famine/emergency	Relief committee (Kuma)
1984–85	Famine/emergency	Relief committee (RC) Sudan Red Crescent (SRC) (Malha)
1986	Emergency	SRC (Kuma)
1987–now	Food-for-work (Kuma)	
1991–92	Emergency (Kuma)	RC and Popular Committee (PC) (Kuma)
1990–99	Government-subsidised food/ strategic reserve (Kuma)	RC, PC and SRC (Kuma)
1990–99	Drought/emergency food aid (Malha)	PC (Malha)
1995	Emergency/drought (Kuma)	RC and PC (Kuma)
2000–03	Emergency/drought (Malha)	PC (Malha)
2002	Emergency (Kuma)	RC and PC (Kuma)
2004–07	Crisis/emergency Government distributions (Kuma)	RC and PC (Kuma)
2005–12	Conflict/emergency food aid (Malha)	PC (Malha)
2007–11	Crisis/emergency food aid (Kuma)	RC and PC (Kuma)
2009–12	Food-for-work (Malha) Government food/strategic reserve (Malha)	PC (Malha)
2011–present	Food-for-work (Kuma)	Area committee (Kuma) Relief committee (Jebel Si – in camps)
2012–present	Targeted food aid (Malha)	PC
2013	Floods/emergency (Kuma)	Area Committee

Source: interviews with focus groups from Malha and Kuma.

Donors limited the quantities of food aid despite more sophisticated food security assessments. From 1996, SC-UK's new food security assessment methods (the Food Economy Approach) incorporated an assessment of different ways of accessing food, which provided lower estimates of food needs than those based mainly on harvest assessments. However, donors still only committed a fraction of estimated needs. For example, in 1997, SC-UK requested 57,519 MT of food aid to save lives and support livelihoods, but DFID only agreed to 5,000 MT for purely life-saving objectives (other donors provided 2,125 MT). Targeting was even more difficult with such limited quantities of food aid – which was usually distributed equally within communities, despite the efforts of SC-UK, which included training workshops with community leaders and government officials on how to target (Osman, 1993; DFID, 1997; Informants 9, 12 and 13, 2012; Informant 29, 2013).

As donors were only prepared to provide food aid when lives were demonstrably at risk, the main tool for early response to support livelihoods became food-for-work. Food distributed through food-for-work schemes ranged from 5,000 to 10,000 MT per year, provided by WFP and implemented by a number of INGOs (Bush, 1996; Informant 30, 2013). WFP started its food-for-work activities in Darfur in 1987 with the aim of rehabilitating drought-prone areas. In these projects, communities built *hafirs* (water reservoirs), repaired dams and dug shallow wells, prepared water-spreading dykes and cultivated gum arabic in the north-east of North Darfur and Kordofan (WFP, 1988b; Informant 37, 2013). By 1998, over 250 *hafirs* had been constructed (WFP, 1998a). Informants who had been involved in food-for-work projects considered them to be more effective in targeting than emergency food distribution, as only those most in need would work for the amount of food aid offered (Informants 37 and 43, 2013). No evaluations of the food-for-work programmes could be found.[17] A 1997 general progress report for WFP's development programmes mentions that the earlier food-for-work project was superseded by emergency operations, and later ones suffered from insufficient and late supply of cereals due to government suspension of local purchase of sorghum (WFP, 1997). According to one informant, the later food-for-work projects were not evaluated due to the outbreak of conflict in 2003 (Informant 37, 2013). Judging from Figure 3.2 (Chapter 3), the amounts of project food aid throughout the 1990s were minimal.

There is little evidence that international food aid during the livelihoods regime of practices in Darfur in the 1980s and 1990s had its intended impact of saving lives or improving nutrition, food security or coping strategies. Only in 1986, when SC-UK had its own transport system, did large quantities of food aid successfully reach rural populations. The Sudan government resisted declaring an emergency in 1985 and 1991, and donors were late to respond. From 1990, donors committed only minimal quantities of food aid for fear of supporting the Islamist regime. Within Sudan, transporters delayed deliveries and failed to deliver to remote areas, and local committees spread the small quantities of food delivered amongst large numbers of people. The practices of the livelihoods regime did influence government food aid practices and the emergence of a class of professional aid workers in Sudan, as discussed in the following sections.

Government food aid in the 1980s and 1990s

During the 1980s and 1990s, the Sudan government provided food at subsidised prices through local committees or cooperatives and emergency food aid in response to food shortages and famine. It also started building up a state-level strategic grain reserve. This reserve was probably the most important government food aid activity in Darfur, although it was rarely used for the most drought-affected. The first state-level strategic reserve was established in 1988 when the EC funded the Ministries of Finance and Agriculture to buy 2,000 MT of millet in North Darfur and 1,500 MT of sorghum in South and West Darfur (Informant 43, 2013). In distribution, however, the government's priority was to provide food for prisoners, traditional leaders or others whose political support was needed by the new regime. Some food was sold at subsidised prices to those facing shortages, but the EC did not make further funding available. Strategic reserve initiatives continued in North Darfur throughout the 1990s, although ad hoc and without donor support. These initiatives were a key component of the Salvation government's aim to be self-sufficient and free from international food aid (Elbashir and Ahmed, 2005). Other initiatives included local or regional purchase of food. In 1990, the Darfur state government imported 48,000 MT of wheat flour from Libya to be bartered for Darfuri livestock (Buchanan-Smith and Davies, 1995b). In 1993/94, a government initiative encouraged banks and businessmen to fund Darfur's State Ministries of Agriculture to purchase grain for Darfur: 9,000 MT for North Darfur and 4,500 MT each for South and West Darfur. Some was sold to government employees at cost price as a relief measure, but large quantities arrived during the rainy season when market prices were already decreasing. Some 4,500 MT was stored in Al-Fashir as a strategic reserve (Diraige, 1994). According to an SC-UK evaluation report, this was released onto the market too early and by 1996, another drought year, only 1,000 MT was in stock (Bush, 1996). The strategic reserve stayed dormant from 1996 to 2000, but was reactivated in 2001, when the federal government adopted the Strategic Reserve Act (see Chapter 3). In that year, the federal government dispatched 4,858 MT to North Darfur for free distribution and 3,100 MT for monetisation.[18] SC-UK staff viewed the revival of the strategic reserve as one of the few positive things to come out of the 2001 crisis, especially as the food appeared to have been targeted to the areas worst affected by drought (Tanner, 2002). These government initiatives in the 1980s and 1990s can be seen as a response to the large international food distributions of the mid-1980s, as well as a means of meeting its obligations to government employees and supporters during times of food shortage. The government's policy of meeting the needs of urban residents and employees first was maintained.

INGOs as new welfare providers?

During the livelihoods regime of practices in the 1980s and 1990s, INGOs took responsibility for managing the lives and livelihoods of drought-affected populations in Darfur. They established new methods for assessing need and for targeting food aid to the most vulnerable, prioritised rural populations and established participatory relief committees at village level. Village-level community-based relief committees, consisting of village leaders and notables, were formed to distribute and later target food aid. Despite the limited quantities of international food aid distributed to drought- and famine-affected communities in the 1980s and 1990s, villagers would go to the offices of SC-UK rather than the government when they needed help. One informant recalls: 'Delegations came from rural areas when they faced food problems ... we kept a book of the delegations, where they came from, etc.' (Informant 9, 2012). Another recalls how this came to form part of an informal food security monitoring system: 'Villagers coming to WFP or INGOs in search of assistance was a kind of early warning system' (Informant 4, 2012). In addition to limited quantities of food aid, SC-UK and other INGOs provided health care, education, water and agricultural services.

Throughout the 1990s, SC-UK played an important role in lobbying government and donors about the food needs of Darfur's populations and advocated for appropriate responses to drought and food insecurity. Using results from its information system, it advised the State Food Security Committee (established in 1990) on the allocation of food aid. This sometimes meant challenging the Sudan government. When it introduced new assessment methods in 1991, for example, SC-UK faced extensive scrutiny from state government, as it was suspicious about NGO work. In other cases, government officials tried to change the findings of SC-UK food security assessments if they contradicted their self-sufficiency policy (SC-UK, 1993). In keeping with food aid objectives in the livelihoods regime, SC-UK requested food aid to support livelihoods as well as save lives, although donors did not agree. By the end of the 1990s, North Darfur had a group of experienced Darfuri aid professionals, who were experts in assessments, information systems, food distribution and a range of other food security interventions and who knew how to negotiate their way around the highly politicised context. Despite the limited impact of the food aid operations they managed, they represented drought- and famine-affected populations, and these populations sought their help when they needed it. In this way, the livelihoods regime provided a sharp contrast with the later resilience regime, when the close relationship between aid workers and crisis-affected communities was broken because of risks to aid workers, remote management and reliance mainly on quantitative assessment methods.

Control of food aid at community level

International food distribution at community level was largely managed through local leaders or committees. The practices of international agencies at first supported local government or traditional leaders, but bypassed them in the 1980s through the establishment of new village committees, a practice which the government built on to extend its control down to village level. In 1985, international food aid was distributed through sheikhs or village councils. The sheikhs welcomed this responsibility as it gave them a chance to re-establish their authority after the introduction of local councils. However, when agencies saw that sheikhs were using food aid to increase their own power, a new system of distribution committees at village level was established (SC-UK, c. 1986; Informant 27, 2013). This in turn increased the power of committee members and may have influenced the development of Popular Committees, as one aid worker explains:

At village level, those who have been part of the relief committee were the ones who had experience of organisation, of how to deal with resources ... they became like leaders. In most cases the members of the relief committees found ways through their role to support the communities to play other type of roles. Like being elected in political committees ... You know, people consider someone who is working for them, who is helping them, who may be nominated to be part of parliament. ... When the government started thinking about subsidising sugar and cereals, in most cases the ... main contact person [would be the one with experience of relief committees] ... [M]ost of the members [of the government committees] first worked on the relief committee, then on the [government cooperatives], and then on the Salvation [Popular] Committees. (Informant 4, 2012)

The Sudan government has used food to bolster reforms in local government and attract political support since Nimeiri's consumer committees. It was Al-Turabi, Sudan's leading Islamist, who intro- duced them when he was the Darfur Political Overseer of the SSU (Khalid, 2009: 38). Not many consumer committees were estab- lished at village level during Nimeiri's time, but relief committees during the 1986 food distribution were widespread, thus providing an example to the government for the future Popular Commit- tees. Every food distribution in the 1990s, whether international or government food aid, was done through the Popular Committees (see Table 4.1). This has political implications. According to the Malik (King) of Al-Fashir:

During Nimeiri's time, there was [international] food distribution directly from donors to beneficiaries. But after Nimeiri's time, the government says that they should receive the food and distribute it ... Q: Why? A: The government wants to build trust between the government and the citizens ... The people do not know that it is WFP or other agencies, they just think that it [food aid] is coming from the government. Q: How was it done? A: Through the Popular Committees in each neighbourhood. (Informant 64, 2013)

According to Darfuri key informants, the political role of the committees was greater in towns than in villages, as each village committee consisted of the same elite (teachers, merchants, tradi- tional leaders). International food aid distributions in the 1990s were monitored closely (Informants 9 and 26, 2012). While the quantities of international food aid provided were too limited to have an effect on nutrition and livelihoods, the ongoing practices of distribution through the Popular Committees maintained or enhanced the authority of elites and, in some cases, the power of government committees. Most importantly, the regime had now assumed control of food distribution at the local level.

Impoverishment – or were people coping?

In *Famine that Kills*, de Waal (1989a) describes how in 1985, in the face of inadequate relief, rural people in Darfur responded to the threat of famine with a range of coping strategies. These included the collection and consumption of wild foods, seasonal labour migration, other low-status trades (casual labour, selling firewood or charcoal), sale of livestock and migration in search of charity on the edges of towns or out of Darfur to central Sudan (De Waal, 1989a). In fact, he goes back further and describes how some people diversified and changed their livelihoods during ecological and climatic changes in the 1960s and 1970s. For example, the Zaghawa from the far north of Darfur changed their herds from cattle to camels in the face of frequent drought, and most people left their homeland to live and work as farmers and merchants in other parts of Darfur. They also migrated further afield: to Libya and the Gulf countries (De Waal, 1989a: 95–96; Ibrahim, 1998). Men from farming families in Jebel Si migrated for work within Darfur or to central Sudan, a strategy used since colonial times in periods of food scarcity (Niblock, 1987). Famine is also associated with the accumulation of wealth. During the 1985 famine, some traders became millionaires from purchasing livestock at low prices and selling grain at high prices, which increased inequality within the region (Bush, 1988). Livestock became concentrated in the hands of richer pastoralists (De Waal, 1986).

For most people in North Darfur, their reality was that very little food aid reached them during the 1980s and 1990s, and they simply got poorer. In 1986–87, rural populations were worse off than urban populations, and nomadic populations often showed some of the highest levels of acute malnutrition (Maxwell, 1989: 26). Rural populations' coping strategies identified in 1985 continued and intensified. An examination of SC-UK's bi-yearly food security reports and assessments from 1994 to 2001 shows that rural people used largely the same strategies as those identified by De Waal (1989a): collection of wild foods, selling of firewood and charcoal, sale of livestock and migration for work, with an increased proportion of people using these strategies in years when rainfall was low. They were no longer short-term strategies but had become a way of life for many, indicating the collapse of their livelihoods systems. Levels of acute malnutrition in the poorest and most drought-prone parts of North Darfur rose above emergency levels every year during the hungry season, and remained high in years of drought and scarcity (Young and Jaspars, 1995). Information on deaths is limited, but an analysis of data from the 1991 famine concluded that excess deaths had almost certainly occurred (Kelly and Buchanan-Smith, 1994). A DFID evaluation of SC-UK's 1996 food aid operation notes localised crises with excess mortality in some locations (DFID, 1997) and an SC-UK survey in 2001 estimated both acute malnutrition and mortality to be at emergency levels (Collins, 2001).

To conclude, despite the efforts of international agencies in the 1980s and 1990s, most people in Darfur received little or no food aid and instead had to rely on their own strategies and became further impoverished. Government food aid was limited and prioritised government staff or those whose support it needed. Food aid in the livelihoods regime of practices, however, did produce a highly trained group of Sudanese aid professionals, who represented and lobbied on behalf of drought- and famine-affected populations, aiming to improve both government and donor responses. Other than training of Sudanese aid professionals, and government initiatives to provide and control food aid, it appears that the main effect of international food aid in the 1980s and 1990s in Sudan was the economic benefits for central government, traders and transporters discussed in Chapter 3.

The Darfur crisis: food aid in the early years (2003–07)

The humanitarian response to the consequences of conflict in 2003–04 can be seen as the peak of the livelihoods regime in Darfur. Substantial quantities of food aid reached conflict-affected populations, including rural populations from 2005, and helped reduce acute malnutrition and supported livelihoods. The aid operation supported livelihoods by lowering market prices of food, supporting cereal traders and keeping local grain markets functioning. It also provided a safe way of accessing food, thus reducing the risks of attack and rape that people faced when collecting firewood or farming. The creation of camps was a new feature of the post-2003 crisis. Al-Fashir became the site of three of the largest camps in North Darfur (Abou Shook, As Salaam and Zamzam). Smaller towns also had camps for the displaced, and in some the displaced mixed with and overwhelmed the local population (see Map 4.2). Food distribution was done on the basis of group status: IDPs in camps, displaced people with hosts and host families, and resident populations. At first, most food aid went to IDPs in camps and Arab nomadic populations were excluded, which compromised the neutrality of the operation. This section first describes the massive scale of the operation and reviews its effect on nutrition, livelihoods and power relations. In 2004–05, aid agencies could work autonomously, but from 2006 onwards government restrictions increased and access became constrained.

Effect on nutrition, food security and livelihoods

WFP delivered food aid in Darfur post-2003 in what became the largest food aid operation that Darfur has seen, not only in terms of scale but also reach: in 2005 it was able to effectively reach people in rural areas for the first time with distribution to over 3 million people at more than 300 distribution points (Young, 2007). The quantity of food aid provided was massive compared with earlier operations in Darfur; almost 450,000 MT was distributed in 2005, more than five times the amount distributed by SC-UK in 1985 and sixty times as much as that distributed in 1997.[19] The ration now included six commodities – cereal, oil, pulses, sugar, salt and corn–soy blend – instead of cereals only as in earlier operations (WFP, 2006). The number of food aid beneficiaries escalated dramatically early in the first years of the operation, from 1.2 million in April 2004 to 3.25 million by June 2005. Food aid and other humanitarian assistance were initially focused on IDPs and expanded to remote rural areas in 2005, when food distribution reached its peak (WFP, 2006). By 2008, the number of beneficiaries was close to 4 million (WFP et al., 2009). Although WFP struggled to meet needs in 2004, due to a lack of logistics capacity and of implementing partners at the start of the operation, coverage improved in 2005 (WFP, 2006) (see Figure 4.1).

The objective of WFP's relief operation was to save lives and protect livelihoods and, initially, the large quantities of food aid distributed brought down malnutrition and mortality, lowered grain prices and supported trade. In September 2004 the prevalence of acute malnutrition in Darfur was 21.8%, which declined to 11.9% in September 2005 (Young, 2007: S49)[20] and remained at a

Figure 4.1: Increase in WFP food deliveries to Darfur from 2003 to 2005

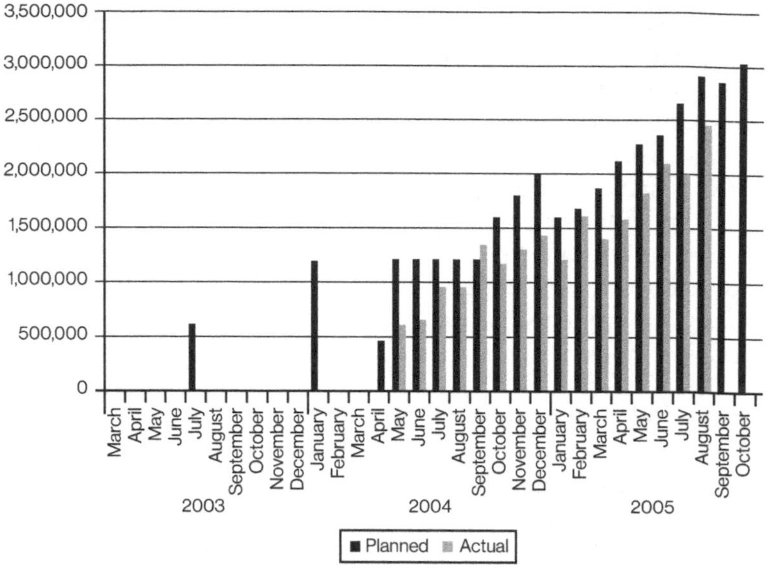

Source: Young (2007) © 2007 Helen Young. Journal compilation © Overseas Development Institute, 2007.

similar level (12.9%) in 2006 (WFP et al., 2007). Mortality levels also fell (Young, 2007).[21] According to WFP's 2006 evaluation, all stakeholders agreed that WFP food flows into Darfur had averted a serious humanitarian catastrophe. The relief operation provided a safe way of accessing food and reduced the need for people to engage in income-earning strategies that increased the risk of rape or attack, such as the collection of firewood or labour on distant farms. A WFP study found that the receipt of food aid put IDPs in a stronger position when negotiating their daily labour rates and eased relationships between IDPs and their hosts. In contrast, when food aid was cut back or stopped (because of good harvests or loss of access), people had to adopt a range of damaging strategies – for example, begging, firewood collection (risking exposure to attack), migration or taking children out of school (Buchanan-Smith and Jaspars, 2006). In 2005, WFP Sudan made a policy decision to integrate protection into its activities by targeting areas of high poverty and vulnerability to prevent displacement and by registering displaced populations. The registration done in 2005 reduced the risk of diversion and the exclusion of some groups by IDP leaders (Mahoney et al., 2005).

Food aid improved food security not only by providing food directly to conflict-affected households, but also by lowering the price of cereals in the market and by indirectly providing trading opportunities. Food aid impacts on markets because beneficiaries commonly sell part of their rations to meet other needs. In 2005, WFP added market and income support as an explicit objective of its food aid operation. Sugar was added to the ration (as this was a key source of expenditure) and higher than usual quantities of cereals in the ration kept the market prices of cereals affordable for non-beneficiaries, as beneficiaries sold it to meet other needs. In 2005, 43% of food aid beneficiaries reported selling part of their rations (WFP and UNICEF, 2005). As food aid was sold, it indirectly supported traders, transporters and cereal markets. Cereal traders could trade in food aid when local cereal production and rural markets had collapsed due to the large-scale displacement of farmers. Food aid trade increased dramatically with the large food distributions from 2005 to 2008 and benefited Darfuri traders, as well as central Sudan traders. In Al-Fashir, a group of traders estimated that the number of grain traders increased from about 150 to over 1,000 between 2005 and 2007 (Trader focus group, 2014). For many displaced people, trading in food aid was a new activity. It provided IDP women with an opportunity to engage in petty trading as they bought food aid direct from beneficiaries and sold it on to mid-level traders, who in turn sold it to bigger traders or their agents in Al-Fashir. Food aid was also bought as livestock feed by dairy and poultry farms around Darfur's main towns, which had been established during the conflict to feed the growing urban population (Informant 88, 2013; Trader focus group, 2014). Food aid also supported North Darfuri transport companies, which increased in number from one to twelve during the conflict (Informant 86, 2013). Some owners of the newly established companies had previously worked as agents for the bigger Khartoum-based companies (Informants 85 and 87, 2013). Food aid was a means of maintaining or even expanding local transport business as other trade collapsed.

Central Sudan traders and transporters benefited by exporting large amounts of cereals from Darfur to central Sudan, as the price of cereals was lower in Darfur than in Khartoum or in Sudan's grain-producing areas. In late 2004 and early 2005, sorghum was cheaper in Darfur than in the sorghum-growing areas of central Sudan (Hamid et al., 2005). In 2006, the same was true for wheat: seven to ten trucks (25–30 MT capacity) of wheat food aid left Al-Fashir for Khartoum every week (Buchanan-Smith and Jaspars,

2006: S69).[22] In 2008, price differentials were small, but the export of sorghum continued because the transaction costs were low; the trucks which delivered food aid to Darfur could also take it back to Khartoum (Buchanan-Smith and Abdulla Fadul, 2008). Sometimes, private transporters contracted by WFP could buy food aid in Darfur and deliver this for distribution. They took food from Port Sudan (where food shipments arrived) to Khartoum, then flew empty bags and paperwork (and sometimes the truck licence plates) to Darfur, bought food aid in Darfur, placed it in WFP bags, and delivered it to WFP. This made a much larger profit as the transporter profited on the food exchange as well as saving on transport costs (WFP, 2006). Some transporters brought back cash crops, in particular ground-nuts and sesame from South Darfur, but it appears that food aid transport back to central Sudan was by far the bigger business from 2005 to 2007 (Informant 49, 2013b; Informant 82, 2013).

Not everyone received food aid or indirectly benefited from it, however; the coverage of food distribution was uneven. WFP's initial focus was almost entirely on IDPs, which led to a perception of polit-ical bias towards certain ethnic groups, in particular those supporting the rebellion (Mahoney et al., 2005). The initial exclusion of Arab nomadic groups was instrumental in creating a perception that the humanitarian operation was not impartial. WFP's expansion of food distribution to rural areas in 2005 was never able to overcome the initial impression of bias towards IDPs. It took until 2007 for some Arab groups to be included in assessments and distributions, although aid agencies sometimes provided food aid to Arab groups as protection payments when passing through areas they controlled (Young and Maxwell, 2009; Informant 29, 2013). The needs of Arab or nomadic populations were never fully considered in food security or humanitarian assessments, although research in 2009 revealed their needs particularly in health care and education. These needs were not addressed because food aid was the entry point for other assistance, and therefore being excluded from food aid meant being excluded from other assistance (Young et al., 2009b). The govern-ment provided its own food aid to Arab groups to maintain their support. As international food aid to camps supported IDP leaders and the rebellion, food aid fed directly into the dynamics of conflict.

Food aid as support for IDP leaders

Food Relief Committees (FRCs), established by WFP in 2006, had close links with the IDP leadership, which in some cases supported the political agenda of the rebellion.[23] For some time and to varying degrees, food distribution in the largest camps for displaced people remained outside of government control. International aid agencies established new leadership in the camps as the interface between them and the IDPs. IDP leaders were sometimes traditional leaders but were often newly elected. Many traditional leaders had been killed, or had become separated from their communities (if part of the population had fled and another part stayed in the village) or had moved to towns because they were linked to government and rejected by their community. The new leaders were also called omdas and sheikhs and were selected on the basis of respect for their actions during the conflict or their skills (Buchanan-Smith and Jaspars, 2006; Young and Maxwell, 2009). In contrast to traditional leaders, their power derived from their interaction with international agencies and the distribution of resources, in particular food aid. The FRCs had close links with the newly elected leaders, either because IDP sheikhs were on the FRC or because the FRC members were appointed by them (Young and Maxwell, 2009; Jaspars, 2010).

IDP leaders sometimes benefited from being involved in food distribution. After registration, some IDP sheikhs had multiple ration cards or required payment from IDPs for their role in food distribution (Pantuliano and O'Callaghan, 2006; Kahn, 2008). WFP informants gave the diversions of food aid by IDP sheikhs as an important reason for shifting from food aid to food vouchers (Informant 7, 2012; Informant 56, 2013). Even after the switch to food vouchers in 2011, IDP leaders retained some benefits, as some were paid by traders to direct beneficiaries to their shops (Pattugalan et al., 2012; Informant 91, 2013), or kept the vouchers and took a cut from their value when redeemed (Group 8, 2013). Mahoney et al. (2005) and Kahn (2008) suggest that any diversion was mainly for the personal benefit of camp leaders rather than providing a contribution for the armed factions. In some camps, however, the IDP leadership was highly politicised and their involvement in food distribution, and the role of food aid in maintaining the camps, helped further their political agendas, in particular that of SLA-Abdel Wahid. In this case, the role of the IDP sheikhs included mobilising IDPs to insist on a peace agreement that included compensation for human and material loss, bringing perpetrators to justice and disarmament of all armed groups (El-Mekki, 2007). IDP camps in government areas thus functioned as a show of strength of political support for the rebellion (Kahn, 2008), and some camps were inaccessible to government representatives for many years. Furthermore, as WFP was the only agency to have registered IDPs, food aid was directly linked to claims for protection and political entitlements (Young and Maxwell, 2009). When WFP tried to re-register IDP populations in 2011, IDP leaders considered it a political act and strongly resisted registration in some of the most politicised camps. It could only be achieved by stopping food distributions until IDP leaders gave in. In Kalma camp, for example, WFP stopped food distribution for eight months (WFP, 2013b: 54). In contrast, the IDP leadership (including the Food Relief Committees) in some of the camps or settlements in smaller towns or villages was often controlled by the local administration and higher government agendas (Young and Maxwell, 2009: 19).

The early days of the Darfur crisis was the only time in the region's long history of food aid that it either directly or indirectly improved nutrition, food security and livelihoods. However, Arab nomadic groups were excluded and food aid boosted the political agenda of the rebellion in some of the large IDP camps, thus compromising the neutrality of the humanitarian operation and feeding into the conflict dynamics. As the following section will show, by 2013 this situation was reversed, with rebel-held areas virtually excluded from food distribution and the government increasing its influence in the larger camps.

The later years (2008–14): reduced food aid and access restrictions

In the later years of the Darfur crisis response, conflict became protracted, food aid decreased and malnutrition increased. WFP's new assessments, using the quantitative food security indicators, showed that food security remained stable or decreased, while other indicators reflected ongoing crisis. Government restrictions on access reduced food aid further for some conflict-affected populations, and even when access was not denied, numerous checkpoints, fees and taxes made transporting food aid almost impossible. From 2008, food aid practices in Darfur reflect the resilience regime: remotely managed quantitative assessments reduced food aid, vouchers and specialised nutritional food products and feeding programmes.

Reduction in food aid
From 2008 onwards, the quantity of food aid distributed in Darfur decreased. In the first half of 2008, food dispatches to Darfur were reduced by half because of attacks and hijackings of trucks (WFP,

2008b). At the same time, both WFP and ICRC considered that some conflict-affected populations were able to meet part of their food needs themselves. The decrease in quantities of WFP food aid distributed is shown in Figure 4.2.

WFP reduced food aid by introducing seasonal distributions for rural populations, cutting rations and reducing the number of commodities provided, by targeting only a percentage of the population and finally by stopping food distributions to some populations altogether. WFP introduced seasonal rations in 2008, in which rural populations would receive food aid only during the four months prior to the harvest. In 2009, rations for displaced populations were reduced by 40% and rural residents received only half-rations of sorghum and oil. WFP attempted to introduce greater targeting but

Figure 4.2: WFP food distributions in Darfur from 2004 to 2012

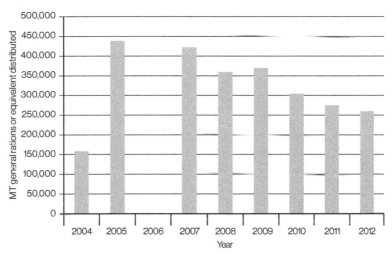

Source: Buchanan-Smith et al. (2014).

Note: These are actual amounts for general rations distributed rather than planned. The amount for 2004 is an estimate, as 60% of the planned amount for November 2003–March 2004 was added to the actual amount distributed from April–December 2004. The figures for 2011 and 2012 are estimated from graphs provided in the 2013 country evaluation, which include general food distribution (GFD) equivalent for beneficiaries receiving vouchers (see WFP, 2013: xiii). The actual amounts for general rations distributed are 220,491 MT for 2011 and 166,105 MT for 2012. The amount of food aid distributed in 2006 could not be found in evaluation reports or WFP records in Khartoum.

was unable to do so because the INGO expulsions in March meant there was no capacity to implement it (Cosgrave et al., 2010).

By 2011, IDP rations were also reduced to only cereals and oil. Food vouchers were introduced for 260,000 beneficiaries in North Darfur, including Abou Shook camp in Al-Fashir (WFP Sudan, 2011). Although intended to provide more appropriate foods and a greater variety, some beneficiaries saw it as a reduction in food assistance as inflation led to rapidly rising prices, which meant they could purchase less food with the vouchers (Group 7, 2013). For rural populations, WFP introduced two levels of targeting: geographical and household. In Malha, for example, WFP aimed to target only 60% of the population from 2012 onwards (Informant 45, 2013). Seasonal support was changed to food-for-recovery in places where the harvest had been good. Food-for-recovery projects focused on short-term activities that communities could complete with little technical supervision, and were implemented when WFP considered free food distribution inappropriate and where food-for-work was not possible because of limited implementation capacity (WFP, 2008b). These approaches reduced the quantity of food aid distributed, but at the same time the number of beneficiaries increased to about 4 million in 2008 and remained at this level until 2011 when WFP re-registered its beneficiaries. The re-registration reduced the number of beneficiaries by 27% (WFP, 2013b). A profiling exercise of displaced populations in 2015 reduced food aid further, as those with access to land and/ or assets (e.g. a cart) or employment were no longer considered in need of food aid (WFP, 2015a).

As food aid decreased, but conflict worsened, nutrition deteriorated again. The prevalence of acute malnutrition in Darfur increased from 12.9% in 2006 to 16.1% in 2007, with higher levels in North Darfur at 16% and 20% respectively (WFP et al., 2007, 2008). From 2008 onwards, WFP switched to regular food security monitoring (which used a different measure of acute malnutrition) and from 2011 supplemented regular monitoring with annual comprehensive food security assessments which focused on non-conflict causes (see Chapter 2). Emergency assessments had shown little change in food security status, and WFP felt that ongoing monitoring would provide more timely information for the kind of programming decisions discussed above. The monitoring excluded the mortality data, which the government considered highly sensitive.

Food security information was contradictory, as WFP assessments indicated a reduction in food insecurity from 2008 but other food security and conflict information suggested otherwise. WFP's assessments show that the percentage of food-insecure households in Darfur did not change between 2005 and 2007: almost 50% of the conflict-affected population remained severely food-insecure. The percentage of severely food-insecure people decreased to 23% only when the timing of the assessment changed from the pre-harvest to the post-harvest period in 2008. The survey report was released in November 2009, by which time WFP had already reduced rations because of constraints on getting food to Darfur. The report recommended that reduced rations should be maintained and a number of safety nets implemented, including food-for-work. The 2011 comprehensive food security assessment was also done after the harvest, but findings are not comparable to those from 2008 because the indicator of household food insecurity was changed[24] – 23% were found to be food-insecure in North and West Darfur and 11% in South Darfur (WFP et al., 2007, 2008, 2009, 2011). The 2012 comprehensive food security assessment, also done in December after a good harvest, was finally released in May 2014 and showed an even lower prevalence of food-insecure households: 17% in North Darfur.[25] As discussed in Chapter 2, it is likely that these assessments of the percentage of food-insecure households are under-estimates. Information on food prices, conflict and ongoing threats to livelihoods indicate ongoing acute food insecurity. WFP's own 2012 food security assessment shows an increase in the cost of food in the four years since 2009. The assessment also showed that most households bought a large proportion of their food, and that in North Darfur more than half of households could not afford to buy the food they would normally consume (WFP, 2014a). The harvest was poor or failed from 2009/10 to 2011/12 and again in 2013/14. Food prices even increased after a good harvest in 2012, because of shortages of labour and high fuel costs. USAID's Famine Early Warning System, and DRA's Market and Trade monitoring system, also showed an increase in cereal prices in North Darfur from 2011 to 2014.[26] Food security deteriorated for most protracted IDPs from 2015 to 2016 but food aid was reduced following the profiling exercise (WFP, 2016). Since 2009, few studies have examined ongoing threats to livelihoods in Darfur. The available information, however, indicates renewed violence causing destruction, displacement and ongoing harassment and assaults on farmers.

Evaluations in Darfur's resilience regime provide limited information on the effectiveness of general food distribution or new food-based resilience practices, and attribute ongoing high levels of acute malnutrition to behavioural practices. The 2010 evaluation simply states that 83% of planned tonnage was delivered but provides no information about distribution or timing, and the 2013 evaluation reports only that almost all beneficiaries were reached but with decreased rations. In terms of impact, the 2010 evaluation notes that humanitarian indicators of mortality below 1/10,000/day and acute malnutrition below 15% had largely been met (but without providing data), and – using WFP quantitative data discussed earlier – that food insecurity had not increased with ration reductions. At the same time, the evaluation report notes persistently high levels of acute malnutrition which were considered normal for parts of Darfur and were attributed to poor hygiene practices (Cosgrove et al., 2010). Acute malnutrition levels were considered 'nothing exceptional' even though the prevalence for Darfur in 2007 was above the emergency threshold. The 2013 evaluation found it impossible to determine the impact of food aid because of inconsistency in the use of the FCS. Despite the lack of evidence, the evaluation considered WFP's plans for greater targeting appropriate and did not question assumptions that people found new ways of accessing food and that high levels of acute malnutrition were not linked to food insecurity (WFP, 2013b). Information on the effectiveness of the new food-based resilience practices is also limited. Evaluations of voucher programmes have been positive about creating choice in theory, but in practice people prioritised quantity and cheaper food items (WFP, 2013b). With high inflation and the need for functioning markets and local food availability, its implementation in North Darfur is questionable. WFP also established a number of different safety nets, including food-for-assets programmes and a number of different feeding programmes. According to WFP's 2013 evaluation, however, only 2% of WFP beneficiaries received food-for-assets. At the same time, ongoing high rates of acute malnutrition meant that by 2012, WFP had four different types of supplementary feeding in place, including integrated blanket supplementary feeding in areas of persistently high levels of acute malnutrition. Integrated supplementary feeding is typical of the resilience regime in that it consists not only of specialised nutritious foods but also nutrition and hygiene education (WFP Sudan, 2012). By 2015, this had been transformed into a community-based nutrition programme incorporating specialised nutritional products, micronutrient powder and social and behaviour change communication (WFP, 2015b). For most crisis-affected populations in Darfur, it appears that the resilience regime was characterised by a decrease in food aid, increase in food prices and ongoing threats to livelihoods. The practices of the resilience regime also coincided with a dramatic reduction in access to crisis-affected populations.

Constraints: access and insecurity

Insecurity and denial of access from 2006 onwards posed major constraints for all food aid practices in Darfur: assessment, transport, distribution and monitoring, as well as assessment, and reduced food aid receipts by conflict-affected populations even further. In 2006, access decreased for areas controlled by rebels who did not sign the Darfur Peace Agreement, and from 2011 for areas held by those who did not sign the Doha Document for Peace in Darfur. For INGOs, attacks and hijacking of trucks were increasingly problematic, and from 2008 transport of food aid within Darfur was managed by WFP using either commercial transporters or its own trucks.

WFP's access for emergency assessments deteriorated. It had no access to newly displaced populations in rebel-held Jebel Marra for more than eight months in 2010 (WFP Sudan, 2010) and access to displaced populations in Abu Gamra in early 2013, following conflict over access to gold mines, was repeatedly denied. In contrast, access for regular assessments and monitoring appeared to improve as for these assessments food security data were collected by the MoA, the MoH and sometimes local NGOs (in rebel-held areas), with the dual objectives of training government officers in food security (Informant 5, 2012). Reports of regular surveys and monitoring, however, have often taken many months to be released, if at all.

Food deliveries into much of rural North Darfur have been particularly difficult since 2010 (when SLA-Minnawi returned to the opposition). WFP food convoys had to obtain security clearance from HAC, National Security and Intelligence Services (NISS) and Military Intelligence, whereas previous food deliveries just required notification (Informant 53, 2013). Even UNAMID, which sometimes provided security escorts for WFP food convoys, asked government permission for its movements (Loeb, 2013). According to local transporters, Military Intelligence effectively controlled the movement of food trucks in North Darfur from 2013 (Informants 61, 76 and 85, 2013). In some parts of North Darfur, Military Intelligence only allowed dropping points where it had a presence, which meant that aid agencies had to combine distribution points, and beneficiaries had to walk much longer distances to get food. A further problem was delays in security clearance, which meant that the crucial hungry season for seasonal distributions was often missed

(Informant 45, 2013). In rural North Darfur, aid agencies had to renegotiate distributions with large numbers of rebel commanders, thus delaying distributions further (Informant 48, 2013). Security clearance also delayed food transport from Khartoum or Al-Obeid to Al-Fashir. With the (in 2013) almost completed new tarmac road, the journey time should have decreased from five to two-and-a-half days, but in 2013 trucks could sometimes be held up for as long as twenty days waiting for escorts (Informant 67, 2013).

In early 2013, only 61% of the planned distribution could be delivered in the first half of the year because of denial of access to parts of North Darfur. Similarly, in August 2013 WFP managed to deliver only 470 out of 5,700 MT (Informant 67, 2013). Food-for-recovery could be even more difficult to implement. Interviews with two local NGOs revealed that insecurity could completely prevent programming in rural areas, that determining feasible activities was difficult and that many rural people had migrated out of their villages. Even where food-for-recovery was possible, for example in the more stable areas of Al-Fashir or Kuma localities, food deliveries were often delayed. In addition, the quantities of food provided for food-for-recovery were only a fraction of the quantities of WFP's development programmes of the 1990s: about 90 tonnes per *hafir* in 2013 compared with 225 tonnes in the 1990s (Informants 99 and 100, 2014).

It is likely that, from 2010, people in rural North Darfur received very little food aid. However, information on food receipt is limited as monitoring was difficult for the same reason of limited access. Each distribution point covered a large area and aid agencies considered it dangerous for monitors to travel to outlying settlements (Informants 59, 63 and 93, 2013). The 2013 WFP country programme evaluation concluded that 'the scale and impact of the food inputs, the changing nature of the conflict, ... official restrictions, and the lack of WFP's (and others') access to all or parts of the affected population inter alia contribute towards a certain lack of direct control and relevance over programming decisions' (WFP, 2013b).

Checkpoints, fees and taxes

Throughout the conflict, transporting food aid (and other goods) in Darfur was subject to an increasing number of taxes, fees and other demands for payment. Together with denials of access this made food aid transport almost impossible. The government imposed a number of new taxes: income tax for federal government and a local *Borsa* tax of SDG 100 per truck to the state MoF. Traders also reported having to pay taxes and bribes to security officials in order to continue trading in food aid (Informant 88, 2013). Informal fees depended on the destination and the road taken. On Janjaweed-controlled roads, private transporters paid protection escorts and checkpoint fees. Moving through Janjaweed areas became particularly costly in 2013, security escorts and checkpoint fees often making commercial transport too expensive for WFP (Informant 73, 2013). From 2008 rebels imposed annual fees, called 'movement support fees', ranging from SDG 1,000 to 2,000, and checkpoint fees (Informants 61 and 76, 2013).

One transporter gave the following information on fees:

Al-Fashir – Mellit: government taxes in Al-Fashir.
Al-Fashir – Taweila: government taxes, security and rebel fees.
   Two checkpoints.
Al-Fashir – Kebkabiya-Seref Omra: government and rebel fees
   many times. In addition, in Kowra, there are many militias to
   be paid.
Al-Fashir – Dar-es-Salaam: Many checkpoints and many rebels.
Al-Fashir – Kutum and Dar Zaghawa: three checkpoints from
   Al-Fashir to Kutum, and one more between Kutum and Dar
   Zaghawa. There are many Janjaweed stations between Al-
   Fashir and Kutum and between Kutum and Dar Zaghawa.
   (Informant 76, 2013)

The fees and taxes imposed on food aid convoys increased as the conflict progressed, which one transporter attributed to the decrease in food aid, as less income could be gained from food aid itself (Informant 76, 2013). Traders also thought that annual fees in rebel areas were imposed from 2008 as a result of declining assistance (Trader focus group, 2014). Checkpoint fees in some areas increased five-fold (Informant 76, 2013), and on some routes the number of checkpoints also increased. For example, the number of checkpoints along the Al-Fashir–Kutum route rose dramatically in 2014; from fourteen to thirty-four between March and May, and to forty-two by August as other routes closed (Darfur Development and Reconstruction Agency, 2014a, 2014b). Many of the risks and constraints associated with food aid transport were dealt with by local transporters, and Table 4.2 illustrates their perceptions of the changes in food transport during the conflict. At the same time, however, security escorts and checkpoint fees are a new source of income for many. Transport companies might pick up escorts of six to ten people in main towns. One Khartoum transporter estimated that

50% of escorts are organised by local people (Informant 61, 2013). It makes sense therefore that the number and size of fees increased as food aid, and other humanitarian assistance, decreased.

The international food aid practices of the resilience regime emerged at a time of severe difficulties in transporting food aid in Darfur from 2008 onwards. The switch to vouchers provided a way of overcoming the logistical constraints faced by WFP, and of transferring responsibility and risk on to local transporters and traders. Less emergency food assistance is needed if high malnutrition rates are interpreted as being due to poor hygiene, and standardised nutrition practices do not need a detailed analysis of the context-specific causes. Regardless of their effectiveness, therefore, food-based resilience practices served a function in that they allowed the aid operation to continue under the guise of the positive ideology of promoting resilience. The next section discusses some

Table 4.2: Transporters' views on differences in food aid transport before 2000 and in 2013

Before 2000	2013
• Trucks transporting food aid moved all the time without taking travel permits • No checkpoints • Security situation was good, no hijacking of trucks • No taxes imposed on food aid transportation • WFP or INGOs provided fuel for trucks transporting food aid • Certain percentage as advance payment was made by WFP or INGO to the transporter • Transport could be part of another business or contracts could be made with individual truck owners	• Movement of trucks only during daytime • Travel permits should be obtained from Military Intelligence for transportation of food aid to any location • Many formal and informal checkpoints • Insecurity, looting, hijacking and confiscation of trucks by rebel groups/bandits • Payment of 17% of the transportation value to the taxation department • Income tax taken by the government on yearly basis estimated by the taxation department • The transporter is responsible for supplying fuel for his truck • Any transporter should have legal status: a business name and a registered transport company • Permission is needed from the rebel group controlling the area for entrance of food aid to the area or location

Source: interviews with five Darfuri transporters.

of the other alternative functions of the reduction in food aid from 2008 onwards.

Indirect effects of reduced food aid

The decline in food aid had indirect effects on trade and on the government's counter-insurgency strategies. As food aid volumes decreased, so did trade in food aid. The switch to food vouchers benefited mainly large traders. More importantly, reductions in food aid in rural areas helped the government's counter-insurgency strategy and the reduction in food aid in camps helped its policies of emptying the camps and encouraging return. It also enabled the government to attract or maintain support with its own food aid, and to penetrate the large urban IDP camps.

Effects on traders and transporters

The decline in food aid affected traders and transporters at all levels, while vouchers provided opportunities mainly for large traders. Traders in Al-Fashir town estimated that the quantity of food aid fell by 70–80% from 2009 to 2013 (Informant 88, 2013; Trader focus group, 2014). The price of food aid increased accordingly; between 2005 and 2008, traders in Al-Fashir could buy one bag of sorghum for SDG 7–8, which increased to SDG 40 by 2009, and SDG 100–105 by September 2013. The number of food aid traders decreased, in particular the number of women petty traders, but middle traders also left the market (Informant 90, 2013). By 2013, the business opportunities linked to food aid were in the hands of larger traders and transporters, but even for them income had decreased (Trader focus group, 2014). Some found other business opportunities, used their savings or moved business elsewhere (for example South Sudan) (Informants 76 and 89, 2013).

Other business opportunities linked to the transport or trade of food aid have also declined. Transporters reported that by 2013 people in rural areas were selling little (food aid, or assets such as goats or cash crops) and that trucks delivering food aid usually went back empty (Informants 76, 85 and 86, 2013). Other reasons for trucks returning empty included companies' prohibitions on carrying goods while on contract to deliver food aid, the quick turn-around required by WFP (which was now managing all food aid transport), the risk of goods being confiscated by armed groups and the high taxes and fees. In addition, if drivers brought back firewood, charcoal and bricks to sell, they had to pay high fees imposed by the Forest National Corporation.

Food vouchers provided new opportunities for traders, but the quantities of food that they were contracted to supply were small. They had to provide fourteen different commodities (sourced in different places) and the constraints on transporting anything within Darfur have become ever more numerous. WFP's criteria for selecting voucher traders and the time it takes for WFP to make payments mean that the voucher programme has been dominated by larger traders (Harrison and Wagabi, 2011; Bizzarri, 2013). It became increasingly difficult for smaller traders to put in bids to become voucher traders in 2013, when harvest failure in Darfur meant that much of the cereals for vouchers had to be purchased outside of the region. Traders sometimes bought food aid distributed elsewhere in Darfur or Chad. In 2011 and 2012, traders bought food aid sold by beneficiaries in Zamzam camp (in Al-Fashir) and sold it to voucher beneficiaries in neighbouring Abou Shook camp (Informant 90, 2013). Similarly, traders supplying voucher beneficiaries in Seref Omra and Kebkabiya bought food aid sold by Darfuri refugees in Chad. On the return journey they supplied oil and onions to Tina on the Chad border (Darfur Development and Reconstruction Agency, 2012). When Zamzam switched to vouchers in January 2014, at a time when North Darfur was suffering serious food shortages, only larger traders could bring food from central Sudan. Within Darfur, some traders bought food rations sold by government soldiers. To conclude, reductions in food aid meant that the alternative economic benefits mainly went to large traders and government.

Effect on counter-insurgency and government policy

The decrease in food aid facilitated government counter-insurgency tactics and policies of dismantling the camps for displaced populations. From 2010, food convoys within North Darfur had to be authorised by Military Intelligence, and from 2011 the government imposed further restrictions on the movement of goods into areas held by groups which had not signed the Doha Document for Peace. Food aid was once again going mostly to IDPs in camps and almost entirely to government-controlled areas. This meant that between 2004 and 2010 the way that food aid influenced conflict dynamics shifted dramatically. In 2004 food aid practices excluded Arab populations but from 2010 they excluded those in rebel-held areas. In other words, the exclusions shifted from those perceived to be supporting the government to those opposing the government, highlighting the fact that the government had taken control of food distribution.

Although WFP has attempted to negotiate access to rebel-held areas, and has sometimes gained access to parts of rural North Darfur, it has not challenged the government's denials when security is given as the justification (Informant 5, 2013). The government's own Darfur strategy of 2010 states that it will only facilitate humanitarian access to *secure* places (Government of Sudan, 2010), thereby giving it the means of restricting food deliveries on the basis of security. The denial of access includes information. The release of WFP food security assessment and monitoring reports has often taken a year or more, and localised nutritional survey results in Darfur may not be released at all. Most importantly, however, conflict-affected people fear talking about their situation to outsiders, due to the now pervasive presence of Sudan's security apparatus and mistrust of anyone not well-known to them. According to one person who did not want to be interviewed: 'Inside [camp X] it is very dangerous. Many national security are living inside the camp now. If they see you talking to outsiders then they think you are talking to foreign spies.' A WFP consultant also noted that she was under close surveillance:

In Al-Fashir, no visit to the camps was possible without armed escort. Close patrolling and accompaniment by assigned police officers was not only en-route, but also within the camps during FGDs [focus group discussions] and in-depth household interviews. Though unavoidable, this affected the atmosphere of confidentiality and trust the team attempted to create with community members. From a practical point of view, this also resulted in less time available for data collection, as escorts could only be available for a certain number of hours each day. (Bizarri, 2013: 19)

Most INGOs working in Darfur find it extremely difficult to get travel permits for international staff, a problem I also experienced. By 2013, Darfur was largely closed to the outside world.

The government's policy of emptying the camps and encouraging return of IDPs to their areas of origin is facilitated by the reduction in food aid. In the government's view, 'return' does not necessarily mean return to areas of origin: it could also mean going anywhere that is not a camp, for example peri-urban settlements. Central government officials have made it clear that they view camps as a magnet for international agencies and that they think distribution of food aid in camps contributes to keeping the IDPs there (Informants 96, 2014). One long-term aid worker put it like this:

> There is convergence between the government and agency strategies. Agencies are not getting sufficient resources so they are reducing food aid and engage in longer-term livelihoods. But people are not returning to their original villages and support for urban livelihoods is very difficult. For the government, this strategy fits quite well with draining the camps. (Informant 75, 2013)

The government's Darfur strategy of 2010 placed emphasis on the return of displaced populations and a shift from relief to development and self-reliance (Government of Sudan, 2010), which converged with aid agency recovery and donor resilience strategies. The shift from general food distribution to food-for-recovery is part of UNDP and Darfur Regional Authority's recovery and reconstruction strategy (UNDP and Darfur Regional Authority, 2013). The government had a number of initiatives to facilitate returns. First, since 2009 it has used funds from Arab states to create model villages, with all services provided, to encourage people to leave the camps and return home. However, IDPs who went to these villages usually returned quickly to the camps because they were attacked and looted in the villages (Informant 51, 2013). More recently, from 2011 the Darfur Regional Authority has planned to construct 'service centres' as part of the returns strategy. These centres, funded by Qatar and in which Qatari NGOs provide services, are to be close to people's original villages so that they can commute to their village before they eventually return there. The first service centre in North Darfur (in Tabit) had to be moved because of insecurity, however (Informant 75, 2013). Second, HAC and the Darfur Regional Authority have a policy to provide food aid to rural areas, but this is often contradicted by Military Intelligence, which blocks food deliveries to these rural areas if rebel movements are thought to be there (Informants 63 and 75, 2013; Informant 62, 2014). Despite government strategies of providing services and assistance in some rural centres, displaced populations did not return to areas that were not safe. An alternative government strategy has been IDP resettlement on the edges of towns or changing IDP camps into residential quarters. For example, in Nyala, South Darfur, the authorities allocated land to some IDP families on the peripheries of the town in 2011. Housing and services were provided, but they no longer received food aid (Informant 51, 2013). By 2013, this strategy appeared to have expanded to other parts of Darfur. For example, in West Darfur the Mornei IDP camp was due to be 'restructured' in early 2014, and HAC informed IDP sheikhs in Sirba locality that the camps were no longer recognised (Radio Dabanga, 2014c). If they agreed to move out of camps, IDPs would change their status from IDP to urban poor or returnee and they would lose their claims to assistance and protection, as well as the political claims by the rebel movements for compensation.

The reductions in international food aid made it easier for the government to maintain or attract the support of certain population groups or individuals. Government food aid from the strategic reserve was distributed in Darfur throughout the 2000s but, unlike in South Kordofan and Blue Nile, this was a small proportion of overall food aid provided in the early years of the conflict. In North Darfur, allocations ranged from just under 2,000 MT in 2003 to almost 13,000 MT in 2005 (Asfaw and Ibrahim, 2008), which was allocated according to government priorities. Kuma received government food aid from 2004 to 2007 (Group 4, 2013). It had been excluded from WFP distribution but, as some of Kuma's population are Arab nomads, they were an important source of government support. Informants from Kuma said that whenever they requested assistance the government would respond. In 2009, HAC provided food aid in areas held by rebel movements which had signed the DPA, and to areas of voluntary return (Humanitarian Aid Commission, 2009). Malha received allocations from the strategic reserve from 2009 to 2012, when WFP food aid allocations declined (Group 6, 2013; Buchanan-Smith et al., 2014). With part of Malha locality being in rebel hands, it was important for government to keep control of Malha town. Using food aid to support government employees remained a government priority. When interviewed in September 2013, staff at the Ministry of Finance in Al-Fashir reported distributing 10–15 kilograms of cereal and sugar to about 500,000 people and were planning a distribution for all employees in the state (Informant 70, 2013). The government also organised food distributions in 2013 in response to floods (for example in Kuma) (Informant 62, 2013), and in 2014 to people in parts of North Darfur that had been attacked by rebels, and to people affected by soaring food prices in North, South and East Darfur (Radio Dabanga, 2014b; Sudan Vision, 2014). Food aid remained an important way of maintaining government support during the conflict. It also appears that government food aid is increasing as international food aid diminishes.

Part of the government's strategy is to bring its opponents, including IDPs, over to its side. As with all politics in Sudan, this can be done with food or financial incentives. As one aid worker commented:

> The government is not just sitting there and seeing what INGOS and UN agencies are doing. They have their own business also. They are working with those communities just to get them to feel that sense of what the international community is talking about is nonsense. Those are the people they are talking about, those are the IDPs. They are settled, they have their land, their homes. They attract them to their side. They give them money, they talk to them. We shall do for you this, and this, and this. So kind of IDPs [that are] government-affiliated people. (Informant 51, 2013)

Or IDPs themselves:

> The government sometimes distributes food [in the camps] during Ramadan or Eid. It distributes something for the fasting people. But not for all. Maybe only for the people that have their approval. They also bring sheep during Eid Al-Adha. We did not get any. Q: Why is the government distributing food to some people in the camp? A: Because the government grows its people inside the camp.

As displaced populations receive less WFP food aid and have few alternative strategies (see the next section), they will be more susceptible to government strategies intended to win them over to the government's side. Some IDP leaders were reported to be receiving financial incentives or even a government salary. Government penetration of the large IDP camps in towns is also apparent from the number of taxes that have to be paid, and licences required, to trade in IDP markets. Until 2011, IDP camps were tax-free havens where traders paid no rent, taxes or licence fees (Darfur Development and Reconstruction Agency, 2011). By 2013, the government had infiltrated some of the largest and most politicised camps.

The indirect or alternative effects of reduced food aid include benefits to large traders and government officials (whereas a range of traders benefited in the early days of the response). It has facilitated government strategies of denying aid to people perceived to be rebel supporters and policies of emptying the camps. It has also improved the effectiveness of government food aid in maintaining its political support and attracting people over to the government side, particularly given the limited livelihoods options for most people in Darfur.

Are people still coping?

Many of the strategies that people use to cope with the threat of food insecurity or famine are blocked during conflict. Risk of attack and rape, as well as restrictions in movement between government and rebel-held areas, limit wild food collection, migration for work, collection of firewood (a common income-earning strategy for poor people) and access to markets for large numbers of people. Those who could leave Darfur early in the conflict largely did so. For those who remained behind, remittances from earlier migrants to Khartoum or elsewhere became an important source of income, although the closure of the border with Libya temporarily halted the remittances from Darfuris working there (Young et al., 2005). Families often split to maximise their options, with some members living in camps, others in their village of origin, or in Khartoum or abroad. Over time, displaced populations developed new strategies, for example brick-making or petty trading in food aid, agricultural or other casual labour, and in some cases people would travel back to their farms on a seasonal basis. Sale of firewood and charcoal remained an important income-earning strategy (Jaspars and O'Callaghan, 2008; Young et al., 2009a; WFP et al., 2011).

A whole new range of militarised or criminal 'coping strategies' developed during the Darfur conflict. These included demanding protection payments or joining militia or paramilitary groups such as the border guards and popular defence forces. Janjaweed militia not only demanded protection payments for food aid or other transport, but also that farmers continue to farm their own land or take their produce to the market (Jaspars and O'Callaghan, 2008). The number of paramilitary groups has increased in recent years, and these have provided an important source of income for young men in strategic government-held towns such as Malha and Kuma (Abdala Fadul and Mohamed Ahmed, 2011). Villagers have also been able to earn an income from setting up checkpoints or providing security escorts for truck convoys. Other strategies have included the hijacking of vehicles, or the theft and diversion of other aid commodities and materials. Young et al. (2009b: 70–71) called these kinds of strategies 'mal-adaptations' as they are short-term, war-related or illegal strategies that negatively impact the livelihoods of others.

The reduction in food aid from 2008 onwards is likely to have led to an increase in marginal, militarised and illegal strategies and strategies which are damaging and risky. Interviews and discussions with groups of displaced people for this research indicated that competition for casual labour, such as brick-making, seasonal farming or domestic work, increased and wages decreased (Groups 5 and 7, 2013). Trading opportunities decreased except for larger traders, some of whom found work in South Sudan or in WFP's food voucher programme. Others mentioned an increase in crime and begging (Group 5, 2013; Informant 51, 2013). It appears, therefore, that displaced people are becoming part of a large, poor urban or agricultural labour force. In rural areas, people's strategies depend on where they live, who controls the area and what their former livelihoods were. The incomes of some of those who fight in the government's militia or paramilitary groups have increased. For example, Malha, historically one of the most food-insecure places, has seen an inflow of money because of the number of people working for the Popular Defence Force and the Border Guards (Abdala Fadul and Mohamed Ahmed, 2011). However, not everyone in Malha has become better off: those with increased income have been able to invest in camels and sheep, but others have been reduced to herding and domestic labour (Abdala Fadul and Mohamed Ahmed, 2011). WFP assessments show that production and sale of crops, casual labour and firewood collection remain important sources of income.

For those unable to find new ways of 'coping' in Darfur, outmigration to Khartoum or abroad by one or more family members appears to be one of the few remaining options. In South Darfur, for example, camp sheikhs reported increasing numbers of people leaving the camps in 2013 to look for work, due to the failure of the agricultural season, the lack of food provided by humanitarian organisations and the lack of security in the region. Women stayed to work on the farmlands or in brick factories, and men went searching for work in Khartoum, Gedaref in eastern Sudan and South Sudan (Radio Dabanga, 2013d). One transporter reported a similar situation for North Darfur in the previous two years: 'People are leaving for economic and security reasons. There are no projects, no work in Darfur. So they come to find work in Khartoum. The situation is very bad in Darfur. Many people move, particularly since last year [2012]' (Informant 76, 2013). Others reported that more people were leaving to look for work (Group 7). The effect of ongoing conflict and reduced assistance is likely not only to drain the camps but to drain Darfur.

These marginal and mal-adaptive strategies do not constitute coping – defined as short-term responses to an immediate and unusual decline in access to food, and which protect livelihoods. The strategies adopted by conflict-affected households in Darfur are long-term and often entail risks to safety and livelihoods for themselves and/or others. Migration can expose refugees to more danger and is often done out of necessity rather than choice. Within Darfur, information on human rights abuses and the risks that people face is limited. Agencies no longer collect mortality data, and food security information mostly reflects long-term chronic rather than conflict-related causes. Information from national nutritional surveys indicates that acute malnutrition levels are alarmingly high in parts of Darfur. In the 1990s, malnutrition rates in parts of North Darfur were often above 15%, but they went down after a good harvest. Since the start of the conflict, state-wide surveys have shown an increase in acute malnutrition from 2006 to 2007, and the 2013 national survey showed prevalences as high as 27–37% in the poorest and most conflict-affected rural areas of North Darfur (Federal Ministry of Health, 2014). Darfur's 'actually existing development' has left most people in Darfur facing permanent emergency.

Conclusions

Despite almost continuous food aid since the mid-1980s, food aid operations have had little impact on the nutrition and food security of drought- and crisis-affected people in North Darfur. During the 1980s and 1990s, food aid was always too little and too late and could not be targeted at only the poorest in rural areas. WFP's 2004–05 operation in response to the conflict-induced humanitarian crisis can be seen as the peak of the livelihoods regime in Darfur: the massive food aid response was effective in reducing malnutrition, supporting markets and increasing people's safety. Despite the ongoing conflict, however, food aid levels soon decreased for reasons of reduced access, insecurity and a desire to move towards recovery and resilience programming. The effect has been that people in Darfur have become increasingly impoverished. In the 1980s and 1990s, a rising proportion of people adopted a limited range of precarious strategies such as collecting firewood or making charcoal to earn income and migrating for work. During the 1990s livelihoods regime, the main economic benefit of food aid was for central government and traders and transporters from central Sudan. In Darfur, it had the

effect of professionalising aid agencies, including training Sudanese aid workers, and influenced government food aid initiatives.
In attempting to provide assistance, and representing impoverished
rural communities, international agencies rather than local government came to be seen by these communities as welfare providers.
Government food aid, in contrast, was intended mostly for urban
populations and government employees.

The response to the 2003 Darfur crisis was different from earlier
food aid operations in Darfur. Food aid quantities were many
times larger and agencies were able to reach remote rural areas.
Malnutrition decreased and for a brief period Darfuri traders and
transporters benefited from the large amounts of food aid distributed, even if transporters from Khartoum made large profits buying
food aid sold by IDPs. From 2008, however, aid agencies decreased
food aid as they considered crisis-affected populations could meet
part of their needs, and beneficiaries received even less because of
attacks on food convoys, numerous checkpoints and informal taxes
and government restrictions on access. Malnutrition increased and
conflict continued to limit livelihoods options. In the 2000s, a large
urbanised displaced population became dependent on casual labour
or other low-income activities, while others farmed what land they
could access, adopted a range of militarised or criminal strategies
or left Darfur. New practices in the resilience regime were perfectly
suited to an environment in which it was difficult to transport and
distribute food aid. Vouchers reduced the need for WFP to transport food directly, a focus on behaviour change does not require any
material assistance and quantitative assessments no longer require
on-the-ground presence of highly experienced staff who can interpret the findings. The actual effect of reducing food aid has been
to help government counter-insurgency strategies and policies to
empty the camps and bring IDP leaders over to the government side.

One of the main impacts of long-term food distribution has been
the creation of a group of highly experienced and knowledgeable
aid professionals (both government and non-government), traders,
transporters and beneficiaries. The following chapter analyses their
perceptions of food aid, and how the regimes of truth they created
enabled an 'actually existing development' in which government and
private sector benefited but crisis-affected populations were abandoned to permanent emergency.

5
Perceptions of food aid: politics, dependency and denial of permanent emergency

Long-term food aid has led to extensive knowledge and experience of food aid practices by government, private sector, aid agencies and beneficiaries. This chapter analyses their views and perceptions of food aid and its beneficiaries, and the regimes of truth they have created. The practices of the Sudan government and international agencies created two dominant regimes of truth in the resilience regime. These have allowed the development of the government and private sector, permanent emergency and the abandonment of conflict-affected people to exist at the same time. The Sudan government's regime is that food aid, both international and national, is a political tool. International agencies have created a regime of truth in which malnutrition and food insecurity is due to people's own behaviours, and in which conflict is invisible. This has allowed the Sudan government to control food aid, and international agencies to work in a highly politicised environment. Food aid beneficiaries and long-term Sudanese aid workers contest these dominant regimes of truth. Their perception is that all food aid is political, but also that the international community is withdrawing food aid while the Sudanese people continue to face threats and constraints in accessing food.

Government officials are well aware of the political and trade aims of some forms of international food aid, which they have learnt through experience or education. They view international food aid and the agencies that provide it as a political tool of the West or, echoing food aid aims from the 1970s, as a means of disposing of US agricultural surpluses and creating overseas markets. Over the years, the Sudan government has absorbed the objectives, language and strategies of international agencies and can challenge the international community on its own terms. Its long-term experience of food aid has enabled the establishment of a food aid apparatus modelled on that of the West.

International aid agencies see food aid mainly as a cause of dependency, particularly for IDPs, and have aimed to move towards recovery and resilience programming, despite the ongoing conflict and high levels of acute malnutrition. In their regime of truth, IDPs and other conflict-affected populations become malnourished because of their culture, food and hygiene behaviours rather than because of limited access to food. International agencies can sustain this belief because remote programming and assessments using universal indicators make conflict and its effect on people invisible. It is a fantasy which requires constant denial of permanent emergency and a belief that the practices of the resilience regime represent progress.

The beneficiaries, Sudanese aid workers, traders and transporters interviewed all perceived food aid as having political and economic as well as life-saving effects. Beneficiary representatives saw food aid as being closely linked to national and international politics, and reductions in international food aid over time as motivated by aims of shifting to development or of reducing dependency rather than by improvements in access to food. Long-term Sudanese aid workers showed extensive knowledge of food aid programming and of the international and local politics of food aid. For some, the continued need for food aid to save lives combined with its effect of providing benefits for the government which continues to fight wars with its own people have created a moral dilemma.

The analysis in this chapter is mainly based on interviews with aid workers, government officials, traders, transporters and beneficiary focus groups. Some information or quotes are not cited because cross-referencing may lead to identification. The chapter starts with information on the nature and length of experience gained by different people involved in food aid, which is followed by an analysis of the views and perceptions of government officials and international agencies and by alternative perceptions of food aid by beneficiary representatives, long-term Sudanese aid professionals, traders and transporters.

A country of food aid experts

Many Sudanese involved in food aid have been so for a long time, including aid professionals, government officials, transporters, traders and beneficiaries. The long-term Darfuri aid professionals I interviewed had all had experience with international agencies since the 1980s or early 1990s and held senior positions in donor and UN agencies or NGOs, or worked as consultants. All moved between agencies over time and most were still working on food security in Darfur, although not always directly in food distribution. They received training on food security in emergencies while they worked for international agencies. Local NGOs also had previous experience; even the volunteers assisting in food distribution in Darfur had done so many times before (Informants 81, 2013). Some had knowledge of Western literature on aid; for example, a UN official travelling to Nairobi heard representatives from the Sudan umbrella agency for local NGOs (Sudan Council of Voluntary Agencies) talking about an article by Mark Duffield in which he argued that the focus of aid was becoming the intervention rather than the problem (Informant 10, 2013).

The government officials I interviewed also had long experience of food aid. They had often worked for RRC and HAC[1] for many years, sometimes starting off at state level and moving up the ranks to federal level in Khartoum. As part of their work, they came into regular contact with international agencies (donors, the UN and INGOs) and learnt through experience. According to one aid worker, the best training of government officials probably came through working for INGOs:

> these people [in HAC] ... when humanitarian intervention
> started, they had no idea. But as time went on, they started
> learning things, and even some of the government staff was
> employed by INGOs, they left, and then they bring them to
> HAC. Some of the HAC people they are former INGO staff.
> So they started to know what assessment, evaluation, log frames
> are and you know every year they come with a new strategy.
> That is why, these years, they want to be involved in everything.
> (Informant 51, 2013)

The current Director-General of HAC worked in senior capacities for INGOs such as Accord and CARE and is very familiar with food aid programming, as was apparent from his summary of the issues:

> Food aid is very important and it has different dimensions. Of
> course there are people in need and it is a life-saving intervention.
> So there is no question about it. How to deliver it – there are
> different approaches ... food-for-work, or food assistance, school
> feeding, monetisation, vouchers, also there are impacts of ...
> unless properly approached, it may create some dependency, and
> affect the local production system and it may affect the taste of
> food. (Informants 96, 2014)

Government officials have learnt the language of international food aid and have used this to challenge the international community on its own terms, often to reduce food aid. The Humanitarian Aid Commissioner from 2004 to 2010 (for much of the duration of the Darfur crisis),[2] for example, was trained by SC-UK in the Food Economy Approach (FEA) and sponsored to follow a food security course at the Institute of Development Studies at Sussex University in the UK. When he became Commissioner, he challenged WFP on the change in method and argued for the use of the FEA on technical grounds, although the reduction in food aid he expected from the FEA would also have had the political effect of reducing support for IDPs in camps and thus potentially for the rebellion. Similarly, at my research presentation at Al-Fashir University, the head of the NISS commented: 'There is often confusion about what is the right intervention at the right time. Food may arrive during harvest time. This raises issues of impartiality and neutrality. The right intervention is to think of a way to improve production' (Informant 68, 2013). This also supports the government policy of reducing international food aid in Darfur. The statement is all the more interesting because food aid was often delayed because of the failure to get clearance from the NISS and/or Military Intelligence.

Government officials have also used knowledge gained through familiarity with Western literature to argue against aid. Two former senior government officials (whom I interviewed) had PhDs from Western universities. They, and others, were familiar with the literature criticising food aid in the 1970s and early 1980s and used this to justify their own position against international food aid. For example, the former Under-Secretary at the MoF commented: 'During the 1970s there were lots of studies on the negative impact of the American food aid, there is lots of literature' (Informant 20, 2012). A former Relief Commissioner referred to Lords of Poverty by Graham Hancock (1991), which criticises official aid (donor, UN, World Bank) for benefiting the aid organisations rather than the poor of the Third World (Informant 17, 2012). Almost all government officials mentioned that food aid was a way of dumping US food surpluses and of creating overseas markets, and that wheat food aid had made the country dependent on imported wheat. They used their knowledge of the criticisms of programme food aid to argue against the provision of emergency food aid in Sudan in the 1990s and 2000s.

Traders and transporters involved in food aid have often had many years of experience too. The three main grain traders who purchase grain locally for WFP had all had a relationship with WFP since the 1980s. The largest grain trader had farmed commercially since the 1950s and had the biggest agribusiness in Sudan. Of the other two, one started as a farmer in 1987 and sold grain to WFP's contractor before he established his own trading company, and the other was contracted by WFP to transport in-kind food aid from 1984 onwards and started a new company for procurement in 1996. Of WFP's two main Khartoum-based transporters, one had worked with the agency since the 1970s and the other since the 1980s. All had detailed knowledge of the food aid business, the changes in international and government policy and how this affected their own businesses. One Khartoum trader/transporter described the changes as follows:

> In terms of the changes, there are two periods. The first one is the Nimeiri era, 1983/84. People and the government were welcoming of food aid. When General Bush [US Vice President] came he declared famine here. He asked the international community to come and help. ... Maybe the government was a little bit reluctant but they were forced to accept it. Relations between US and government were good at that time. The second period is from 1984 to now. But can divide this again in three. First is 1989–93, when there was war between north and south [Sudan]. The government made big problems for NGOs and WFP. I had no business at that time ... The second era is from 1994 to 2005. The war stopped [in 2005]. There were many tenders to transport food to the south at this time. I contributed to this ... The government signed the [peace] agreement [and] thought that relations between government and Western donors would develop. Then the last period is after separation [of South Sudan in 2011] to now. These are times of hostility between the government and NGOs. People think that the presence of food aid has prolonged the conflict in Darfur. That without food aid, the conflict could have been solved early on; food aid attracted people to the camps, to find food, to find health care. For me this is not true, for the government to say so. People have a problem, others come to save them. But it also has a negative impact. Dependency. It changes consumer behaviour. In Darfur, people are used to millet, not sorghum. Sorghum and wheat have changed their behaviour. This in turn affects the budget of the government because they need to import wheat. (Informant 46, 2013)

This account is noteworthy because it contains a number of different discourses around food aid. First, food aid as part of global politics, and how it affects government policy and its relation with Western organisations. Second, food aid as creating dependency, whether through changing consumption habits or through assisting in the creation of camps. Third, food aid as assisting rebel movements and prolonging conflict. And fourth, food aid as good for business and the impact of the government's strategies on business, in particular the restriction of food movements to the south and their relaxation following the peace agreement. Both Darfuri and Khartoum transporters had long-term experience and in-depth knowledge about international food aid practices, government policies and their effect on crisis-affected populations as well as on their own businesses.

Sudanese experience of food aid is not only acquired through direct involvement in programming; receipt of food aid is a common experience for almost everyone in Sudan. The first time US aid, including food aid, was accepted is remembered as an event of historic significance by many because it was highly political (see Chapter 3). The demonstrations and military coup at the time of the first US food aid intervention were often referred to spontaneously in my interviews, and the subject was brought up by the Military Intelligence representative in HAC when I applied for my travel permit. He also mentioned the first humanitarian assistance in South Sudan from churches, saying that he had been taught these things at the military academy. More personal experience of food aid includes school feeding. When discussing the research with Sudanese friends, this was often the first thing they mentioned. The current HAC Director-General referred to his own experience of receiving food in school as an example of the positive effects of food aid, as he believed that without school feeding many of Sudan's professionals would not be where they are today (Informants 96, 2014). Some Darfuris also remembered receiving emergency food aid in response to famine in the 1970s.

To conclude, almost everyone in Sudan has knowledge or experience of food aid, and many of those involved directly have been so for many years. This means that Sudanese aid professionals, whether government, aid agency staff, traders or transporters, can engage the international community on its own terms, using food aid language to their own advantage. This knowledge and experience of food aid programming is one of the real but unintended developmental effects of long-term food aid.

The government view of food aid

Government representatives[3] always referred to international food aid as a political tool that provides support to rebel movements, threatens the government's sovereignty and makes the country dependent on food imports. As discussed in Chapter 3, government officials saw food distribution during ongoing conflict in the 1990s as the start of the politicisation of international food aid (Informants 17, 20 and 23, 2012). They viewed food aid distributed as part of Operation Lifeline Sudan (OLS) as direct support for rebel movements, which later influenced the government's position on food aid and international agencies operating in Darfur, Blue Nile and South Kordofan. One former government official commented: 'Food aid until the early 1980s was mainly development. From 1972 to the early 1980s there was peace. In evaluations at that time, we looked at efficiency. Now we just look at how much moves across lines. We do not want the enemy to get it or people on the other side' (Informant 20, 2012). According to one former HAC commissioner: 'Of course the food aid itself has its own power; if you give, or you don't give, it influences the situation' (Informant 41, 2013). In Darfur, long-term provision of food aid was seen as a key factor in maintaining the camps for displaced populations, which thereby supported the rebellion and prevented the return of displaced populations to their villages (Informant 24, 2012; Informant 94, 2013; Informants 96, 2014).

Government officials also linked the politicisation to more subtle ways of undermining the Sudan government. Humanitarian intervention was twice referred to as a Trojan horse, first during OLS and later during the Darfur crisis. Food aid was perceived as a means of infiltration that allowed the enemy, Western governments, to weaken Sudan's government. A former Relief and Rehabilitation Commissioner referred to the effect of OLS food aid in this way: 'They create dependency for the community, imposed by the international community. It is the same as a Trojan horse. After the war stopped, the government would be very weak' (Khalifa, 2006). Similarly in 2004 Sudan's representative to the UN Assembly asked whether the UN Security Council's 'lofty humanitarian objective' in Darfur was a '"Trojan horse ... embraced by other people who are advocating a different agenda"' (quoted in Williams and Bellamy, 2005: 36). The most direct reference to the use of food aid to impose Western forms of governance and weaken the Sudan government was made by the Chairman of the Darfur Regional Authority:

The government thinks food aid is a policy mechanism from the
West. It is a means to implement their own [the West's] policies
over time in marginalised areas. I.e. they [the West] want to
change the perception of people towards the government, and
turn them against government ideology. To convince them of
the necessity of civil society, democracy, human rights. The
government is very sensitive to this. (Informant 94, 2013)

Similar comments were made by the Director-General of HAC
in 2014:

It is like a family level … .Rather than the family seeing me as
the main breadwinner, now they see another important person
coming in at the time of my inability to play that role. Q: So it
undermines that kind of relationship? A: Absolutely. And we
can take it further. The fact that this is always done by external
actors, whether national or international, today there is some
displacement in an area which used to be very stable and all of
a sudden they see some national or international NGO doing
delivering and all that, at a time when the local government also
seems to be in crisis, not able to deliver. (Informants 96, 2014)

This view that international food aid gives foreign nations
power over Sudanese populations was to some extent confirmed by
interviews with beneficiary focus groups who named food distributions after the political leaders of countries who provided it, such
as Reagan or Gaddafi (see beneficiary views later in this chapter).
Rejecting emergency food aid is also a matter of pride or self-respect.
Sudanese professionals, whether government or aid agency, remembered with pride the period of the 1970s when Sudan did not need
external food aid, and aspired to a time when the country will be free
from it. Government officials considered the most positive aspects of
food aid to be those that can contribute to development, for example
school feeding and infrastructure projects, such as road or railway
rehabilitation, in the 1970s and 1980s (Informant 23, 2012).

Senior government officials linked food aid with the disposal of
US agricultural surpluses (Informants 20 and 24, 2012; Informants
96, 2014). One former HAC Commissioner remembered that American donor representatives informed him that they had to support
their own farmers rather than purchase locally and support production (Informant 24, 2012). Government officials, and other Sudanese
professionals, felt that wheat food aid had changed food habits and

in doing so had created markets for imported wheat. Wheat imports into Sudan certainly show an increase over time (see Figure 5.1), but whether this is due to food aid is difficult to prove. For the purpose of this research, however, the important point is that many Sudanese believe that US food aid has made their country dependent on imported wheat and that this had been intentional on the part of food aid donors.[4]

International agencies involved in food aid or other forms of emergency aid are under suspicion of gathering intelligence. This came to a head after President Al-Bashir was indicted for genocide, war crimes and crimes against humanity and the ICC issued a warrant for his arrest in March 2009. INGOs were suspected of having sent information to the ICC and of working as spies under cover of providing humanitarian assistance. A study by the Middle East and Africa Studies Centre reviewed documents confiscated from

Figure 5.1: Sudan per capita wheat imports and food aid

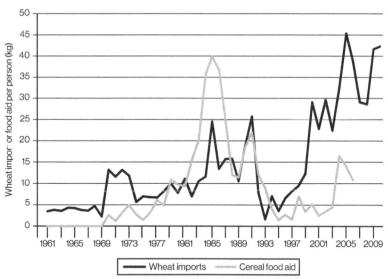

Source: FAOSTAT (FAO, 2012c).

Notes: This graph presents wheat imports and cereal food aid per capita, because the population of Sudan increased significantly between 1961 and 2009, from around 12 million to 43 million in 2010 (Sudan before separation of South Sudan). Data on population, wheat imports and cereal food aid are all from FAOSTAT. FAO confirmed by email that the wheat imports would include wheat food aid.

the offices of the expelled agencies after President Bashir's indict-ment. As evidence for intelligence gathering, it not only considered the monitoring of protection and human rights abuses but also information in agency technical and medical reports about aerial bombardments, Janjaweed attacks, displacement, rape, ill health and threats to food security and livelihoods (Middle East and African Studies Centre, 2013).[5]

Government officials also saw international agencies as businesses that needed to maintain their sources of income. They believed that it was in aid agencies' interest to exaggerate the numbers of people in need or food aid requirements, as their funding is linked to tonnage distributed (Informant 24, 2012; Informants 96, 2014): 'most of [the money] is not going to beneficiaries, it is going for other things, administration, consultants, logistics, distribution, re-distribution, evaluation, assessment, re-assessment' (Informant 12, 2012). This view was echoed by others (Informant 19, 2012; Informant 41, 2013). Research on perceptions of aid by armed non-state actors in Somalia and Afghanistan, namely Al-Shabaab and the Taliban, had similar findings: they were concerned that international agen-cies worked as spies for enemy countries and that they were in the country for their own economic benefit (Jackson, 2014). As in Sudan, this had major implications for access by international agen-cies. With a government view of international NGOs as political tools of the West, it is not surprising that the Sudan government wants to establish stricter control over international agencies and manage food distribution itself.

Government views are that food aid supports the agriculture of donor countries and that it has made Sudan dependent on imported wheat. International food aid is also seen as undermining the Sudan government by supporting rebel movements, and by undermining its relationship with its citizens. International agencies are seen as working mainly in their own financial interest and to provide intel-ligence to their governmental donors. As discussed in the previous chapters, Sudan has developed its own food aid apparatus, modelled on its knowledge and experience of international food aid.

International agencies: de-politicisation and abandonment

International agencies currently working in Sudan believe that behaviour is a key cause of food insecurity and malnutrition. The resilience regime was a response to the failures of past practices and

to changes in global politics, and is maintained because of the political sensitivity of indicators of humanitarian crisis and a remoteness
from the conflict-affected Darfuris that aid agencies have come to
assist. This in turn facilitates reductions in food aid on the grounds
of dependency and an abandonment of populations to deal with the
effects of conflict themselves. Limited information and claims of
dependency have facilitated the reduction in aid.

I interviewed aid workers[6] in international agencies currently
working in Darfur about their policies on food aid. Policies ranged
from complementing food aid with other food security and livelihoods interventions to switching from food aid to food assistance
and attempts at greater targeting. The limited access to some population groups, however, meant that these changes have to be made
without regular and timely information on people's food security
and nutritional situation, and particularly on the conflict threats
faced by different population groups and on their vulnerability.
This lack of information came through when I asked what strategies
people could use to access food or about the implications of food
aid reductions:

> [T]argeting should be done, but there will be some inclusion
> and exclusion error. In IDP camps we will discuss with field
> staff. There are some people who are wealthy but still receive
> food. This is creating dependency. If we could identify the other,
> then we can provide properly. Q: So what else can people do?
> A: We are having a consultation meeting – but have to do the
> camp profiling first. We are thinking of doing garbage collection
> as food-for-work. Get food in return for collecting garbage.
> Otherwise, I have no answer, maybe they will do some trade.
> But the poor – I don't know. (Informant 92, 2013)

> Q: I think Kalma did not receive food for a long time. A: I think
> eleven months or so ... Q: What were they doing to get food?
> A: It was a question for us, even for us. But we are yet to have
> any kind of assessment to see what was happening. Because even
> during this time we did not have full access to the camp ...
> Q: It is difficult to see what people were doing. A: Very difficult,
> unless there is study. Q: are you planning to do this? A: I am
> not sure. Q: UNICEF did a survey after three months and the
> malnutrition levels went up. You wonder what happened eight
> months later. But nobody knows? A: Nobody knows. (Informant
> 51, 2013)

WFP's assessments provide much of the information on food security in Darfur. Its 2011 and 2012 annual comprehensive food security assessments show a lower percentage of food-insecure households than before, but they were done after the harvest – thus reflecting the time of year when food is available – and their food consumption indicator is likely to under-estimate food insecurity (see Chapter 2). The December 2012 assessment showed only 17% of people in North Darfur to be food-insecure (WFP, 2014a). The assessments provide information on people's economic strategies to access food, such as the sale of crops or livestock or livestock products, wage labour, sale of firewood and grass, and petty trade. Food security is analysed by residence group and state, and, at the individual level, by education, gender and employment of heads of household. Other information includes the natural and economic aspects of food security, such as the harvest and food prices. Both food security assessments and nutritional surveys gather information on child feeding practices and morbidity, and national nutritional surveys also collect information on hygiene practices, sanitation and health-seeking behaviour. Assessments provide little information on the nature of conflict, threats to livelihoods, political vulnerability, and how this affects food insecurity. These assessments create a reality, or truth, in which it is considered that people have ways of accessing food, most households are food-secure and, if their children are malnourished, it is due to their own behaviour. Conflict is invisible. Such a reality is also acceptable to government authorities. As the section on government views showed, assessments which provide information on the conflict lead to accusations of intelligence gathering for Western governments. WFP's regular monitoring uses the same quantitative indicator of food insecurity and also reports information on food prices, income sources and expenditure. These reports have shown a deterioration in food security for displaced populations since 2014 but give no analysis or recommendations (see for example WFP Sudan, 2015, 2016). The national nutritional survey carried out in 2013 in Sudan shows an acute malnutrition prevalence of 28.3% in North Darfur (in all areas except the capital Al-Fashir). High prevalences of malnutrition in Sudan generally have been linked to poor feeding or hygiene practices and mothers' knowledge and education (Federal Ministry of Health, 2014). This has created a belief that parents do not know how to look after their children, as shown in the views of some of the aid workers currently working in Darfur:

Mothers do not know how to cook ... It is a desert area, people breed animals only for cultural aspects. They do not know how to farm. Sometimes they only drink milk. They have a child every year, which means they are weaning their children too early. (Informants 63, 2013)

People in Kebkabiya have many wives and have too many children. Water dries out in the dry season. Work is only seasonal. Many men have more than one household ... We distributed a half ration for two months. This has not changed anything. We need to consider hygiene practices. (Informant 65, 2013)

The result is that the solution to malnutrition in Darfur can be standardised and be the same as elsewhere in Sudan, or in other countries: improved hygiene and sanitation practices, increasing mothers' awareness of good infant feeding practices, vaccination and vitamin supplements and the provision of specialised foods to malnourished children. This regime of truth removes government responsibility for creating food insecurity and malnutrition through its war strategies and denial of access, and removes international responsibility for protecting civilians from large-scale loss of life at the hands of their own government.

This regime of truth, in which food aid is not needed to tackle malnutrition, also addresses concerns about food aid dependency in Darfur's protracted crisis. The need to decrease food aid to reduce dependency and encourage self-reliance was mentioned in all seven interviews carried out with INGO staff currently working in Darfur and in interviews with WFP staff. This converged with government perceptions that long-term food aid for drought- and conflict-affected people had created dependency, and that food aid had made their country dependent on food imports – particularly wheat (Informant 20, 2012; Informants 41 and 94, 2013). INGO staff and long-term Sudanese aid workers talked about long-term food aid making IDPs lazy or unwilling to work, and said that IDPs now saw IDP status itself as a livelihoods opportunity, which justified the need for recovery-based or developmental approaches (Informant 12, 2012; Informants 48, 63 and 93, 2013). One aid worker in Darfur expressed the sentiment as follows:

People got used to sitting, just waiting to get food. Up to two years ago, there were IDPs with multiple ration cards. There is high dependency on free food, free services ... [We need to] start food-for-recovery. Get them back to production. Otherwise, there are work opportunities with the peace-keeping forces, people have developed new skills, and have some coping mechanisms. (Informants 63, 2013)

Beneficiary representatives had also adopted the dependency discourse and expressed feelings of shame about receiving food aid for a long time or about having to rely on others. When asked about views on long-term food aid, beneficiary representatives would often say, like international agencies, that it created dependency and that people had stopped working and were just doing nothing. When questioned further, however, they would elaborate that children no longer knew how to farm and that they themselves had of course not stopped working. Others felt bad about simply relying on others (Groups 4 and 7, 2013). While beneficiaries' views reflected some of the negative associations of food aid with dependency, by 2013 they were receiving very little food aid and had to rely on their own strategies to access food.

Linking people in the category 'IDP' with the concept of dependency provides further justification for the withdrawal of food aid. At the start of the Darfur crisis, being displaced was explicitly linked with the need for protection, first by the international community and then by the displaced themselves. In 2004, Darfur was called the 'first protection crisis' because of the nature and severity of the violence, including violent deaths, rape and destruction leading to large-scale displacement (Pantuliano and O'Callaghan, 2006). In interviews I carried out in 2012 and 2013, a narrative about the need for protection had been replaced by one about the risk of dependency. This change in discourse is reinforced by the international aid community's inability to monitor and report protection risks following the NGO expulsions of 2009 and the restrictions imposed on INGOs that remain. Long-term IDPs were seen as cheats and their leaders as particularly troublesome.[7] In camps, IDPs were seen as enjoying the free goods and services provided and as choosing to stay in camps rather than going back to their farms to work.[8] These views were expressed by donors, aid agencies and government alike. Viewing IDPs as lazy or dependent facilitated the withdrawal of aid because they were seen as unworthy of receiving it. The removal of the need to protect IDPs gave Western governments a further excuse for inaction.

To conclude, international aid workers in Darfur in the second decade of the 2000s have little access to conflict-affected populations and have to rely on simple quantitative indicators to get a picture of what is happening. These practices have created a regime of truth in which conflict is invisible, people are malnourished because of their own actions, food insecurity is minimal and displaced people are dependent on food aid because they are lazy. In this regime, food aid can be reduced and neither the Sudan government nor Western governments are responsible for causing the emergency or for protecting civilians. Conflict-affected populations have been abandoned to address the effects of conflict and of the failures of aid themselves.

International agencies: the denial of permanent emergency

As discussed in the previous section, in Darfur's resilience regime food aid practices have created a regime of truth in which conflict-affected people are food-insecure and malnourished because of their own actions. This regime of truth is a fantasy which requires the denial of permanent emergency. This means being able to talk about food aid dependency despite most conflict-affected populations receiving little food aid since 2008. It involves maintaining aims of recovery, while at the same time knowing that it is impossible to implement most recovery interventions because conflict is ongoing, and while having evidence of the negative consequences of withdrawing food aid. It means believing that levels of acute malnutrition that are twice the emergency threshold have nothing to do with lack of access to food, while at the same time knowing that many people's access to land remains limited and that food prices have been rising. In this fantasy, food vouchers can be provided to increase choice and can be implemented in a context where markets do not function, inflation is rampant and conflict limits local food production. These contradictions are present throughout INGO and WFP programming in Darfur.

The Darfur fantasy is similar to the one Marriage (2006) described for South Sudan, where aid agencies created a fantasy about principled and sustainable programming by denying the effects of protracted conflict and violence. In the South Sudan fantasy, aid agencies attributed the limited impact of programmes to aid dependency or lack of participation, and if access was limited, or civilians and aid workers attacked, they interpreted this as non-compliance with humanitarian principles. The inadequacies of aid programmes had to be denied to maintain funding levels, but also to 'provide psychological protection to aid workers and political protection to the institution of assistance' (Marriage, 2006: 490). The exclusion of politics was necessary to maintain the fantasy. In the case of Darfur, a fantasy was created in which food aid was no longer needed because of the difficulties of gathering information and of providing material assistance in the face of persistent denial of access and ongoing violence. Using Cohen's (2001) analysis in his book *States of Denial*, this fantasy involves two forms of denial. The first is interpretive denial: things are given a different meaning. A prevalence of acute malnutrition above 15%, for example, is considered normal, and therefore does not need an emergency response. The second form of denial consists of simultaneously knowing and not knowing about the permanent emergency and failure of aid in Darfur. Aid workers continue to justify recovery programming, or aims of reducing dependency, while at some level knowing that conflict or violence is ongoing and that some people continue to face difficulties in accessing food. The creation of the Darfur fantasy has elements of Walkup's (1997) aid worker strategies for coping with the stress and moral dilemmas of working in humanitarian crises. The impossibility of meeting needs with limited assistance in complex environments has led – according to Walkup – to four stages of coping strategies: overwork, detachment, transference and reality distortion. Practices of the resilience regime facilitate these strategies because detachment is already a result of remote management.[9] Similarly, resilience practices facilitate transference, or blaming aid recipients themselves, and reality distortion, creating a truth in which people themselves are considered responsible for their malnutrition and food insecurity, and only minimal material assistance is needed.

In Darfur, aid workers maintained a concern about long-term food aid creating dependency (and other negative aspects of food aid) in the face of evidence that the withdrawal of food aid had negative consequences, and that conflict created ongoing risks for many people. One aid worker's explanation of the consequences of withdrawal of food aid from some IDPs shows how this can be seen as success and failure at the same time:

> They cut off the food distribution to free them from the dependency. Q: Who? A: The government, the strategy was to let them live as citizens in that place. This is the good thing about it – they had their own land, they started taking care of themselves. And some initial needs, like the health, water

and kinds of services, but as a family you have to work to gain
your livelihoods. But on the other side, maybe I don't know
... how can I say ... because like right now, for example, it is
very difficult for someone to go there after sunset. The rate
of crimes and all these kinds of things. Q: So there is a lot
of crime? A: Yes. Q: Why do you think that is? A: Basically
because of the needs. If you cannot cover your livelihoods for
your family, you will think of other ways of getting money.
(Informant 51, 2013)

Another aid worker talked about dependency while at the
same time referring to the shortfalls in distributions in early 2013,
somehow combining the perceptions that food aid is bad for IDPs in
camps and that no food aid is bad for people in rural areas:

People got used to sitting, just waiting to get food. Up to two
years ago, there were IDPs with multiple ration cards. There is
high dependency on free food, free services. ... [We need to] start
food-for-recovery. Get them back to production. ...

Access was denied to all rural areas in XXX. So the situation
worsened. In the first half of the year, we only distributed
61% of the planned allocation of food aid – only in the camps.
(Informants 63, 2013)

Other aid workers talked negatively about food aid keeping
people in camps, while at the same time acknowledging the
ongoing insecurity and displacement: 'If we speak about the beneficiaries, the food aid is definitely a big pull factor to the camps.
Other basic services also influence the mechanism of movement.
And all the time, there were still insecurity incidents that were
causing displacements' (Informant 48, 2013). In a similar vein, aid
workers could explain high levels of acute malnutrition as the result
of cultural or behavioural factors, while at the same time having
little information about the kinds of livelihood strategies that were
actually feasible for different population groups in Darfur. They
assumed that people survived despite the lack of food aid, and that
conflict-affected or displaced people had developed new livelihood
strategies over time:

In Kalma, the biggest camp in South Darfur, the leaders refused
to be verified for one year [and food distribution was stopped

until they agreed to verification]. But they survived. Q: How
do you know they survived – was there a mortality survey?
A UNICEF survey in Kalma three months after the food
distribution was stopped showed an increase in malnutrition.
A: It is true that in Dar Zaghawa, when the food was cut,
malnutrition increased to 30%. (Informants 63, 2013)

Why do you think there are persistently high levels of acute
malnutrition? A: Well, it is no longer an acute crisis. People have
developed new livelihoods in the camps. Pastoralists [in places
like Malha] have access to milk. (Informant 60, 2013)

The latter quote was part of my discussion with a nutritionist
about the possible reasons for a high prevalence of acute malnutrition,
particularly in older children in pastoral populations, using weight-
for-height measurements. According to this nutritionist, the most
likely explanation was that pastoralists have a different body shape so
they are not malnourished. There are technical arguments against this
theory (see for example Young and Jaspars, 2009: 30, 52–53, 62, 66–68,
72), but for agencies working in Darfur this provides another reason
for not responding with food aid or other emergency food security
interventions. It was only through further, informal discussions with
aid workers about a nutritional survey in Kebkabiya that it became
apparent that aid agencies were reluctant to investigate or talk about
causes they could not address. The survey examined the causes of
persistent acute malnutrition by comparing the characteristics of IDP
households with well-nourished and those with malnourished children. Displaced populations with well-nourished children had access
to land and regular employment. Health, water and sanitation were
similar for both groups of IDPs (Ibrahim, 2011). When discussing the
survey, aid workers at first emphasised the ability of a mother to care
for her children, but after some time acknowledged that differences
in access to resources (which could be linked to social and political
status) were probably an important cause of malnutrition and that
this would in turn influence caring behaviours. However, while they
could not address differential access to land, they could educate on
feeding and hygiene practices, which they felt were at least a contributing cause. Aid agency actions as well as analysis focused on what is
possible in a highly politicised environment.
     In the aid agency regime of truth, the introduction of vouchers also
becomes possible despite supply failures and political interference
in markets. Food vouchers aim to provide greater choice, culturally

suitable food and a quicker response than in-kind food aid (which often has to be shipped from the US). In Darfur, secondary aims were to revive markets and stimulate production, and to undermine the power of corrupt IDP sheikhs (WFP Sudan, 2011; Informant 56, 2013). WFP's own evaluations have shown that beneficiaries appreciate the choice but usually only buy two or three commodities, and that large traders dominate the voucher system. Evaluations also highlighted the risks of providing vouchers in a context of market concentration, political interference and low production (Harrison and Wagabi, 2011; Bizzarri, 2013). The programme has been mainly implemented in North Darfur, the state with traditionally the lowest production even before the conflict, and was expanded in 2014 when the whole of Darfur faced extreme food shortages. As a consequence, some food bought by voucher traders was the same food aid that WFP had distributed to IDPs or refugees elsewhere but who had sold part of their ration. Diversion by IDP sheikhs has not stopped completely and voucher traders sometimes charge higher prices than for the same goods in the regular market (Pattugalan et al., 2012; Groups 7 and 8, 2013). Yet voucher programmes are generally presented in positive terms.

In conclusion, international food aid practices in the resilience regime produced a truth in which it became acceptable to withdraw food aid and to expect conflict-affected populations to change their behaviour to deal with permanent emergency. This requires the denial of the ongoing risks that populations face and of the failures of aid. It allows aid agencies to remain present but also unintentionally makes them complicit with the actions of the Sudan government because their practices make the impact of war strategies and the use of food aid as a political tool invisible. As in Keen's (2014) study in Sri Lanka, the language – or practices – of aid provided a smokescreen behind which abuses could be carried out. The regime of truth of international agencies also suppresses the alternative views, perceptions and experiences of aid beneficiaries and conflict-affected people, of long-term Sudanese aid workers and of the private sector.

Alternative perceptions of food aid: politics, war and economic benefits

The beneficiary view

The beneficiary perception was that all food aid is political and that international agencies are reducing food aid, but also that they continue to face threats to their livelihoods and their access to food remains severely constrained. In focus group discussions with long-term beneficiaries, I or my research assistant asked them about their perceptions of international food aid, government food aid and their perceived reasons for change.[10] The beneficiary view of food aid as political was reflected in their associations of food aid with leaders of foreign nations, their own presidents or aid agency staff in charge

Table 5.1: Timeline with food distributions according to long-term beneficiaries

Time period	Why/what	Who – examples of associations
1970s	Emergency	Foreigners
1970s–now	School feeding	Foreigners
	Subsidised food	Nimeiri
1980–84	Famine/emergency	Nimeiri Arab countries Libya/Gaddafi
1984/85	Famine/emergency	Reagan Malaysian aid Kuwaiti Red Cross
1991–92	Emergency	Reagan
1990–99	1. Subsidised food/strategic reserve 2. Emergency/drought 3. Food for training	1. Government, Bashir. 2. Oxfam, 'Holland aid', John (Malha). 3. Anke (Shagra)
2000–03	Emergency/drought	Ahmed Suleiman (Malha)
2004	Crisis/emergency.	Government (Kuma) WFP (Jebel Si – in camps)
2005–12	Conflict	Ahmed Suleiman (Malha)
2007	Crisis/emergency	WFP (Kuma)
2009–12	Subsidised food/strategic reserve	Government (Malha)
2011	Food for training	Mohamed Siddiq (Shagra)
2013	Floods (Kuma)	Government/Sudan Red Crescent

Source: interviews with representatives from Malha, Kuma, Jebel Si and Korma.

of distribution locally. They used the names of political leaders or local INGO representatives to describe food distributions at different points in time. Everyone in Sudan calls US sorghum food aid, first distributed in 1984–86, 'Reagan'. In the 1980s, Cold War politics meant that the US was a key supporter of first Nimeiri's and later Al-Mahdi's regime. In some places, beneficiaries associated distributions in 1983/84 with Gaddafi, Libya or the Arab League (Beneficiary 3, 2013; Groups 2 and 3, 2013). As Chapter 4 showed, Libya was an influential player in Darfur from the 1970s, and in the early 1980s food aid was given along with military assistance (Prunier, 2008). Government distributions were linked with Presidents Nimeiri or Al-Bashir. Naming the distributions after political leaders not only highlights beneficiary perceptions that food aid is connected to national and international politics, but also confirms the government's view that food distributions can boost or undermine its power. Representatives from Malha and Shagra also named food distributions after the person in charge of distribution locally, for example Ahmed (Ibrahim) Suleiman, who had worked for INGOs in Malha in drought and conflict responses. Food aid is remembered for those who provide it, thus enhancing their status and authority within that community. Examples of these associations for some of the communities from which representatives were interviewed are shown in Table 5.1.

The perception of food aid as having governmental functions was also shown by answers to questions about the reasons why aid agencies and the government provided food aid. Most focus groups or beneficiaries answered that the international community gave food aid to save lives, as drought or famine relief, or in response to displacement. The reasons why government gave food aid, in contrast, were generally perceived to be to strengthen relations between the government and its citizens, to maintain security and to attract votes. Government food aid was clearly seen as political. No one mentioned addressing hunger, food shortages or assisting the poor as government objectives of food aid. Some of the reasons given for government provisions of food aid were:

> The government distributes for the stability of its citizens. To feel they are secure. If people are not hungry, they become satisfied. It calms the criminality. (Group 4, 2013)

> To strengthen the relationship between the people and the government. (Group 1, 2013)

To build trust ... It uses food aid as a pull for voting. To create a huge number of people around them. (Group 3, 2013)

The government distributes food ... to announce to the others that the government is doing something. (Group 6, 2013)

Beneficiary groups also had clear views on why the quantities of international food aid had decreased. Reasons they gave included: an increase in the population in need, new displacement or new emergencies and insecurity and banditry on the roads, which increases the cost of transport (Groups 4, 5 and 7, 2013). Two groups said that they thought the reduction in international food aid was due to government policy, to put pressure on them to return to their villages (Groups 7 and 8, 2013). They also thought that aid agencies reduced food aid as a way of shifting to development or to make them do things, such as return to their villages, or work:

The change especially happened in the last time, food for work, is to induce people to work and not rely on others. (Group 3, 2013)

[I]f people receive aid for longer, they cannot work. Finally, it is to encourage people to work. (Group 5, 2013)

The government decided to reduce the amount [of international food aid]. Q: Why? A: They reduced the amount to encourage us to return. But there has been no change. Where can we go? We lost our house, our property, and there is no security. (Beneficiary 1, 2013)

At the same time, one beneficiary group questioned whether the actual interventions provided could lead to development:

They [the international agencies] think that with emergencies, usually, later the emergency is finished. We found something to do, work. Some people are working in town, some in brick-making. Q: So was it the right thing to do, to reduce food aid? A: actually, this [the emergency being finished] is not the real reason. There are emergencies in other countries. Also the conflict in Darfur is taking a long time. This is also the reason why food aid has reduced. Also during transportation, there are armed groups. The fourth reason is to change to development, for example school feeding, skills training. But this is not

development; neither are donkey carts, fuel-efficient stoves. It
is not development because it is very small. Most people are
farmers and herders. How can they develop? They have no
land to cultivate. No water. In 70,000 people, maybe 60 receive
development aid. No one goes back to Jebel Si. (Group 7, 2013)

None of the beneficiary focus groups said that food aid had
decreased because they were now able to access their own food. The
quotes show that beneficiaries understood that, in terms of changes
in food aid practices, the dominant regime of truth was to reduce
food aid to move towards recovery and development. At the same
time, however, they contested the appropriateness of reducing food
aid, because they continued to experience ongoing risks to safety,
and questioned whether limited household-level assistance could
help achieve development. Food-for-work was seen as something to
make them work, rather than a way of providing food or creating
community assets. This contrasts with official agency objectives of
food-for-work, which are to meet food needs and create community
assets, but more closely matches the aid agency discourse of food aid
creating dependency and the need to get people out of the mentality
of just 'sitting and waiting for food' (Informant 92, 2013). The beneficiary focus groups that were interviewed as part of this research
contested the dominant international agency regime of truth that
food aid was no longer needed. Their own perception of truth was
that access to food remained a concern for many, because of limited
access to land and dependence on a small range of precarious strategies to meet their needs. The distance between international aid
workers and beneficiaries in the resilience regime, however, means
they have little influence over food distribution other than trying to
capture as much as possible. Trying to capture aid might include
making requests to government or aid agencies if they appear
sympathetic, and/or keeping family members in a displaced camp
while others try to find work or farm. In rural communities, representatives often distribute food aid equally despite agency requests
to target only the most vulnerable.

These views and perceptions of beneficiary groups contrast sharply
with the stereotypes produced in international agency discourse, of
ignorant people who do not know how to cook or look after their
children. The practices of the resilience regime, and the distance that
remote programming produces between international aid agency
staff and food aid beneficiary households, makes it possible for their
respective regimes of truth to remain separate. Beneficiaries saw both

international and national food aid to be political. Their perception of truth was that reductions in food aid were aimed at changing their behaviour, to make them work harder or return to their villages, but many cannot return and are dependent on a limited number of precarious strategies to meet needs.

The long-term Sudanese aid worker view

Long-term Sudanese aid professionals are experts in international food aid programming and in the intricacies of local politics and how to navigate between the two. In this study I mainly interviewed Darfuris with experience of working for international agencies,[11] but Sudanese professionals working in Kordofan or Red Sea State have similarly long experience. They were familiar with multiple food aid discourses, and saw food aid issues from a technical and political perspective. The government's promotion of the Food Economy Approach in Darfur during the conflict, for example, could be explained on the grounds of the technical superiority of the approach, or of the political motivation to reduce food aid in Darfur. Similarly, government food distribution in government-held areas only, in South Kordofan in 2012, could be interpreted politically as supporting only people on the government side, or technically as the government not having the logistical capacity or the methods to distribute according to need.

The recognition that international food aid had been needed to save lives on a regular basis since the mid-1980s, coupled with knowledge about the long-term negative social and political impacts, led to moral dilemmas about continued involvement in food aid. One aid worker explained how concerns about creating dependency and harming farmers and markets were key concerns amongst African aid workers in the early 1990s:

> [When I first joined agency X] the African debate was about food aid creating dependency. Secondly, that food aid objective is to create a market in Africa for Europe and the US, especially the US ... [I]t means that you provide food aid, you change the taste of the people from cassava, from millet from sorghum to wheat and then after that you do not give it for free ... [S]o those are the two hot debates at the beginning ... within the Sudanese and Africans also. Then [in] Sudan – two additional issues came into this. 1. ... create harm to local producers, especially when food aid is being pumped into an area where there are some parts ... which have good production and some parts which do

not have very good production ... [P]eople like me were very
much influenced by [these] three, the creation of dependency,
the creation of a market for Europe and the States and [causing]
harm for the local producers. And [2] ... the government of
Sudan adds [another] element ... that this is political twisting.
And this is the debate when I joined agency X ... [W]hen we
make the assessments and we make our recommendations there
is a very heated conversation between us, internally, about are
we doing these things. We are grilling ourselves to answer these
questions, before we agree to the report and we start publicly
advocating and championing for the report.

The same aid worker also ultimately aspired to a Sudan free of
international food aid and for the government to be independent,
using the *zakat* (Islamic tax) collected to ensure no Sudanese family
went hungry: 'this is what most of us Africans are looking for'. As
Chapter 2 showed, the negative impacts of food aid the 1980s and
1990s were also topics of discussion and debate amongst international aid workers. This included not only the use of food aid to
create overseas markets and its impact on production, but also how
food aid could become part of the political economy of war.
    A number of Sudanese aid workers mentioned their concerns that
food aid had enabled the government to use more of its resources to
fight wars against its own population. One aid worker explained in
relation to Darfur:

I think politically the government benefited [from food aid]
... [W]e have been [supporting] ... millions with food aid,
and taking completely the responsibility of the government
... There have been dilemmas on how you can use food aid
as a political tool but I think for the government in Darfur
for a long time, in most of the 1980s the agencies ... took the
responsibility for feeding the people. Where [the government]
use the money that should have gone to the people ... is a big
dilemma, which we always discuss, have we really freed the
government from responsibility ... [allowed] killing the people,
displacing them, destroying their livelihoods, bringing them to
a big camp, to the urban centres and we are feeding [conflict-
affected] for the past ten years, and the government is still
continuing ... this is a big dilemma for me. I cannot say stop
food aid because people will die.

The key difference between these issues in the 1990s livelihoods regime and the 2000s resilience regime is that in the resilience regime it is only the Sudanese professionals who acknowledge the moral dilemmas of distributing food aid in conflict. For the increasingly remote international staff, the politics of distributing food aid in conflict situations has become invisible. Even decisions on how to measure food insecurity, and its analysis, are increasingly made by those who are not based in Darfur or even Sudan. Many of the Darfuri aid professionals who had gained their expertise in the 1990s are now employed by WFP and INGOs, but the analysis of quantitative data no longer requires their detailed contextual knowledge and could be undertaken in Rome or Khartoum. Decisions about the food security indicators used in WFP's assessments are made in Rome. In USAID, national staff monitor the situation in Darfur but decisions are made in Washington and Nairobi.[12] These changes represent a disempowerment of Sudanese professionals working for international agencies. Two long-term Sudanese aid workers expressed their concerns about the changing relationship between national and international staff within INGOs. They felt the relationship had changed from long-term relationships of equals in the 1980s and 1990s to short-term relationships marked by distance and distrust (because of the possibility that national security agents had been planted in INGOs). As a consequence, they feared there would not be a new generation of Sudanese professionals able to take up senior positions within international agencies in the future.

Those with long-term experience understood the dominant international agency and government discourse, and the political motivations and effects of government, donor and aid agency food aid practices. Long-term Sudanese aid workers perceived that food aid continues to be needed to save lives but also that food aid is used as a political tool and can have negative effects on the economy and enable conflict to continue. Like beneficiaries, they are becoming further removed from decision-makers in international agencies.

The private sector view

Food aid traders and transporters also had a very clear view of the life-saving, economic and political effects of food aid. As traders and transporters in Al-Fashir were affected by the crisis themselves, they were more likely than their Khartoum counterparts to mention the life-saving aspects of food aid for their communities.[13] Food aid was also seen as a source of income and helped establish community infrastructure and management capacity through food-for-work

projects. All were very clear about the importance of food aid for
their business:

> The massive increase in food aid increased the number of food
> aid traders in the camps, especially women like me ... Food aid
> has helped me to find opportunity in supporting my livelihood
> and food security while I am in the camp. (Informant 90, 2013)

> My own view about long-term food aid, it allowed my company
> to continue the business. It also allowed my company to engage
> with other institutions, e.g. UNAMID, in transporting materials
> to their stations (sand, gravel, cement) as well as involvement in
> construction works for UNAMID. (Informant 61, 2013)

Traders and transporters, in both Darfur and Khartoum, felt that
food aid had replaced some of the government's responsibility (Informants 49a and 86, 2013), and that Darfuri communities were now
relying on WFP and other donors for assistance or relief (Informant
61, 2013), but that at the same time the government had benefited
from food aid through the various taxes and fees it imposed for food
transportation and trade.

Khartoum traders and transporters were more likely to bring
global politics into their view as they were closer to government
and were more likely to focus on the economic and political effects
of food aid than the life-saving ones. Not surprisingly, some gave
similar views on food aid to those of the government, such as the
motivations of donors to support their own farmers. One Khartoum
trader summarised the divergent effects of food aid as follows:

> Politically I am against [food aid]. It influences the decisions of
> the government and the local people. In [1984], USAID food
> came to Sudan. In the past [before 1984] attitudes to the US
> were negative, because of Palestine, but when food aid arrived
> this changed. They started to sing for Reagan and Nancy. The
> people do not know the complications. This is the political
> side. Economically, it has affected the attitudes of the people as
> consumers. For myself, it is good business. (Informant 46, 2013)

Another wished that, despite the business that food aid offered,
Sudan did not need international food aid (Informant 40, 2013).
As shown in Chapter 3, the impact on Khartoum grain trading and
transport companies was massive, and they now no longer depend on

response to the Darfur crisis. These companies preferred contracts to transport food aid over commercial contracts because food aid provided regular work and the payment was fast (Informant 49a, 2013). On the whole, the reality for traders and transporters was that they benefited from the food aid operations in Darfur, but also that it had political repercussions for the government.

To conclude, in the resilience regime, the perceptions of food beneficiaries, aid professionals and the private sector reflect an alternative to the dominant regimes of truth. Their perception is that food aid is used as a political tool and that it has indirect political and economic effects, but it is also needed to save lives because access to food remains constrained due to conflict. These perceptions are subordinate to the dominant regimes of truth of international agencies and the government of Sudan.

Conclusions

In the resilience regime in present-day Sudan, two discourses on food aid dominate and create different but converging regimes of truth. One dominant regime is that of the government of Sudan, in which food aid and international aid agencies are political tools of the West and therefore need to be restricted and controlled. In the other, created by international agencies, malnutrition and food security is not the result of conflict but of people's own behaviour, actions and ignorance, and the situation is conducive to recovery interventions. These two regimes of truth allow for Sudan's 'actually existing development' in which there are indirect benefits of food aid for the Sudan government and private sector but which abandons conflict-affected populations to become resilient in a context of permanent emergency. The international community justifies a reduction in food aid on the grounds that it makes IDPs and other conflict-affected people lazy and unwilling to work, that malnutrition is linked to behavioural practices, and because their quantitative food security assessments show food insecurity to be minimal or stable. Their regime of truth is a fantasy, as it requires the denial of permanent emergency. This denial is possible because remote programming limits contact between staff working for international agencies and conflict-affected people and assessments do not cover conflict-related causes. This fantasy is also convenient because it resonates with the current resilience agenda and it adopts the most recent scientific developments in nutrition and food security.

Food aid has also indirectly created a group of experienced Sudanese aid professionals, traders, transporters and beneficiaries who know the practices of food aid. Everyone I interviewed was clear about the political as well as the life-saving effects of international food aid. Beneficiaries thought that reductions in food aid were attempts to make them work or return home, or part of a switch to development. They also saw that government food aid was given mostly to government supporters. Beneficiaries, Sudanese aid professionals and private sector actors understood both the government's and international agencies' regimes of truth. Their own perceptions contested the dominant regime of truth but were subordinate. Darfuris' perception of truth is that food aid is being reduced but also that conflict produces ongoing threats to livelihoods – such as displacement and lack of access to land, markets and employment. They experience a war economy in which the only possibility of becoming food-secure is to leave Darfur, engage in corrupt or criminal activities or join the army or closely linked militia, but in which most people can only just survive through marginal activities. Their perception is also that the continued provision of food aid produces a dilemma because it saves lives but at the same time helps sustain a regime that is intent on fighting wars with its own population. Those with the most direct experience of both the conflict and of food aid are not part of the dominant discourse.

In the resilience regime, international agencies' practices have created powerful regimes of truth around malnutrition, food insecurity and food aid, in which reductions in food aid, vouchers and behaviour change improve food security and nutrition and promote resilience. Conflict and politics are invisible, so international aid workers do not need to consider the possibility that food aid supports an oppressive regime, or that the withdrawal of food aid increases the risks faced by conflict-affected populations. The Sudan government perceives food aid as a political tool, and so restricts international food aid and provides its own food aid to those who support the regime. Beneficiaries, experienced national aid workers and private sector actors understand the dominant regime but have little power to influence it. Conflict-affected populations are left to survive in a state of permanent emergency. The next, and final, chapter pulls together the main conclusions, including the role of criticism in bringing about changes from one regime of practices to another and the implications for future regimes.

6
Conclusions

This book started by introducing Sudan as experiencing one of the world's most protracted emergencies and as one of the countries receiving the largest amounts of food aid and for the longest. It also presented the 2014 context in Darfur as one of ongoing threats to livelihoods and persistently high levels of acute malnutrition, but where aid agencies were nonetheless reducing food aid. At the same time, the Sudan government has established its own food aid apparatus, which has mainly assisted its supporters, and a semi-governmental trade and transport private sector has blossomed. In attempting to explain this incongruous situation, I have explored the governmental functions of food aid by examining regimes of practices, how food aid has co-evolved with other forms of governance in Sudan over the past fifty years, its power effects, and the implications for livelihoods and social welfare.

Over fifty years, international food aid has changed from a tool to promote the foreign policy and economies of donors, to a tool mainly used by the UN and international NGOs in emergencies to save lives and protect livelihoods, to one which – by the early 2000s – was considered largely redundant when the focus of aid became to promote resilience. While resilience approaches were intended to improve people's ability to cope with repeated crises, they can also be seen as an effective abandonment because they excluded the social and political causes of malnutrition and food insecurity and made individuals responsible for their own malnutrition and food security problems. The distance between aid workers and beneficiaries introduced by declining access and remote management has led to further abandonment. By 2013, international aid workers were no longer really present and could not interact and communicate with crisis-affected populations in a way that enabled ethical decision-making based on sympathy, equality and respect (Slim, 2015). Furthermore, this distance has helped maintain a regime of truth in which food insecurity is minimal, malnutrition can be addressed through specialised food products and behaviour change, and in which conflict is invisible. The resilience regime has enabled the government to continue to deny access and use food aid as a political tool but has suppressed the views and perceptions of Darfuri beneficiaries and long-term aid professionals.

This disconnect between aid workers and beneficiaries would perhaps not have mattered so much if food aid had its intended effect of saving lives and supporting livelihoods. However, food aid in the early years – the 1960s to the 1970s – hardly reached Darfur, adding to its marginalisation in Sudan's existing development process. Evaluations done throughout the 1980s and 1990s concluded that food aid had little or no impact on livelihoods (see Chapter 4). WFP's 2004/05 operation in response to need created by conflict was the first time that food aid successfully helped reduce malnutrition and mortality and supported livelihoods. Later, in the resilience regime, the focus was on reducing food assistance and promoting resilience. New voucher programmes were closely monitored and evaluated, but information on the impact of food aid (which remained the main form of assistance) was scarce.

Whether current practices achieve resilience – the ability to withstand or adapt to shocks – is difficult to say. Furthermore, resilience as a humanitarian objective needs to be challenged. Clearly people have had to adapt and respond to ongoing conflict and reduced aid. But at what cost? The prevalence of acute malnutrition in North Darfur remains well above emergency levels. Mortality estimates are not available. Little is known about people's livelihoods options and strategies after 2008. Militia and herder attacks on farmers and displaced populations continue. From 2013 onwards, the conflict in Darfur once again escalated. Battles between government forces and Arab groups over gold mines and attacks and destruction by the Rapid Support Forces resulted in almost 500,000 newly displaced persons in 2013 (UN Security Council, 2014). New displacements continued in the following years, including due to aerial bombardments of the Jebel Marra area in central Darfur. Over 1 million people were newly displaced between 2013 and 2015 (UN OCHA, 2015) and up to 200,000 people in 2016 (UN OCHA, 2017). Unilateral ceasefires declared by the government and SLA-MM (SLA-Minni Minnawa) in early 2017 provided some temporary respite but the latest estimates of the total in need in Darfur remain as high as 3.3 million (OCHA, 2017). Fighting between the two broke out again in May 2017 in North and East Darfur. What does resilience mean in this context other than expecting populations to adapt to ongoing suffering and permanent crisis? It has become people's individual responsibility to keep safe, prevent malnutrition and find food. As Evans and Reid (2013) argue, while it appears common sense to encourage populations to take on these responsibilities, it also has a dehumanising political effect. It removes the power of protest or resistance against the conditions which cause suffering, and inhibits political action to achieve freedom and security (Evans and Reid, 2013; Welsh, 2014). This shift is evident in the changing role of international aid workers from the livelihoods to the resilience regime: they have gone from representing neglected and oppressed populations based on proximity and relationships, and lobbying to address causes as well as provide assistance, to distant bureaucrats who encourage adaptation to existing conditions of protracted emergency. From 2008, Darfur's 'actually existing development' has been informed by the ideology of resilience, which in practice has meant ongoing high rates of malnutrition, threats to livelihoods and limited assistance and protection. Resilience ideology reduced expectations from development and security to adaptation and acceptance of permanent crisis.

Instead of assisting vulnerable populations, international food aid has had a number of wider political and economic impacts. In the 1990s, international food aid provided an increasingly important economic resource for government and the private sector, and its manipulation became an important part of counter-insurgency measures. By the 2000s, the Sudan government had learnt from its experience of international food aid and established mechanisms to control it. It has also established its own food aid apparatus modelled on its perception of international food aid as a political tool. The economic benefits of food aid have evolved over time to facilitate Sudan's uneven development process, its counter-insurgency tactics, and have helped to create a number of multinational transport and grain trading companies. This chapter draws out the main conclusions on the evolution and effects of food aid regimes of practices in Sudan, and provides some thoughts on the way forward.

What brought about change?

Change in food aid practice can be divided into three discrete regimes of practices. These regimes have consolidated and transformed as a result of changes in global politics, food crisis and responses to food aid's failure and its governmental effects, rather than as a result of the accumulation of knowledge and scientific progress. As in Foucault's (1977) genealogical study of the practice of punishment, change has not been due only to external factors but to the power that certain practices produced and sustained. The resistance and adaptation of the Sudan government to the governmental effects of international food aid practices has played a key role in shifts in regimes of food aid practices.

The three regimes of practices have had different aims – state support, livelihoods support and resilience. Each regime of practices has created particular dominant truths, constituted in part through the concepts used by the scientific communities concerned with food aid, food security and nutrition. In the 1970s food security was defined as sufficient food availability and production, but in the 1980s it was defined as individual or household access to food and purchasing power, and since the 2000s food security has come to incorporate nutrition, capacity and knowledge (see Chapter 2). Emergency nutrition has gone from being a global social and political issue to one of individual behaviour and the need for better treatment. From the 2000s, donors and aid agencies have seen both of these as a means to achieving resilience in the context of climate change, protracted crisis and state fragility. These shifts also reflect a progressive de-politicisation of food security and nutrition and wider neoliberal trends in the global economy from the 1980s, which shifted responsibility away from the state and international community and towards the individual.

The change from the state support to the livelihoods regime was brought about by a combination of the failure and critiques of state-led food aid, food crisis and famine, and the end of the Cold War. From the 1950s to the 1970s the state support regime was dominated by programme food aid and influenced by Cold War geopolitics, agricultural surpluses and prevailing models of state-led development. In Sudan, programme food aid was largely aimed at improving production in central Sudan and supported urban bread subsidies. Improving production failed, but food aid ultimately provided support for the government, which in turn provided the West with a buffer against the expansion of Soviet influence given Sudan's socialist neighbours. The 1970s food crisis highlighted the failures of early food aid practices, and led to donor initiatives to strengthen the developmental aims of food aid through more poverty-oriented programming, minimum food aid commitments and support for the multilateral World Food Programme (see Chapter 2). Academics and aid agencies criticised programme food aid for being dominated by foreign policy and trade objectives, and project food aid for benefiting the rich and perpetuating inequality. In Sudan, the country's economic decline from the late 1970s onwards led to weakening and corruption of government authorities, and donors and UN agencies contracted INGOs for refugee and returnee assistance and for emergency food distribution in response to famine in 1984/85. This had three effects. First, it was a step towards the externalisation of welfare provision in Sudan. Second, the experience of INGOs working with refugees and famine victims led to the development of new practices (see below). Third, it led to the first stirrings of resentment and resistance by the Sudan government to external food aid intervention.

In the livelihoods regime, emergency food aid and international agencies dominated. INGOs bypassed government and worked directly with communities to save lives and protect livelihoods of emergency-affected and marginalised populations. Food aid practices proliferated to include assessments of the underlying causes of malnutrition, famine early warning systems, expertise in food security, food aid targeting and community-based distribution, as well as new treatment methods. New practices were also influenced by new theories of famine and development which emphasised individual or household capacity and their ability to access food, rather than that of the state. Repeated or ongoing crisis in countries like Sudan led to ideas of linking relief to development or developmental relief, often manifested in a desire by agencies to reduce relief and to provide it in a way that encouraged self-reliance and reduce dependency. By the end of the 1990s, food aid objectives had expanded to support livelihoods and promote self-reliance. The livelihoods regime was also characterised by the provision of food aid to populations during ongoing conflict. The second Sudanese civil war, from 1983 to 2005, led to one of the longest aid operations based on negotiated access and new practices of minimising the manipulation of food aid by the warring parties. It also led to government suspicion that food aid supported the rebellion. In Sudan, the livelihoods regime was a struggle for control between aid agencies and the Sudan government over food aid and the populations to which it was provided. For the Sudan government, the livelihoods regime posed a threat to its sovereignty: international aid agencies bypassed government, food aid supported rebel movements in the south, and international food aid contradicted the Islamist ideology of self-sufficiency. Initially, food aid was resisted, but by the late 1990s the government had found a way of using international food aid practices to its own advantage and the INGO operating environment was restricted through country agreements and reductions in access.

The shift to the resilience regime of practices was brought about by the failures of the livelihoods regime, the Sudan government's response to the livelihoods regime and the Darfur crisis, and global influences following the 2008 global food crisis and the War on Terror (WoT). By the end of the 1990s, it was clear that new assessment and early warning practices were rarely successful in eliciting a timely and adequate response. It wasn't until the massive 2005 WFP food aid operation in response to the Darfur conflict and humanitarian crisis that food aid successfully reduced malnutrition and supported livelihoods (see Chapter 4). Food aid diversion and its incorporation of aid into the political economy of oppressive regimes were evident. Also, long-term food aid recipients had failed to achieve self-reliance, and donors and aid agencies came to see emergency levels of malnutrition as normal. Ever-higher levels of malnutrition were needed to elicit a response. From 2008, global instability and the expectation of on-going food crises due to climate change led to the formulation of resilience approaches, which included food production, medicalised nutrition and targeted cash transfers as ways of improving people's capacity to adapt to an environment of repeated crises. These strategies intensified the shift towards individual responsibility and towards market-based approaches. New nutrition practices focus on changing feeding and hygiene behaviours, and treatment with specialised nutritional products as cost-effective ways of promoting economic growth and national security. These practices were also well suited to intervening in the Darfur crisis. Presenting malnutrition as a medical rather than a social and political problem enabled aid agencies to work in a highly politicised environment and to remotely manage interventions. These practices converged with the Sudan government's aim to Sudanise the aid industry, by prioritising Sudanese NGOs and encouraging the provision of government food aid. A national strategic food reserve was used to maintain or attract government support and to keep international agencies out of the new conflict areas in Blue Nile and Southern Kordofan.

The resilience regime reflects a shift in both ideology and expectations compared with earlier regimes. Nutrition and food security are seen as medical or technical problems and issues of poverty and inequality are no longer a concern. Emergency levels of acute malnutrition no longer need a general food aid response but people's behaviour can be changed to adapt to permanent emergency. The resilience regime has created a truth in which conflict is invisible and people's own actions are responsible for their malnutrition and food insecurity. The exclusion of the politics of aid also hides aid's ineffectiveness and the ongoing risks that people face. Furthermore, remote management practices increase the physical and emotional distance between beneficiaries and aid workers, which reduces

empathy and facilitates the withdrawal of assistance. This abandonment of crisis-affected populations is sustained by the convergence
of interests between the government, donors, aid agencies, private
sector and to some extent the nutrition and food security scientific
communities. The Sudan government wants to control international
food aid and reduce the presence of international agencies. Donors
facing austerity measures at home want to contain global instability
with limited funds; aid agencies want to maintain a presence in insecure and politicised environments; the private sector wants to use
malnutrition and the need for new aid technologies as a business
opportunity; and the emergency nutrition and food security scientific communities want to implement the latest scientific advances.
In this new resilience regime of practices, the needs and priorities
of long-term Sudanese aid workers and crisis-affected populations
have been lost.

Continuities?

In addition to transformations, some practices and ideas have been
remarkably persistent over time. Nutritional surveys have been
around for a long time; so has food security as a concept. Aid agencies have attempted to target food aid at the poorest households
since the 1980s – often linked as much to fears of creating dependency and attempts to shift from relief to development as to aims of
reaching the most vulnerable. Despite these apparent continuities,
the meaning and function of these practices have changed along
with the changing regimes of truth from the state support to the
livelihoods and to the resilience regime. Some of these changing
meanings and functions are discussed below.

Nutritional surveys have been conducted in emergencies since
the 1970s, but their interpretation has changed over time. Like
other forms of health surveillance at the level of populations, nutritional surveys is a form of biopolitics that aims to maximise health
and requires the development of a norm and determination of the
levels of risk which are considered acceptable (Foucault, 2007).
Through their role in surveillance and emergency response in the
1980s, aid agencies assumed responsibility for managing the lives
and livelihoods of crisis-affected and marginalised populations,
particularly when government failed to assist those they considered
most vulnerable. WHO, and other aid agencies, adopted a threshold
for responding to unacceptably high levels of acute malnutrition.

However, in Sudan, as in other protracted crises, donor and aid agency perceptions of what was normal and acceptable changed over time. By the end of the 1990s, levels of malnutrition well above emergency thresholds were needed to elicit an emergency response. Bradbury (1998) associated this 'normalisation of crisis' with the notion of developmental relief, such as reducing relief to promote self-reliance, or building capacity, in situations of ongoing conflict and suffering. Response to the results of nutritional surveys changed again in the resilience regime. From 2010 onwards, WFP in Darfur did not consider emergency levels of acute malnutrition to require an emergency food aid or food assistance response (WFP, 2013b). In 2011 and 2012, new food security assessments using universal and quantitative indicators had shown food insecurity to be low, and medicalised nutrition approaches focused on behavioural factors as causes and specialised nutritional products for treatment. In the shift from the livelihoods to the resilience regime, international agencies have gone from taking responsibility for improving the lives and livelihoods of crisis-affected populations to expecting them to change their behaviour to adapt to permanent emergency. Although many aid workers knew at some level that continued material assistance and protection continued to be needed, this new regime of truth was also necessary at a psychological and organisational level because it had become almost impossible to deliver food aid in much of Darfur.

Similar changes in meaning can be seen in the practice of targeting. Targeting the most needy or vulnerable has persisted from the early days of international food aid but its method and purpose has changed over time. Difficulties in targeting the most vulnerable is often discussed by aid workers at conferences as one of the most intractable problems, and better targeting is presented as a common solution in evaluations which highlight the limited impact of aid. Food aid has been targeted on the basis of nutritional status or other physiological criteria (such as pregnant and lactating women), social criteria (the elderly, female-headed households) or economic criteria (the poorest or most emergency-affected) (Jaspars and Young, 1995). During the state support regime, Western donors targeted emergency food aid at refugees in camps, and within camps agencies targeted the most physiologically or socially vulnerable. This changed when aid agencies provided food aid to rural populations in response to the famines of the mid-1980s, the start of the livelihoods regime. In the livelihoods regime, aid agencies attempted to target the poorest or worst-affected population groups and, later, the poorest households within communities. Reasons included not only a desire to concentrate assistance on those most affected by famine, but also limited resources and fear of damaging the local economy and creating dependency (Borton and Shoham, 1989). Aid agencies established socio-economic information systems to aid targeting, and village committees to select the poorest households. Throughout the 1990s, SC-UK in Darfur received food aid well below estimated needs and attempted to target the poorest to support their livelihoods. Globally, targeting was part of promoting self-reliance (WFP, 1998a). By the 2000s, in the resilience regime, targeting of food assistance (including specialised nutritional prod-ucts, vouchers, food-for-recovery and food-for-assets) was promoted to achieve resilience in the context of protracted crisis. In 2015, WFP started 'profiling' displaced populations in camps to assist in targeting. All displaced households were assessed and categorised according to their access to land or employment and their asset status (e.g. owner-ship of a cart in Geneina). Only those with high 'vulnerability status' on the basis of these indicators remained entitled to free food aid, and those of medium vulnerability would receive seasonal food aid or food-for-assets (WFP, 2015a).[1] At the same time, a new range of specialised nutritional products was targeted at the malnourished Over time, only the *idea* of targeting remained the same. Like regimes of practices more generally, the objectives of targeting have changed from assisting the most vulnerable to promoting self-reliance and later resilience. Like the resilience regime more generally, targeting strate-gies in this regime have come to be more directly aimed at changing behaviour, and local participation has decreased.

Despite the persistence of the targeting idea, the evidence is that it mostly failed. A review as early as 1989 concluded that targeting of vulnerable households within communities was prob-lematic because it often skewed distributions to those with greater power, and that perceptions of need were often different between agencies and the affected population (Borton and Shoham, 1989). The most vulnerable have often received less. In Darfur in 1985, many of the displaced and nomads were excluded from distribution (Keen, 1991). In later years, limited quantities of food aid were often distributed equally within rural communities. In the 1988 southern Sudan famine politically vulnerable Dinka received minimal levels of assistance, and in the 1998 famine the displaced, smallest clans and female-headed households were excluded (Keen, 1994; SPLM et al., 1998). The conclusions to Keen's seminal book *The Benefits of Famine* are still applicable today: politically weaker groups fail to access sufficient relief because they lack political muscle within their society. He recommended taking a holistic approach, anticipating the needs of the 'oppressor' as well as the victim, the difficulties of targeting the poorest and neediest group, and advocated pushing relief through to all areas in need (Keen, 1994). This strategy worked in Darfur in 2004–05. Despite widespread conflict, destruction and displacement, famine was prevented.

Post-2008, information on the effectiveness of targeting is limited. WFP's 2013 country programme evaluation urges refined targeting for the chronically food-insecure – but provides little evidence that this took place. My own interviews in Darfur indicate that food-for-recovery was only possible in the more stable places close to Al-Fashir. Globally, recent studies on targeting are few but the ones that exist show findings similar to studies in the 1990s: those with political connections received more (Caeyers and Dercon, 2012). The limited information on the social and political constraints in reaching vulnerable groups could be linked to the demise of social nutrition or a shift towards quantitative and digital technologies. So what does targeting actually achieve? It appears that by the time of the resilience regime, the aim had become purely to reduce food aid. In the livelihoods regime, aid agencies worked hard at targeting the most vulnerable, and evaluated and monitored whether they achieved this. It required regular assessment, training and monitoring by INGOs or WFP and the assistance of local committees or leaders. In this way it maintained particular authorities and organisations and functioned as a way of managing vulnerable populations but maintained existing inequalities (see for example Edkins, 2000). In the resilience regime in Darfur, monitoring and evaluation of targeting is rare. At the same time, from a donor perspective, it maintains a fantasy that food aid is only for those who truly deserve it.

In the face of evidence that targeting does not work, the concept of dependency has enabled the practice to continue. Fear of creating dependency has been a common reason for reducing food aid in protracted relief operations (see for example Harvey and Lindt, 2005). In Darfur, by 2013, a narrative that displaced populations had become dependent on aid replaced one about the need for their protection. Reducing dependency on food assistance was an explicit aim of WFP's IDP profiling exercise (WFP, 2015a). A regime of truth in which food aid is not needed to address malnutrition is reinforced by concerns that long-term food aid can create dependency. In Darfur, it has allowed the reduction of food aid during ongoing conflict and crisis and, like other practices of the resilience regime, implies that action is needed on the part of crisis-affected populations themselves. My interviews showed that even crisis-affected populations themselves have internalised dependency discourse and consider long-term reliance on food aid a bad thing. However, a reduction in food aid justified by a concept of dependency fails to examine political vulnerability and the political effects of reductions in aid.

Impact of food aid practices in Sudan's protracted emergency

Food aid has largely failed to meet its intended aims but has had a range of wider political and economic effects. When food aid was first provided to Sudan, it supported the state, but not always in the ways intended. Its biggest impact was probably in supporting a bread subsidy for urban consumers which helped the government cope with the rapid rate of urbanisation and the inevitable riots which followed rising food prices. WFP project food aid failed to improve production but did support wages for labourers on government projects, for example modern agriculture on commercial farms in central Sudan. Although small-scale, these projects supported Sudan's unequal development process, which favoured an economic and political elite at the centre over populations living in Sudan's peripheries. North Darfur received little or no programme or project food aid in the 1960s and 1970s (see Chapter 3).

In the 1980s and 1990s, emergency food aid had little impact on the nutrition and food security of drought- and conflict-affected people because it was too little and came too late. Little food aid reached vulnerable rural populations because at first government priorities of feeding urban populations dominated, and later because Sudan's Islamist regime resisted international food aid. Donors were reluctant to support the Islamist regime in the 1990s and therefore provided only minimal life-saving quantities of food aid (see Chapter 4). Traders and transporters delayed delivery to Darfur in attempts to maximise profits, and aid agencies were unable to target food aid to the poorest or most vulnerable. Emergency food aid in the livelihoods regime was therefore unable to actually support the lives and livelihoods of people in Darfur. The food aid operation in 2005, in response to the Darfur conflict, was an exception in that it delivered far larger quantities of food aid than had earlier operations and it had an unprecedented coverage of rural populations. For the first time, food aid successfully helped reduce malnutrition and mortality and supported livelihoods. WFP's operation in Darfur in 2004–05 can therefore be seen as the peak of the livelihoods regime in Sudan. However, the quantities of food aid distributed decreased from 2006 onwards, due to funding constraints, limited access and agency objectives of moving from relief to recovery. Evaluations from this time provide little information on effectiveness and impact. Acute malnutrition once again increased. Peace agreements failed and the conflict continued, with surges in violence and displacement in 2010 and again from 2013 onwards in different parts of Darfur. Over the thirty years that agencies have distributed food aid in Darfur, most people have become increasingly impoverished and reliant on marginal activities, depend on criminal or militarised livelihoods strategies, or have migrated out of Darfur.

The wider effects of long-term food aid are the economic and political benefits for the government of Sudan and the private sector, and the knowledge and experience of food aid gained by Sudanese professionals, businessmen and beneficiaries. My research shows that the findings by Keen (1994) on government, army and trader manipulation of food aid in the 1988 Bahr Al-Ghazal famine were not an isolated incident. Nor were the findings of the OLS review that promoting self-sufficiency by reducing food aid could have negative social or political consequences. Furthermore, Duffield's (2002a) analysis – that categorisation of people as IDPs or according to wealth groups had a de-socialising effect and facilitated government oppression – still applies today. These were essentially critiques of the livelihoods regime of food aid practices. Like the work of Duffield and Keen, my research shows that food aid had political and economic benefits for government and private sector throughout the 1980s and 1990s, and that this continues up to the present time. Food aid brought in hard currency (through manipulation of official exchange rates) and lucrative contracts for traders and transporters. At the local level, underfunded government institutions diverted international food aid to pay government salaries or for personal gain. The restriction of food aid to populations perceived to support the southern rebellion formed part of the government's counter-insurgency strategy and the displacement that followed helped create a cheap labour force. As discussed in Chapter 3, these strategies intensified in the late 1990s as the government no longer rejected food aid on ideological grounds but increased the ways by which it could benefit from it. It used discourse on international food aid to promote local purchase and benefit its private sector, and it used discourse on moving from relief to development to better control international agencies. These practices were well entrenched by the end of the 1990s, but by that time were rarely examined by either researchers or aid workers as government resistance to international agencies increased.

At the height of the Darfur food aid operation – in 2005 – international food aid provided personal funds for IDP leaders but, more importantly, their role in food distribution enhanced their authority and in some cases helped them promote the political agenda of the rebellion. At the same time, traders and transporters from central Sudan had large contracts to transport or purchase food aid for Darfur, and were able to make even more money from buying food aid sold by Darfuri beneficiaries to meet other needs and transporting it back to Khartoum. Their businesses expanded massively and the largest became multinational. For a short while, even Darfuri transporters and traders benefited. The reduction of food aid in later years, however, fed into government strategies of emptying the camps and gathering political support, including from displaced populations, by distributing its own food aid. This was further facilitated by aid agencies portraying IDPs as lazy and cheats, thus justifying the withdrawal of aid. WFP's recent profiling exercise throws up a potentially divisive political issue: it is those IDPs who were traditionally farmers (Fur, Masalit), and from whom the opposition movements were drawn, who had least access to land and therefore kept their food rations, and Arab or other government-aligned groups had most access to land and lost their rations (WFP, 2015a). This information not only highlights the ongoing occupation of land and constraints on returns, but also that food assistance could either maintain this status quo or feed into ongoing conflict. In Darfur's permanent emergency, displaced populations have become part of a large urban or agricultural labour force. Given the Sudan government's renewed emphasis on modern commercial agriculture, it is not inconceivable that Darfur's displaced populations will become part of Sudan's development strategy. Sudan would be a prime area for investment by the New Alliance for Food Security and Nutrition because the Sudan government is already following an agricultural strategy centred on large-scale modern farming and Darfur has a large reserve of cheap labour. These political effects of food aid, and of changes in food aid practices, are not recognised in the resilience regime. Worse, the practices of the resilience regime make them invisible.

Even though international agencies know that Sudan's crisis continues, and know some of the political and economic effects of food aid, the ongoing crisis can be denied because of their limited contact with conflict-affected populations and because assessments do not reveal many of the risks that people continue to face. The funding available for the new homogenised nutrition and food security makes their fantasy – that technical and behavioural interventions can solve malnutrition – more attractive than a narrative in which malnutrition and food insecurity are a social and political problem they cannot address, and that conflict-affected populations will continue to face risks. They have absolved themselves from responsibility for making difficult decisions about the unintended effects of food aid or food assistance. More importantly, practices in the resilience regime make the government's role in the crisis invisible and they remove the necessity of political or military action by other nations. Instead, food aid has allowed the Sudan government to concentrate wealth and services in the centre at the same time as containing the protracted emergency in Sudan's peripheries.

The knowledge and experience gained by those involved in food aid, whether government officials, long-term aid workers, traders, transporters or beneficiaries, is another aspect of food aid's unintended development effects. Government officials in influential positions often had long-term experience with food aid and some had previously worked for INGOs. Over time, they used this experience to control international agencies and the food aid they provided, and to establish Sudan's own food aid apparatus. The effect of emergency food aid has therefore gone beyond unintentionally strengthening the government, local authorities or rebel movements, as concluded in other studies, whether through diversion, taxation or simply involvement in distribution (see for example De Waal, 1997a). During the resilience regime the learning from long-term international food aid transformed the state through the establishment of a national strategic grain reserve, a network of local NGOs and government food aid. Food aid also created a group of highly trained Sudanese aid professionals outside of government. This group has expertise in food aid programming and in the politics of food aid at national and international levels, as they are the ones who have to navigate between donor and aid agency expectations and the political realities on the ground. In the de-politicised resilience food aid regime, however, their ability to put food security and nutrition into its social and political context, and their knowledge of the politics of food aid and of who benefits, are often no longer needed. However, the programming skills they developed in the livelihoods regime, in the 1990s, can now be replaced by assessments and cash transfers via remote sensing, mobile phones and smart cards. Long-term aid

workers and beneficiaries view food aid as political but also believe
that it continues to be needed to address humanitarian needs. These
views are not part of the dominant regime of truth.

Implications for humanitarian and food aid operations

In this book, I have shown that contemporary food aid practices can
be seen as an abandonment of crisis-affected populations, that food
aid has rarely met its intended objectives, but that it has had a range
of political and economic effects that go well beyond the intended
target groups. As aid practices become medicalised and quantified,
and the distance between international aid workers and crisis-affected populations increases, local populations have little say in what
aid is provided and how. These findings raise issues about humanitarian principles, the role of food aid, and power within the aid
system that goes beyond Sudan. Sudan is not the only country that
has received long-term food aid or where resilience approaches and
remote management have become a way of providing humanitarian
assistance. Sudan, Ethiopia, Kenya, Afghanistan and the Occupied
Palestinian Territories are all long-term humanitarian assistance and
food aid recipients and were amongst the top ten recipients in the
first decade of the 2000s (Development Initiatives, 2011).[2] Food aid
or food assistance is likely to continue to be needed in many of these
countries. In Pakistan, Afghanistan, Sri Lanka, Somalia and Sudan,
restricted access has become the norm and aid agencies have developed a range of remote management techniques. Syria is unique in
that remote management has been the main form of operation since
the start of the crisis in 2011, rather than having been developed over
time (Howe et al., 2015). In this final section of the book I argue for a
more critical attitude towards contemporary approaches, for greater
honesty and transparency about the effects of food aid by those who
provide it, and a rebalancing of power within the aid system through
proximity and solidarity with crisis victims.

Recognising that politics and ideology, rather than simply
scientific progress, played a role in transformations in regimes
of practices makes it possible to revisit the approaches of earlier
regimes. A case can again be made for examining nutrition within its
social and political context, for qualitative methods, and for a livelihoods approach which involves proximity to – and participation of
– crisis-affected populations. Such a politically informed approach
would also lead to a more critical examination of current food-based

resilience approaches and would challenge the fantasy that crisis-affected populations are responsible for their own food insecurity and malnutrition and that food aid is making them dependent or lazy. In contrast to food aid and humanitarian organisations, human rights organisations offer a growing critique of current food security and nutrition practices. They highlight that the private sector is unlikely to solve malnutrition and food insecurity because its primary aim is to create new markets and maximise profit. Furthermore, the promotion of specialised nutritional products diverts attention from government policies and the food industry itself in causing nutritional problems. The potentially negative effects of the involvement of global food and agribusiness in food security and nutrition, they point out, include an accelerated process of land-grabbing in Africa, and changes required by the New Alliance for Food Security and Nutrition in land and seed laws may displace small farmers or make saving their own seeds illegal. As in the 1970s, modern agricultural technologies will most likely benefit the rich. A growing number of social science researchers also argue that alleviating malnutrition through the delivery of nutrients is more about business and profit than about addressing its causes. Food policy analysts have called for a food systems approach to food security and nutrition which 're-embed[s] nutrition in society, nature and politics' (Prato and Bullard, 2014). Part of this would be politically informed approaches to food aid.

Food aid in Sudan has not been neutral and impartial, and none of the Sudanese people interviewed for this research perceived it to be so. Aid agencies cannot claim that food aid has been used to prevent or alleviate suffering wherever it may be found (humanity), that it is provided solely on the basis of need (impartiality), and that agencies have maintained their autonomy (independence) (UN OCHA, 2012). Food aid has often had explicit political aims and has always had political effects beyond the immediate target group, thus compromising any claim to neutrality. This applies to all types of food aid. Western governments have used food aid for geopolitical purposes, from support for Western allies during the Cold War to the current withdrawal of aid from countries in which it may support groups classified as terrorist organisations. Aid agencies have used food aid biopolitically, initially to support the lives and livelihoods of poor and marginalised populations and later to link targeted distributions to food production, self-reliance and – most recently – resilience. Aid beneficiaries interviewed in North Darfur perceived recent reductions in food aid as intended to make them work, to encourage return

to their areas of origin, or as the consequence of needs in other countries, rather than being justified on the basis of improved access to
food. In other words, they perceived these changes in international
food aid as a political decision, and as linked to government policies.
Emergency food aid has been further compromised by the limitations
imposed by access denials and the inability of UN or donors to challenge these. Since 2010, most food aid has gone to government-held
areas irrespective of need. WFP's 2013 evaluation concluded that
because of the conflict, official restrictions and lack of access to parts
of the affected population, WFP had little control over programme
decisions (WFP, 2013b). Transporters in North Darfur considered
that Military Intelligence was in control of how much international
food aid went where and when.

The wider political effects of food aid practices, as summarised in
the previous section, are rarely examined in the resilience regime. In
the shift from the livelihoods to the resilience regime, international
agencies have sought progress through changing from food aid to
food assistance, quantifying assessments, medicalising nutrition and
focusing on behaviour change and agricultural technologies. Rather
than promoting neutrality and impartiality, however, resilience
approaches have reduced understanding of the social and political
context which in turn has enabled the Sudan government to continue
its political use of food aid and made conflict and the political and
economic effects of food aid invisible. To some extent, this makes
aid agencies complicit with the actions of the Sudan government.
The practices of the resilience regime obscured government actions,
reduced international responsibility and discouraged political resistance. Aid agencies have been morally negligent by not recognising
the importance of local knowledge about the political effects of food
aid. Slim (2015) argues that aid agencies are not morally responsible
for the harm created by aid because it usually plays a minor role in a
war economy and that in acute emergencies agencies they may have
little time to gather information. However, in protracted emergencies agencies have time, and in Sudan the political effects of food aid
go beyond a role in the war economy.

A key element of humanitarian reform needs to be honesty and
transparency about the actual impact of food aid, and the political effects of food aid practices in protracted crisis. This includes
recognising that even though food aid can save lives and support livelihoods, mostly it has not done so; that strategies to target the most
vulnerable have largely failed. The only time that food aid reached
vulnerable rural populations in Darfur was when aid agencies set up

their own transport systems and access was unrestricted: in 1986 and in 2004–05. Sudan's private sector has shown little evidence of motivation by humanitarian concerns, except perhaps when they have been directly affected by crisis themselves. All food aid practices have political effects. In some contexts, other forms of assistance may be more appropriate, but the same need to examine the political effects applies. In Sudan, WFP purchased food aid locally from one or two of Sudan's main grain traders, with close links to government. Food vouchers benefited large traders in Darfur and central Sudan. Similarly, in-kind food aid benefits US farmers and agribusiness, grain and shipping companies as well as transporters in Sudan. So the decision about what kind of food assistance and how to provide it needs to be based on an analysis of its political effects, as well as advantages in terms of choice and speed and the severity and nature of the crisis. In today's crises, however, the tendency of aid agencies has been to conceal the political impact of food aid. In the context of the War on Terror, aid agencies have re-emphasised the principle of neutrality to distinguish themselves from the political intent of parties to the conflict and for fear of violating counter-terrorism laws. Such a 'frame' of neutrality, however, also stifles analysis of the unintended political effects of aid through, for example, access denials and distribution through government channels (Martinez and Eng, 2016). This book has shown not only the importance of examining the political effects of food aid, but also of the reduction in food aid, as this can feed into existing political processes such as the emptying of the camps in Darfur. In Sudan, these political effects are known by most actors involved in food aid, including government officials, national aid workers, traders, transporters and beneficiaries. This knowledge and experience needs to inform any decisions about humanitarian programmes.

Making decisions about humanitarian programmes requires a process of deliberation: of evaluating and deciding upon a course of action (Slim, 2015). In Sudan, such decision-making will always pose a moral dilemma: whatever decision is taken will involve some moral loss. There is no right answer or short-term solution to improving aid in protracted crises. Whereas in the 1990s the moral dilemmas resulting from food distribution were discussed between national and international aid workers, in the resilience regime long-term Sudanese aid workers experienced the moral dilemmas resulting from long-term food aid in Sudan alone. On the one hand, they saw that international food aid continued to be needed as crises are ongoing in Sudan. On the other hand, they knew that when aid agen-

cies took responsibility for feeding people affected by conflict and
crisis it left the government with resources to continue conflict in the
peripheries and restrict development to Sudan's centre. All Sudanese interviewed were well aware of the range of wider political and
economic effects discussed in this book. These findings are similar
to those of Haver and Carters (2016: 11) on access and programme
quality in insecure environments: local staff working in Somalia,
South Sudan, Syria and Afghanistan encountered ethical dilemmas
but received little support in making compromises on access because
of a culture of silence on these issues. The same study also found
that agencies with national staff in senior management positions
had better-quality programmes. In some contexts, however, no
acceptable compromise can be found, perhaps because of official
obstruction to providing humanitarian assistance, or because the
risk of complicity with practices that are harmful to vulnerable populations is too great. In this case, refusal must be an option. In Sudan,
for example, MSF-Belgium withdrew in January 2015 because it
was no longer able to access war-affected populations in Darfur
and Blue Nile. In contrast, in South Kordofan, after failure to gain
access to all war-affected populations, WFP decided to continue to
assist people in government-held areas only. In Syria, under similar
circumstances, more than seventy organisations suspended cooperation with the UN because of a concern that the Syrian government
had too much influence over the UN's programme (Beals and
Hopkins, 2016). Discussions with Sudanese professionals in early
2017 made clear they felt that issues of access could only be resolved
at the highest political level. Recent pressure from the US government to improve humanitarian access as one condition for lifting
sanctions shows that it can be done, but at the time of writing the
jury is still out on whether access has actually improved. Even this
action to improve access entails a moral loss as increased trade and
cooperation between Sudan and the US moves attention away from
ongoing violence and human rights abuses.

The difficulties of applying humanitarian principles does not
mean that humanitarian ethics should be abandoned. The basis of
all humanitarian action is a feeling of compassion and responsibility towards others. The principle of humanity – the alleviation
of suffering wherever it may be found – incorporates the value that
human life is a fundamental good and must be protected, and the
virtue of being humane, or reaching out and acting to preserve life
(Slim, 2015). Humanitarianism is more than a technical exercise
of grouping people into particular categories, estimating needs,

feeding the malnourished and treating the diseased. It is also an act of solidarity with the suffering. This can be viewed not only in a general sense but also as relationships between the people who suffer and those who decide to ameliorate their suffering. Such relationships of solidarity are not founded on sentiment or pity but on moral and legal grounds (Reshaur, 1992; Scott-Smith, 2016). Scott-Smith (2016: 17), referring to Norwegian People's Aid, highlights that a solidaristic approach recognises that suffering is rooted in socio-political conditions and aid has socio-political effects. Rather than encouraging crisis-affected populations to adapt, solidarity means not accepting the socio-political conditions that cause suffering. The importance of solidarity in Darfur between aid workers and crisis victims is evident from food aid programmes in the 1990s. Food aid was minimal, and had little impact, yet crisis-affected people still came to national and international NGOs for assistance, which lobbied donors and government on their behalf. Those who managed the relief operations at village level were remembered many years on. The presence of aid workers on the ground showed that people cared, despite the limited impact of aid.

Solidarity requires proximity. In Sudan, however, and other countries where international agencies are programming remotely, humanitarianism is moving in the opposite direction. Sympathy and feelings of responsibility for others are reduced in power by distance (Slim, 2015: 30). As remote management becomes the norm, 'cyber-humanitarianism' is inevitable, encouraged by new digital technologies developed in partnership with private companies (Duffield, 2013). WFP can now carry out food security assessments and monitoring by mobile phone (for example in Sudan, the Democratic Republic of Congo and Somalia). Other aid agencies have used smart cards and mobile phones to provide cash transfers as interventions that are cost-effective and can be remotely managed (Vincent and Cull, 2011). This has created the possibility of virtual assistance where no contact with crisis victims or beneficiaries is necessary. Digital humanitarianism has been enthusiastically adopted by the aid system, as it has the potential for rapidly collecting large amounts of data in remote areas. The Grand Bargain, the outcome of the first global Humanitarian Summit in 2016, commits donors and aid agencies to reducing management costs through the use of mobile and digital technologies while at the same time promoting greater participation of people and communities affected by crisis. This book has shown that these may be two conflicting aims. In Darfur, new remote technologies not only produce an apolitical regime of truth in which the dynamics of conflict are invisible, but they also disempower national aid workers and aid beneficiaries. In remotely managed programmes, national staff may be used to gather data or implement programmes, but their knowledge of the local context and their interpretation of data are no longer required. Similarly, standardised interventions do not need beneficiary participation. This in turn facilitates a situation which is conducive to perceptions by international agencies that IDPs or food aid beneficiaries are lazy or ignorant and responsible for their own food security and nutrition problems. Such stereotypes make it easier to withdraw aid. While some organisations have established remote monitoring and evaluation methods, these are largely aimed at accountability towards donors and rarely involve direct contact between beneficiaries and international agency staff (Howe et al., 2015). As such, the analysis of the resilience regime of practices in this book has revealed the risks to solidarity and compassion with national aid workers and victims of crisis.

This book has provided a critical analysis of the failure of food aid in Sudan, and highlights the need for a radical overhaul of the humanitarian aid industry. Food aid has continued to fail crisis-affected populations because changes in food aid practices have come about more by changes in politics, ideology and economic interests than by a simple process of linear scientific progress. The resilience regime has taken humanitarian intervention in the wrong direction – international aid agencies have become distant from the populations they aim to assist, conduct little critical reflection on contemporary aid practices, and inequality between international and national aid workers and crisis victims has grown. This trend needs to be reversed if humanitarian ethics are to be maintained. The book has also highlighted that food aid practices have rarely had their intended results and have always had political effects, and that in long-term food aid operations the indirect political and economic consequences evolve over time. These consequences need to be acknowledged, analysed and anticipated. In countries which have received food aid for a long time, almost everyone involved in food aid will be an expert on both the technical and political aspects of food aid, whether aid workers, government officials, traders, transporters or beneficiaries. More importantly, in deliberation and decision-making, it is ultimately up to those directly affected by crisis to determine what support they need and what ethical compromises they are willing to accept.

Appendix 1
Chronology of key political events in Sudan

Year	Event
1899	Britain and Egypt sign the Anglo-Egyptian Agreement restoring Egyptian rule of Sudan but as part of a British-dominated condominium.
1913/14	Nationwide famine.
1920	Colonial government introduces Famine Codes.
1922	Colonial (British–Egyptian condominium) government promulgates the Powers of Nomad Sheikhs Ordinance, in pursuit of indirect rule. Establishment of native administration.
1927	Promulgation of Power of Sheikhs Ordinance gives same powers to sedentary sheikhs.
1936/37	Rural councils founded as well as local councils in urban municipalities. Dominated by tribal leaders, but included newly emerging elites.
1943	Country divided into eight provinces, each governed by a Commissioner.
1945	Umma party formed by Sayyid Adb al-Rahman al-Mahdi, and calls for Sudan's independence.
	Umma party wins majority of seats in newly created legislative assembly.
1951	Local government act passed, based on recommendations by Marshall, a British local government finance specialist, to divide councils according to local communities' preparedness to shoulder responsibilities of local governance. Country divided into urban and rural councils with delegation of powers supervised by provincial commissioners.
1952	Pro-Egyptian Sudanese groups form National Unionist Party led by Ismail Al-Azhari.
1953	Egypt signs agreement with Sudanese parties for self-determination within three years. NUP wins elections.
1955	Soldiers mutiny in Torit, followed by eight other mutinies across South Sudan.
1956	Independence (1 January). Ismail Al-Azhari becomes Sudan's first Prime Minister.
	Twenty-one members of the NUP defect and form the People's Democratic Party), forcing Al-Azhari to resign. Abdullah Khalil becomes Prime Minister in Umma–PDP coalition.
1958	Umma party wins national election and forms coalition with PDP.

General Aboud takes power in military coup and dissolves all political parties.

Sudan accepts US food aid as part of general assistance agreement between US and Sudan governments.

1959   Egypt and Sudan sign Nile Waters agreement. Egypt starts constructing Aswan dam.

1962   Southern opposition to Aboud's policy of Arabisation and Islamisation leads to first southern Sudanese opposition political movement and start of civil war.

1963   Anyanya emerges as organised guerrilla force in the south.

1964   Popular uprising (October Revolution) overthrows Aboud's government. Sirr al-Khatim al-Khalifa becomes Prime Minister. Only lasts for four months; Khalifa resigns in February 1965.

Formation of Islamic Charter Front under the leadership of Hassan Al-Turabi.

1965   Umma party wins elections and Muhamed Ahmed Mahjoub becomes Prime Minister of four-party coalition government. Followed by succession of three coalition governments (Umma–NUP under Mahjoub from May 1965 to June 1966; under Sadiq Al-Mahdi from June 1966 to May 1967; Mahjoub returns in coalition with Imam wing of Umma and NUP afterwards).

Influx of Congolese refugees – 22,000 by January 1966.

1967   Influx of 30,000 Eritrean refugees. Continues up to 1970 (leading to 1 million refugees).

1969   May: Nimeiri seizes power in military coup. Establishes Revolutionary Command Council with close ties to the Communist Party.

1971   Nimeiri abolishes multi-party system and makes Sudan Socialist Union the sole permitted political organisation.

Communist Party briefly takes power on 19 July 1971 but Nimeiri returns to power in counter-coup on 22 July.

Native administration is abolished and replaced with elected councils under People's Local Government Act. Provincial administration is established with broad legislative and executive powers (Hamid). Darfur divided into two Provinces, and North Darfur into four Area Councils. At the lowest level are Neighbourhood, Market Area, Industrial Area, Village and Camp Councils; above these Rural and Town Councils followed by Area Councils (ACs).

1972   Addis Ababa peace agreement ends the first civil war.

1973   United Nations High Commissioner for Refugees (UNHCR) announces programme for the repatriation of 180,000 southern refugees back to South Sudan.

1972–74 Famine in Darfur, Kordofan and the East. Refugees from Chad enter Darfur. Famine relief organised locally through SSU and local councils.

1977–78 Nimeiri changes political direction and brings Sadig Al-Mahdi and Hassan Al-Turabi ('Muslim Brothers') into government.

Major influx of refugees from Ethiopia (mostly Eritrea). 390,000 in East Sudan by 1979.

1979 Influx of refugees from Uganda (into Equatoria – South Sudan). Around 200,000.

Sudan agrees to IMF loan terms.

1980/81 Regional governments introduced into North Sudan. Country divided into five regions. Each region has elected governor. Darfur now one region, with two Provinces and Area Councils. Mellit added as AC in North Darfur. Many of the functions of other councils transferred to ACs – to be established by the regions. Responsibilities of People's Provincial Executive Councils transferred to Regional Executive Authority.

Al-Turabi tries to redraw north–south border to include oil fields in the north.

Nimeiri introduces stringent economic measures on recommendation of IMF. Devaluation of the Sudanese pound, tax rises, withdrawal of public subsidies and reduction in public expenditure.

1983 Nimeiri abolishes southern regional government, dividing south into three regions – Equatoria, Bahr Al-Ghazal and Upper Nile.

Nimeiri introduces Islamic law.

Sudan People's Liberation Army (SPLA) is formed. Start of second civil war.

1984–85 Influx of Ethiopian refugees (Tigray), leading to a total of more than 1 million refugees in Sudan.

120,000 Southern Sudanese flee and become refugees in Ethiopia.

Famine in Red Sea Hills, Darfur, Kordofan. Famine relief by international agencies.

1985 April: Nimeiri government falls as result of popular uprising. Transitional Military Council formed.

1986 Sadiq Al-Mahdi elected as Prime Minister. Umma–DUP coalition. National Islamic Front captures fifty-one seats.

1987 Native administration re-established.

Tribal units in north–south borderland armed by the government and start operating as militias against SPLA-controlled areas in the south.

Emergence of the 'Arab Gathering' in Darfur with letter to Sadiq Al-Mahdi claiming marginalisation and lack of representation in Darfur.

First Arab–Fur war in Jebel Marra, which lasts until 1989. First organisation of Arab militia. First Darfur security conference in Al-Fashir in November.

1988 Famine in Bahr Al-Ghazal, South Sudan.

1989   Start of Operation Lifeline Sudan (OLS) – a UN-led operation to negotiate access to war-affected populations.

Clashes between Fur and Arab groups in Darfur, leading to massive displacement.

Omar Al-Bashir and National Islamic Front seize power in military coup.

Establishment of government militia, Popular Defence Force and Popular Neighbourhood Committees by members of Islamic Movement as a way of mobilising grassroots support for the regime. Native administration changed to conform to Islamic orientation of the state.

Establishment of National Congress Party as governing political organ of the Islamist movement.

1990/91 Federal system of governance adopted; Sudan divided into nine states, each with its own government, a number of provinces and local councils.

Popular Committees proposed at conference on new ways of organising the political system in Sudan.

US terminates all military and economic aid to Sudan. IMF declares Sudan non-cooperative in September 1990.

Fighting between government and SPLA (Bolad) in Jebel Marra area of Darfur.

Famine in northern Sudan in Darfur, Kordofan and Red Sea State, eventually leading to international response.

1992   Khartoum regime introduces a programme of economic liberalisation under which the national currency is floated, subsidies on essential goods lifted and most public sector corporations are privatised or disbanded.

1993   Amendment to federal system divides country into twenty-six states. Darfur is now three separate states (North, South and West) and North Darfur is divided into first three and later seven provinces: Al-Fashir, Um Keddada, Kutum, Kebkabiya (1996), Mellit (2000), Tine (2002), Waha (2003). Each province is divided into a number of localities.

1994   Riek Machar forms South Sudan Independence Movement.

1995   Federal structure consolidated by devolving more financial powers to the state.

Role of native administrator redefined as that of a religious leader for each identity group, to lead them in prayer and to prepare youth for jihad (religious war) in the south or in Darfur.

Governor of West Darfur reorganises state into thirty-four emirates, each one headed by a government-appointed amir. The allocation of six Arab emirates threatens the Masalit homeland.

Start of four-year war between Arab tribes and Masalit.

1996   President Bashir elected for a new five-year term. Turabi appointed as Speaker of the National Assembly.

Drought/food scarcity in Darfur, Kordofan, Red Sea State.

1997   Government signs agreement with Machar.

Government declares state of emergency in Darfur.

1998   Famine in Bahr Al-Ghazal, South Sudan.

Turabi becomes NCP Secretary-General.

1999   Oil exports begin.

President Bashir dissolves National Assembly and declares state of emergency after power struggle with Al-Turabi.

2000   *The Black Book*, written by disaffected Darfurians alleging discrimination, circulates in Khartoum.

President Bashir is re-elected for five years.

2001   Organisation of armed opposition in Darfur.

Drought/food scarcity in Darfur.

2002   Machar rejoins SPLM. Warring parties agree to ceasefire. Machakos protocol agreed as overall framework for peace agreement.

Darfur Liberation Front carries out a number of attacks.

2003   New local government act. Provinces within each Darfur state changed to localities (same number and names as provinces). Localities are divided into administrative units.

Formation of Sudan Liberation Army (SLA) and Justice and Equality Movement (JEM). Rebels attack Al-Fashir airport in March, and Mellit, Kutum and Tina in April. Government/militia counter-offensive begins in June.

Start of humanitarian operation in Darfur in August.

2004   First Darfur ceasefire, but immediately broken. African Union military (AMIS) observers arrive in June. Peace talks begin in August in Abuja.

July: Sudan government agrees to fast-track procedure for international agency travel permission to Darfur.

2005   Comprehensive Peace Agreement (CPA) signed on 9 January, ending the second civil war. John Garang becomes first Vice President but dies three weeks later. Abyei Boundaries Commission submits report but this is rejected by Khartoum.

World Bank resumes its support through managing the Multi-Donor Trust Fund.

July: food aid beneficiaries reach 3.25 million in Darfur.

UN Security Council refers Darfur to International Criminal Court.

2006   Darfur Peace Agreement signed by SLA-Minni Minawi faction but not by SLA-Abdul Wahid or JEM. Splintering of rebel movements and Arab militia.

Eastern Front, coalition of rebel groups in the east, signs Eastern Sudan Peace Agreement.

2007   ICC issues indictments against government minister Ahmed
            Haroun and militia leader Ali Kushayb.

2008   UNAMID takes over from AMIS in Darfur.

            SPLA and Sudan Armed Forces clash in Abyei.

2009   NCP and JEM sign goodwill agreement and Qatar backs
            negotiations between the two parties in Doha.

            ICC issues arrest warrant for Al-Bashir. Government expels
            thirteen NGOs from Sudan.

2010   New Darfur coalition: Liberation and Justice Movement (LJM).

            Al-Bashir gains new term as President in national elections. Salva
            Kiir elected as President of South Sudan.

            Minnawi (SLA) returns to opposition. Violence increases in North
            Darfur.

2011   Southern Sudan votes for separation from the north and becomes
            independent in July.

            Doha Document for Peace in Darfur signed by LJM but not by
            other opposition movements.

            Conflict in South Kordofan and Blue Nile between SPLM-North
            and Government of Sudan.

            Darfur opposition movements and SPLM-N form Sudan
            Revolutionary Front demanding national transformation.

2012   Sudan government expels seven international agencies from eastern
            Sudan.

2013   Large-scale displacement in Darfur (ongoing into 2014).

            Sudan government refuses to renew residence permits of twenty
            UNHCR staff working in Darfur.

2014   January: government suspends activities of ICRC.

            November: UNAMID is asked to close down operations in Darfur.

            December: UN Resident Coordinator and UNDP Country
            Director are asked to leave Sudan.

Sources: Norris, 1983; Harir et al., 1994; African Rights, 1997a; Karadawi,
1999; Abdul-Jalil et al., 2007; Assal, 2008; Collins, 2008; Flint and De Waal,
2008; Ryle et al., 2011; Sudan Tribune, 2012; Sudan Tribune, 2013; ICRC
Resource Centre, 2014; Reuters, 2014; Hamid, n.d.

Interviews

Beneficiary 1 (2013) *Interview with displaced person from Mornei.* By SJ and MA on 6 February 2013, Khartoum.

Beneficiary 3 (2013) *Interview with resident from Shagra.* By SJ and MA on 6 February 2013, Khartoum.

Group 1 (2013) *Discussion with six men from Kuma.* By MA on 20 September 2013, Kuma.

Group 2 (2013) *Interview with six women from Kuma.* By MA on 20 September 2013, Kuma.

Group 3 (2013) *Interview with relief committee in Kuma.* By MA on 20 September 2013, Kuma.

Group 4 (2013) *Interview with women from Kuma.* By SJ and MA on 25 September 2013, Al-Fashir.

Group 5 (2013) *Discussion with three male IDP leaders from Abou Shook camp.* By SJ and MA on 26 September 2013, Al-Fashir.

Group 6 (2013) *Discussion with two representatives from Malha (one man and one woman).* By SJ and MA on 27 September 2013, Al-Fashir.

Group 7 (2013) *Discussion with two displaced people (one man and one woman) from Jebel Si.* By SJ and MA on 28 September 2013, Al-Fashir.

Group 8 (2013) *Discussion with four women from As Salaam camp.* By MA on 15 September 2013, Al-Fashir.

Informant 1 (2012) *Interview with former WFP staff member.* By SJ on 8 June 2012, London.

Informant 4 (2012) *Interview with long-term aid worker.* By SJ on 19 June 2012, Khartoum.

Informant 5 (2013) *Meeting with WFP staff members.* By SJ on 3 February 2013, Khartoum.

Informant 7 (2012) *Interview with WFP staff member.* By SJ on 19 June 2012, Khartoum.

Informant 9 (2012) *Interview with long-term aid worker.* By SJ on 21 June 2012, Khartoum.

Informant 10 (2013) *Interview with long-term aid worker.* By on 5 February 2013, Khartoum.

Informant 12 (2012) *Interview with long-term aid worker.* By SJ on 24 June 2013, Khartoum.

Informant 13 (2012) *Interview with long-term aid worker.* By SJ on 24 June 2012, Khartoum.

Informant 16 (2012) *Interview with WFP staff member.* By SJ on 25 June 2012, Khartoum.

Informant 17 (2012) *Interview with former Relief and Rehabilitation Commissioner.* By SJ on 26 June 2012, Khartoum.

Informant 19 (2012) *Interview with former Humanitarian Aid Commission official.* By SJ on 26 June 2012, Khartoum.

Informant 20 (2012) *Interview with former Under-Secretary and Minister of Finance.* By SJ on 26 June 2012, Khartoum.

Informant 20 (2013) *Further discussion with former Under-Secretary and Minister of Finance.* By SJ on 1 October 2013, Khartoum.

Informant 22 (2012) *Interview with former Relief and Rehabilitation Commissioner.* By SJ on 27 June 2012, Khartoum.

Informant 23 (2012) *Interview with former government official.* By SJ on 27 June 2012, Khartoum.

Informant 24 (2012) *Interview with former Humanitarian Aid Commissioner.* By SJ on 28 June 2012, Khartoum.

Informant 25 (2012) *Skype interview with WFP staff member.* By SJ on 11 December 2012, London.

Informant 26 (2012) *Interview with long-term aid worker.* By SJ on 20 December 2012, London.

Informant 27 (2013) *Skype interview with long-term aid worker.* By SJ on 4 January 2013, London/Manchester.

Informant 28 (2013) *Interview with donor representative.* By SJ on 8 January 2014, London.

Informant 29 (2013) *Interview with long-term aid worker.* By SJ on 15 January 2013, Khartoum.

Informant 30 (2013) *Interview with long-term aid worker.* By SJ on 16 January 2013, Khartoum.

Informant 31 (2013) *Interview with WFP staff member.* By SJ on 17 January 2013, Khartoum.

Informant 35 (2013) *Interview with UNICEF staff member.* By SJ on 19 January 2013, Khartoum.

Informant 36 (2013) *Interview with transporter.* By SJ on 20 January 2013, Khartoum.

Informant 37 (2013) *Interview with long-term aid worker.* By SJ on 20 January 2013, Khartoum.

Informant 38 (2013) *Interview with former Humanitarian Aid Commission official.* By SJ on 20 January 2013, Khartoum.

Informant 40 (2013) *Interview with grain trader.* By SJ on 23 January 2013, Khartoum.

Informant 41 (2013) *Interview with former Humanitarian Aid Commissioner.* By SJ on 23 January 2013, Khartoum.

Informant 43 (2013) *Skype interview with long-term aid worker.* By SJ on 17 April 2013, London/Al-Fashir.

Informant 45 (2013) *Discussion with long-term aid worker.* By SJ on 27 January 2013, Al-Fashir.

Informant 46 (2013) *Interview with grain trader.* By SJ on 30 January 2013, Khartoum.

Informant 48 (2013) *Interview with aid worker.* By SJ on 31 January 2013, Khartoum.

Informant 49 (2013a) *Interview with transporter.* By SJ on 31 January 2013, Khartoum.

Informant 49 (2013b) *Follow-up phone discussion with transporter.* By SJ on 3 October 2013, Khartoum.

Informant 50 (2013) *Interview with former government official.* By SJ on 2 February 2013, Khartoum.

Informant 51 (2013) *Interview with aid worker.* By SJ on 2 February 2013, Khartoum.

Informant 53 (2013) *Interview with WFP staff member.* By SJ on 5 February 2013, Khartoum.

Informant 54 (2013) *Interview with grain trader.* By SJ on 20 January 2013, Khartoum.

Informant 55 (2013) *Interview with donor representative.* By SJ on 14 May 2013, London/Khartoum.

Informant 56 (2013) *Interview with WFP staff member.* By SJ on 17 September 2013, Khartoum.

Informant 57 (2013) *Interview with long-term aid worker.* By SJ on 17 September 2013, Khartoum.

Informant 58 (2013) *Interview with aid worker.* By SJ on 18 September 2013, Khartoum.

Informant 59 (2013) *Interview with aid worker.* By SJ on 18 September 2013, Khartoum.

Informant 60 (2013) *Interview with UNICEF staff member.* By SJ on 18 September 2013, Khartoum.

Informant 61 (2013) *Interview with transporter.* By AJ on 19 September 2013, Al-Fashir.

Informant 62 (2013) *Interview with long term aid worker.* By SJ on 24 September 2013, Al-Fashir.

Informant 62 (2014) *E-mail communication with long-term aid worker.* By SJ on 4 February 2014, London/Al-Fashir.

Informant 64 (2013) *Interview with native administration representative.* By SJ and MA on 25 September 2013, Al-Fashir.

Informant 65 (2013) *Discussion with aid workers.* By SJ on 25 September 2013, Al-Fashir.

Informant 67 (2013) *Interview with WFP staff member.* By SJ on 26 September 2013, Al-Fashir.

Informant 68 (2013) *Feedback after presentation at Al-Fashir University.* By SJ on 29 September 2013, Al-Fashir.

Informant 70 (2013) *Interview with official from State Ministry of Finance.* By SJ and MA on 29 September 2013, Al-Fashir.

Informant 72 (2013) *Interview with donor representative.* By SJ on 30 September 2013, Khartoum.

Informant 73 (2013) *Discussion with WFP staff member.* By SJ on 1 October 2013, Khartoum.

Informant 75 (2013) *Interview with long term aid worker.* By SJ on 2 October 2013, Khartoum.

Informant 76 (2013) *Interview with transporter.* By SJ on 2 October 2013, Khartoum.

Informant 77 (2013) *Interview with researcher.* By SJ on 3 October 2013, Khartoum.

Informant 78 (2013) *Interview with donor representative.* By SJ on 3 October 2013, Khartoum.

Informant 82 (2013) *Interview with transporter.* By SJ on 7 October 2013, Khartoum.

Informant 83 (2013) *Interview with representative of chamber of transporters.* By SJ on 8 October 2013, Khartoum.

Informant 84 (2013) *Briefing from WFP staff member.* By SJ on 8 October 2013, Khartoum.

Informant 85 (2013) *Interview with transporter.* By AJ on November 2013, Al-Fashir.

Informant 86 (2013) *Interview with transporter.* By AJ on November 2013, Al-Fashir.

Informant 87 (2013) *Interview with transporter.* By AJ on 9 October 2013, Al-Fashir.

Informant 88 (2013) *Interview with trader.* By AJ on 24 December 2014, Al-Fashir.

Informant 89 (2013) *Interview with trader.* By AJ on 20 November 2013, Al-Fashir.

Informant 90 (2013) *Interview with trader.* By AJ on 23 November 2013, Al-Fashir.

Informant 91 (2013) *Interview with voucher trader.* By AJ on 15 December 2013, Al-Fashir.

Informant 92 (2013) *Interview with aid worker.* By SJ on 9 October 2013, Khartoum.

Informant 93 (2013) *Discussion with aid worker.* By SJ on 5 February 2013, Khartoum.

Informant 94 (2013) *Interview with Chairman of the Darfur Regional Authority.* By SJ on 13 May 2013, London.

Informant 95 (2014) *Phone interview with donor.* By SJ on 8 January 2014, London/Washington.

Informant 99 (2014) *Interview with local NGO representatives.* By AJ on 15 February 2014, Al-Fashir.

Informant 100 (2014) *Interview with local NGO representative.* By AJ on 15 February 2014, Al-Fashir.

Informant 101 (2015) *Interview with Darfur chief negotiator for peace (JEM/SLA).* By SJ on 8 April 2015, Skype.

Informants 21 (2012) *Interview with staff from Strategic Grain Corporation.* By SJ on 27 June 2012, Khartoum.

Informants 63 (2013) *Interview with aid workers.* By SJ on 24 September 2013, Al-Fashir.

Informants 81 (2013) *Discussion with aid workers.* By SJ on 7 October 2013, Khartoum.

Informants 96 (2014) *Interview with HAC Director-General and Director of Emergencies.* By SJ on 10 April 2014, Khartoum.

Informants 98 (2014) *Telecon with donor representatives.* By SJ on 29 May 2014, London/Nairobi/Washington.

Trader focus group (2014) *Discussion with traders in food aid.* By AJ, Al-Fashir.

Notes

Chapter 2

1 PL480 has, since 1966, also been known as Food for Peace (Riley, 2004).

2 The Food Aid Convention (FAC) was part of the International Grains Agreement) to regulate global wheat trade, negotiated as part of the General Agreement on Tariffs and Trade). The Wheat Trade Convention was the other part of the IGA. The FAC could not come into effect until all the signatories of the GATT became party to the IGA as well as the FAC. The purpose of the agreements was therefore to stabilise global wheat markets as well as the provision of food aid. In fact, it was hoped that in the case of future surpluses, the FAC would help in 'supporting the higher prices enshrined in the Wheat Trade Convention' (Parotte, 1983: 11).

3 The eleven countries were Argentina, Australia, Canada, Denmark, Finland, Japan, Norway, Sweden, Switzerland, the United Kingdom and the United States. Spain and Austria joined in 1980 (Parrotte, 1983: 10–13).

4 With the exception of 1999, when large shipments of programme food aid went to Russia (Barrett and Maxwell, 2005).

5 Consolidated Appeals were started in 1991, following General Assembly resolution 46/182, which stated that in emergencies requiring an emergency response the UN Secretary-General should issue a Consolidated Appeal on behalf of all concerned organisations (UN General Assembly, 1991).

6 While other definitions exist, and modifications have been made over time, these are still the most commonly used definitions.

7 Wasting is also referred to as acute malnutrition and is the result of recent rapid weight loss, or failure to gain weight in children. It is measured using weight-for-height, which reflects body weight in relation to height. A child is classified as malnourished if it is two standard deviations (or Z-scores) below the median. Wasting is also measured by mid-upper arm circumference, although until recently this was mostly used for medical screening rather than population surveys. Acute malnutrition includes children with both wasting and nutritional oedema (Young and Jaspars, 2009).

8 This is just a sample of the new PPPs to improve food security and nutrition; there are many more.

9 It should be noted, however, that much humanitarian assistance remains food aid.

10 This was a group composed mainly of staff from US universities, but some from UK and developing-country universities (Pakistan, Mexico, Chile, South Africa), and UN agencies (UNICEF and WHO).

11 Chronic malnutrition is also called stunting or low height-for-age. It is generally used in non-emergency contexts because it reflects long-term processes of underdevelopment and poverty, and therefore develops slowly. Acute malnutrition, or thinness, or low weight-for-height is the preferred indicator in emergencies as it reflects rapid or recent weight loss and responds quickly to changes in food intake or disease (Young and Jaspars, 2009).

12 WFP's assessments also include quantitative information on

production, food prices, source of income and food assistance.

13 ActionAid has defined land grabs as land deals that violate human rights. Land grabs take place without free and informed consent of the affected land users, are not based on thorough assessments of the social, economic and environmental impacts and are without independent oversight and local participation (ActionAid, 2014).

Chapter 3

1 Sudan received more than 60% of its total official development assistance (ODA) as humanitarian assistance and was the top recipient of humanitarian aid in the first decade of the 2000s (Development Initiatives, 2011: 24–25).

2 I extracted data from WFP's food aid information system to identify the main food aid recipients globally (WFP, 2009b).

3 The overall prevalence of wasting was 16.4% < −2 Z-scores for weight-for-height. Northern Province, Khartoum and Gezira were below the emergency threshold of 15%, and the highest rates (>20%) were found in Red Sea State (28.5%), Sinnar (21.6%) and North Darfur (21.6%).

4 Native administration was established as a form of indirect rule by the colonial government and was based on pre-existing traditional tribal leadership (Abdul-Jalil et al., 2007).

5 Administrative divisions have undergone frequent changes in Sudan. In 1943, the country was split into eight provinces, which were divided into rural and urban councils in 1951. In 1971, further provinces were created (for example North Darfur and South Darfur), and Area Councils as divisions within provinces. Regional governments were introduced in 1981, with

Darfur becoming one region and two provinces. A federal system of governance was adopted in 1990, dividing Sudan into five states. This was amended in 1993, splitting the country into twenty-six states, and Darfur into three separate states: North, South and West Darfur (Abdul-Jalil et al., 2007). In 2011, Darfur was divided into five states. I will use the word 'state' to describe administrative divisions at all times, so I will only refer to Red Sea State, but this was formerly Red Sea Hills and Red Sea Province. When referring to Darfur, I will refer to the correct state, or refer to the Darfur states or region.

6 Popular Committees are also known as Salvation Committees.

7 A ration of wheat, milk powder, oil and dried and canned fruit (Shaw, 1967).

8 The OECD's data for food aid expenditure as a percentage of humanitarian assistance by country are not reliable before 2000, but from the evaluations of emergency operations in 1991 and 1997 and the review of Operation Lifeline Sudan it can be concluded that most humanitarian assistance was emergency food aid. From 2000, food aid as a percentage of total commitments was between 28% and 56%. From 2011, data become more difficult to interpret because of a change from food aid to food assistance and a lack of standardised donor reporting on the latter, and because of the independence of South Sudan.

9 Azza transport company airlifted food to Geneina, West Darfur, in 2001. The company was later subjected to US economic sanctions for contributing to the conflict in Darfur (US Department of the Treasury, 2009). Specifically, it was accused of supplying arms to Sudan government forces and Janjaweed militia (Axe, 2007).

10 I was part of this team, with responsibility for reviewing food aid and food security programmes.

11 Even MSF-Belgium announced in January 2015 that it was leaving Sudan because it was not able to access war-affected populations in Darfur and Blue Nile.

12 I could not interview a representative from Kiir because the company went bankrupt after taking on large contracts in cooperation with government and attempting to expand beyond its capacity. The company now works in South Sudan.

Chapter 4

1 A prevalence of 28.3% acute malnutrition for rural North Darfur in 2013 (Federal Ministry of Health, 2014).

2 The Northern Rizeigat is the name for a group of smaller Arab tribes such as the Iraygat, Mahamid and Mahriyya.

3 In addition, exclusive *hakura* was granted to notables and religious dignitaries, which gave them all rights for taxation (Abdul-Jalil, 2006: 11).

4 The Darfur Sultanate was briefly re-established from 1989 to 1916, after the British defeated the Mahdist army, which had overthrown the Sultan of Darfur in 1882.

5 The Omda or Nazir was the intermediary of the tribal paramount chief and is the head of a tribal sub-section and the Sheikh was the village headman. The paramount chief was the highest authority in the native administration system (Abdul-Jalil, 2006: 16).

6 The use of impoverished Arab nomads to fight wars had already been tested in South Kordofan, where the Misseriya Arabs had formed militia fighting the Sudan People's Liberation Movement (SPLM) in South Sudan by destroying the livelihoods of Dinka

in Bahr Al-Ghazal. Southern Rizeigat in Darfur had been used for the same purpose (see, for example, Keen, 1994: 92–98, and Flint and De Waal, 2008: 23).

7 An International Commission on Intervention and State Sovereignty, reporting to the UN, developed principles and approaches on the Responsibility to Protect in 2001. It followed the Rwandan genocide in 1994 and ethnic cleansing in the Balkans in 1999. One of the basic principles states that: 'where a population is suffering serious harm, as a result of internal war, insurgency, repression or state failure, and the state in question is unwilling or unable to halt or avert it, the principle of non-intervention yields to the international responsibility to protect.' The 'just cause' thresholds for military interventions were 'large scale loss of life' as a result of deliberate state action or neglect and 'large scale ethnic cleansing' whether by killing, forced expulsion, acts of terror or rape (ICISS, 2001: xi–xii). The UN General Assembly adopted the principle in 2005.

8 When UN Security Council Resolutions demanded in 2004 that the government disarm the Janjaweed, Arab militia were incorporated into government paramilitary groups, such as the Border Guards and Central Reserve Forces. The RSF picked the best (El-Basri, 2014).

9 The RSF may in part have been created to diffuse the threat to the Khartoum regime from disillusioned Arab militia. The RSF was not only deployed in Darfur, but was also used to fight the insurgents in Kordofan and to quell riots in Khartoum in September 2013 when subsidies were removed (International Crisis Group, 2014).

10 This food came from the stocks of the Agricultural Bank of Sudan,

to be replenished by WFP once its food aid arrived (Pearson, 1986).

11 In addition to this quantity of Title II (emergency) food aid, USAID provided a further 396,000 MT of Title I and Title III (programme) food aid (Pearson, 1986).

12 Administrative division in Darfur at the time. Darfur consisted of two provinces: North and South Darfur, and thirteen Area Councils.

13 Arkel-Talab, the Sudanese-American company contracted to transport USAID food aid, used the railways until July 1985 and started trucking to North Darfur after that. The MoF, who had to release the counterpart funds, had insisted on using the railways (Pearson, 1986; SC-UK, c. 1986).

14 Some of the consumer committees from Nimeiri's days changed into cooperatives. Sugar was the most commonly distributed government-subsidised food, hence the name 'sugar cooperatives'.

15 As part of rehabilitation activities following the 1985 famine, the RRC had established a national early warning system (EWS) in 1986, and in Darfur the Ministry of Agriculture established the Agricultural Planning Unit (APU), which monitored food security and, combined with the Red Crescent's Drought Monitoring Programme and Oxfam's nutritional surveillance programme, formed Darfur EWS (Buchanan-Smith and Davies, 1995b).

16 The 1993 FAO/WFP crop and food supply assessment mission estimated the food deficit to be 94,500 MT (90,000 MT in North Darfur); donors committed 38,800 MT, and SC-UK distributed 37,087 MT (Diraige, 1994).

17 I searched in WFP and the SC-UK archives, asked staff who had been involved in food-for-work programmes in Darfur and wrote to people who might have been evaluators. It is possible that evaluations were done and that reports are to be found elsewhere.

18 Note: other sources give slightly higher amounts – e.g. 9,420 MT according to Asfaw and Ibrahim (2008).

19 The quantity distributed in 1985 was 90,3761 MT (De Waal, 1989), and 7,460 MT in 1997 (DFID, 1997)

20 Note that the coverage of these surveys was different, but this gives an indication of improvement in nutritional status. Young (2007) also plots the results of localised surveys carried out by INGOs, which give an overall trend of decreasing prevalence of malnutrition.

21 'Crude mortality rates fell from 0.72 per 10,000 per day in February to August 2004 to 0.46 per 10,000 per day. Similarly, mortality rates for the under-fives fell from 1.03 per 10,000 per day to 0.79 per 10,000 per day' (Young, 2007: S42).

22 Wheat was the main cereal distributed in 2005 and accounted for about 30% of food aid cereal in 2006 (Dorosh and Subran, 2009).

23 Despite WFP aims to establish FRCs in rural communities as well, evidence from this and other studies show that in some communities in government-held areas, the Popular Committees continued to have a role in food distribution, thus potentially assisting in their political and military roles. Food distribution in SLA areas will have been different again. According to Kahn (2008), IDP camps in rebel-held areas were largely under military control and food aid in such circumstances was likely to provide support for rebel movements.

24 From 2011, the household food security indicator included information on a household's ability to afford at least two

minimum healthy food baskets, in addition to the food consumption score and expenditure included in the previous indicator. In addition, the threshold for identifying households with poor consumption was raised: in earlier surveys households with an FCS of 21 were classified as having poor consumption, whereas in 2011 those below an FCS of 28 were considered to have poor consumption. In 2011, the indicator also no longer included an estimate of the household's reliance on food aid.

25 The quarterly food security monitoring system was established in 2009 and no annual surveys were done until 2011. Quarterly monitoring was soon changed to three times a year (February, May and September), and twice a year when the annual surveys restarted. The February 2013 monitoring could not be done for security reasons, and the May 2013 monitoring had still not been released by September that year.

26 USAID's Famine Early Warning System (FEWSnet) monitors food security at national and local level, and the Darfur Rehabilitation and Reconstruction Agency (DRA) has a Market and Trade monitoring system for each of the Darfur states.

Chapter 5

1 The Relief and Rehabilitation Commission (RRC) changed to the Humanitarian Aid Commission (HAC) in 1996. See Chapter 4 for changes in role and function.

2 I interviewed him as Minister of Tourism, Antiquities and Wildlife in 2012, and in 2013 he was appointed as one of the Vice Presidents.

3 I interviewed four of the longest-serving RRC or HAC Commissioners out of the total of thirteen (in 2014). Their tenure covered the start of the RRC, and therefore the 1985/86 relief

operations and the start of aid to conflict-affected populations in South Sudan, the 1991 famine and the start of the Islamist regime, Operation Lifeline Sudan and the 1998 famine, and the recent Darfur crisis. I also interviewed the current Director-General and Director of Emergencies in 2014, and four other RRC or HAC staff who served in key positions for a long period of time.

4 From 1997, imported wheat was from Australia and Canada, as the US imposed a trade embargo. The trade embargo was imposed because of Sudan's ongoing support to terrorism, destabilisation of neighbouring countries and human rights violations (Office of Foreign Assets Control, 2013).

5 In the same way that government was suspicious of INGOs as political tools of the West, the rebel movements were suspicious of national NGOs as political tools of the Sudan government. No national NGOs were allowed access to rebel-held territory, as according to the movements' humanitarian coordinator they were sponsored by the NISS. Even for INGOs, all Sudanese staff had to get authorisation to travel into rebel-held areas due to fear of government infiltration (Loeb, 2013). For the same reasons, national NGOs initially faced difficulties when starting to work in the IDP camps (Jaspars, 2010).

6 The references to and quotes from aid workers in this section are from both national and international aid workers in agencies currently working in Darfur. Their views reflect those of agencies or people who have only spent limited time in Darfur, compared with the long-term Darfuri aid professionals who are speaking from the perspective of long-term and personal experience.

7 Expressed in seven interviews: two with aid workers, three with donors and two with government.

8 Expressed in eleven interviews: one with a trader, three with former government officials, one with government, seven with aid workers.

9 In Walkup's analysis, burnout is a reason for detachment.

10 We held eight focus group discussions in total, and interviewed five individual beneficiary representatives.

11 I interviewed fourteen long-term Darfuri aid professionals with experience of working for international aid agencies. I tried to interview representatives from Islamic Sudanese agencies through the Sudan Council for Voluntary Agencies (SCOVA), but when I tried to contact them in 2013 they were busy responding to the floods in Khartoum.

12 On each of my three PhD fieldwork visits to Sudan I tried to interview USAID officials in Khartoum. I met with experienced national staff, but they said they could not talk about USAID policy as they did not make decisions. I was eventually told I had to discuss policy with staff in Washington, with whom I set up a phone interview in January 2014.

13 In total, my research assistant and I conducted interviews with three Khartoum-based traders, four Al-Fashir-based traders and one food aid trader focus group, three Khartoum-based transporters and five Al-Fashir-based transporters.

Chapter 6

1 Only the Geneina profiling report is available on WFP website.

2 I extracted data from WFP's food aid information system (WFP, 2009b) to identify the main food aid recipient countries.

References

Abdala Fadul, A. and Mohamed Ahmed, I. (2011) *Research Study on Pastoralists Food Security in North Darfur State*, Al-Fashir: World Food Programme.

Abdul-Jalil, M. (2006) 'The dynamics of customary land tenure and land resource management in Darfur', *Land Reform. Settlement and Cooperatives*, 2: 8–23.

Abdul-Jalil, M., Azzain Mohamed, A. and Yousuf, A. (2007) 'Native administration and Local Governance in Darfur: Past and Future', in: De Waal, A. (ed.) *War in Darfur and the Search for Peace*, Ithaca and London: Justice Africa and Harvard Global Equity Initiative, 39–68.

Abrahamson, R. (2004) 'The power of partnerships in global governance', *Third World Quarterly*, 25 (8): 1453–1467.

Action Aid (2014) *Our Land. Our Choice. The Great Land Heist. How the World is Paving the way for Corporate Land Grabs*, London: Action Aid.

Africa Centre for Biosafety (2013) 'Modernising African agriculture: who benefits?', available at https://acbio.org.za/modernising-african-agriculture-who-benefits-civil-society-statement-on-the-g8-agra-and-the-african-unions-caadp/.

African Rights (1997a) *Food and Power in Sudan. A Critique of Humanitarianism*, London: African Rights.

African Rights (1997b) 'Origins of the Disaster: 1978-84', in: African Rights (ed.) *Food and Power in Sudan. A Critique of Humanitarianism*, London: African Rights, 10–39.

Ahmed, A., Abdelsalam, S. and Siddig, K. (2012) 'Do grain reserves necessarily contribute to prices stability and food security in Sudan? An assessment', *Journal of the Saudi Society of Agricultural Sciences*, available at http://dx.doi.org/10.1016/j.jssas.2012.03.002.

Aiga, H. and Dhur, A. (2006) 'Measuring household food insecurity in emergencies: WFP's household food consumption approach', *Humanitarian Exchange Magazine*, 36: 36–39.

Alcock, R. (2009) *Speaking Food: A Discourse Analytic Study of Food Security*, University of Bristol Working Paper No. 07-09, Bristol: University of Bristol.

Alertnet (2012) 'Conflict-hit Sudanese may go hungry despite aid deal', available at https://www.hhrjournal.org/2012/07/alertnet-conflict-hit-sudanese-may-go-hungry-despite-aid-deal/.

Ali, T. M. (1989) *The Cultivation of Hunger. State and Agriculture in Sudan*, Khartoum: Khartoum University Press.

Alinovi, L., Hemrich, G. and Russo, L. (2008) *Beyond Relief: Food Security in Protracted Crisis*, Rugby: Practical Action Publlishing.

Anderson, M. (1999) *Do No Harm. How Aid Can Support Peace or War*, London: Lynne Rienner.

Appleton J, Borrel A, Duffield A, Frankenberger, T., Gostelow, L., Grellety, Y., Jaspars, S., Maxwell, D., Taylor, A., Toole, M. J. and Young, H. (2000) 'Chapter 5: Nutrition of refugees and displaced populations', in: ACC/SCN (ed.) *4th Report on the World Nutrition Situation. Nutrition Throughout the Lifecycle*, Geneva: UN Administrative Committee on Coordination/Sub-Committee on Nutrition (ACC/SCN) with International Food Policy Research Institute.

Arnold, T. and Beckmann, B. (2011) *Update on Scaling up Nutrition (SUN) and the '1000 Day' Movements*, Field Exchange 41, Oxford: Emergency Nutrition Network.

Asfaw, A. and Ibrahim, S. (2008) *The Strategic Reserve Corporation of Sudan. Learning from Best Practices*, Technical Discussion Paper 1, Khartoum: FAO and the Ministry of Agriculture and Forestry.

Assal, M. (2008) *Is it the Fault of NGOs Alone? Aid and Dependency in Eastern Sudan*, Sudan Working Paper 5, Christian Michelsen Institute.

Axe, D. (2007) 'Grounding Sudan's Air Force', available at http://www.wired.com/2007/05/grounding_sudan/.

Ayers, A. (2010) 'Sudan's uncivil war: the global–historical constitution of political violence', *Review of African Political Economy*, 37 (124): 153–171.

Barnett, M. (2011) *Empire of Humanity: A History of Humanitarianism*, New York: Cornell University Press.

Barnett, T. (1988) "Introduction: the Sudanese Crisis and the Future", in: Barnett, T. and Abdelkarim, A. (eds.), *Sudan; tate, Capital and Transformation*, London: Croom Helm.

Barrett, C. and Maxwell, D. (2005) *Food Aid After Fifty Years: Recasting its Role*, London: Routledge.

BBC (2004) "Mass rape atrocity in west Sudan", available at http://news.bbc.co.uk/1/hi/world/africa/3549325.stm.

Beals, E. and Hopkins, N. (2016) 'Aid groups suspend cooperation with UN in Syria because of Assad "influence"', available at https://www.theguardian.com/world/2016/sep/08/aid-groups-un-syria-concern-assad-united-nations.

Béné, C., Godfrey Wood, R., Newsham, A. and Davies, M. (2012) *Resilience: New Utopia or New Tyranny? Reflection about the Potentials and Limits of the Concept of Resilience in Relation to Vulnerability Reduction Programmes*, IDS working paper 405, Brighton: Institute of Development Studies.

Benson, C. and Clay, E. (1986) 'Food aid and food crisis in Sub-Saharan Africa: statistical trends and implications', *Disasters*, 10 (4): 303–316.

Bhutta, Z., Ahmed, T., Black, R., Cousens, S., Dewey, K., Giugliani, E., Haider, B., Kirkwood, B., Morris, S., Sachdev, H. and Shekar, M. (2008) 'Maternal and child Undernutrition 3. What works? Interventions for maternal and child undernutrition and survival', *Lancet*, 371: 417–440.

Bickersteth, J. S. (1990) 'Donor dilemmas in food aid. The case of wheat in Sudan', *Food Policy*, 15 (3): 218–226.

Bizzarri, M. (2013) *Comparative Evaluation of Cash Voucher and In-Kind Activities in North and West Darfur*, Rome: World food Programme.

Black, M. (1992) *A Cause for our Times. Oxfam the First 50 Years*, Oxford: Oxfam.

Black, R., Allen, L., Bhutta, Z., Caulfield, L., de Onis, M., Ezzati, M., Mathers, C. and Rivera, J. (2008) 'Maternal and child Undernutrition 1. Maternal and child undernutrition: global and regional exposures and health consequences', *Lancet*, 371: 243–260.

Borrel, A. and Salama, P. (1999) 'Public nutrition from an approach to a discipline: Concern's nutrition case studies in complex emergencies', *Disasters*, 23 (4): 326–342.

Borton, J. and Shoham, J. (1989) 'Experiences of non-governmental organisations in the targeting of emergency food aid. A report on a workshop on emergency food aid targeting at the London School of Hygiene and Tropical Medicine,

London, 4–6 January 1989',
Disasters, 13 (1): 77–93.

Boudreau, T. (1998) *The Food
Economy Approach: A Framework
for Understanding Rural Livelihoods*,
HPN Network Paper 26, London:
Overseas Development Institute.

Bradbury, M. (1998) 'Normalising
the crisis in Africa', *Disasters*, 22
(4): 328–338.

Brigg, M. (2002) 'Post-development,
Foucault and the colonisation
metaphor', *Third World Quarterly*,
23 (3): 421–436.

Bryce, J., Coitinho, D., Darnton-Hill,
I., Pelletier, D. and Pinstrup-
Andersen, P. (2008) 'Maternal and
child Undernutrition 4. Maternal
and child undernutrition: effective
action at national level', *Lancet*,
371: 510–526.

Buchanan-Smith, M. (1989)
*Evaluation of the Western Relief
Operation 1987/88. Final Report*,
Wokingham: MASDAR (UK) Ltd.

Buchanan-Smith, M. (1990) *Food
Security Planning in the Wake of an
Emergency Relief Operation: The
Case of Darfur, Western Sudan*, IDS
Discussion Paper 278, Brighton:
Institute of Development Studies.

Buchanan-Smith, M. (2006) *The
Darfur Early Warning System and
Food Information System. Final
Evaluation of Phase III*, London:
Save the Children-UK.

Buchanan-Smith, M. and Abdulla
Fadul, A. (2008) *Adaptation and
Devastation: The Impact of the
Conflict on Trade and Markets in
Darfur. Findings of a Scoping Study*,
Boston: Feinstein International
Center, Tufts University.

Buchanan-Smith, M., Abdala Fadul,
A., Rahman Tahir, A., Adam Ismail,
M., Ibrahim Ahmed, N., Zakaria,
M., Yagoub Kaja, Z., Abdulrahman
Aldou, E.-H., Hussein
Abdulmawla, M. I., Ali Hassan, A.,
Awad Elkarim, Y. M., James, L. and
Jaspars, S. (2014) *Against the Grain:
The Cereal Trade in Darfur*, Boston:
Feinstein International Center,
Tufts University.

Buchanan-Smith, M. and Davies,
M. (1995a) *Famine Early Warning
and Response – The Missing Link*,
London: Intermediate Technology
Publications.

Buchanan-Smith, M. and Davies,
S. (1995b) 'Chapter 5: Sudan',
*Famine Early Warning and
Response – The Missing Link*,
London: Intermediate Technology
Publications, 84–110.

Buchanan-Smith, M. and Jaspars,
S. (2006) *Conflict, Camps and
Coercion: The Continuing Livelihoods
Crisis in Darfur*, Khartoum: World
Food Programme.

Buchanan-Smith, M. and Jaspars,
S. (2007) 'Conflict, camps and
coercion: the ongoing livelihoods
crisis in Darfur', *Disasters*, 31
(Supplement 1): S57–S76.

Buchanan-Smith, M. and Maxwell,
S. (1994) 'Linking relief and
development. Introduction and
overview', *IDS Bulletin*, 25 (4):
1–15.

Buckley, R. (1988) 'Food targeting in
Darfur: Save the Children Fund's
programme in 1986', *Disasters*, 12
(2): 97–103.

Bush, J. (1996) *Sudan: Evaluation of
the Darfur Early Warning and Food
Information System*, London: Save
the Children-UK.

Bush, R. (1988) 'Hunger in Sudan:
the case of Darfur', *African Affairs*,
87 (386): 5–23.

Caeyers, B. and Dercon, S. (2012)
*Political Connections and Social
Networks in Targeted Transfer
Programmes: Evidence from Rural
Ethiopia*, CEPR Discussion Paper.

Cannon, T. and Muller-Mahn, D.
(2010) 'Vulnerability, resilience
and development discourse in the
context of climate change', *Natural
Hazards*, 55: 621–635.

CARE (2001) *Benefit-Harms
Facilitation Manual*, Atlanta: CARE.

Cathie, J. (1982) *The Political
Economy of Food Aid*, Aldershot:
Gower Publishing Company.

Chambers, R. (1988) 'Sustainable
rural livelihoods: a key strategy

for people, environment and development', in: Conroy, C. and Litvinoff, M. (eds.) *The Greening of Aid. Sustainable Livelihoods in Practice*, London: Earthscan.

Chambers, R. (1989) 'Vulnerability, coping and policy (editorial introduction)', *IDS Bulletin*, 20 (2): 1–8.

Chandler, D. (2013) "Human-centred' development? Rethinking 'freedom' and 'agency' in discourses of international development', *Millennium: Journal of International Studies*, 42 (1): 3–23.

Charlton, M. (1997) 'Famine and the food weapon: implications for the global food aid regime', *Journal of Conflict Studies*, 17 (1), available at https://journals.lib.unb.ca/index. php/jcs/article/view/11736/12493.

Chatterjee, P. (2004) *The Politics of the Governed. Reflections on Popular Politics in Most of the World*, New York: Columbia University Press.

Chhotray, V. and Stoker, G. (2009) *Governance Theory and Practice. A Cross-Disciplinary Approach*, Basingstoke: Palgrave.

CIJ (2006) *Soil and Oil: Dirty Business in Sudan*, Washington, DC: Coalition for International Justice.

Civil Society Forum (2014) 'Social movements statement on nutrition', *Development*, 57 (2): 305–309.

Civil Society Organisations (2014) *Public Interest Civil Society Organizations' Statement on ICN 2 process*, Rome: Civil Society Forum.

Clapp, J. (2012) *Hunger in the Balance. The New Politics of International Food Aid*, Ithaca and London: Cornell University Press.

Clapp, J. and Clark, S. (2012) 'The 2012 Food Assistance Convention: is a promise still a promise?', available at http://triplecrisis. com/the-2012-food-assistance-convention-is-a-promise-still-a-promise.

Clay, E. (2006) *Food Aid and the Doha Development Round: Building on the Positive*, Overseas Development Institute Background Paper, London: Overseas Development Institute.

Clay, E. (2010) *A Future Food Aid or Food Assistance Convention?*, ODI Background Paper on Food Aid No. 6, London: Overseas Development Institute.

Clay, E. (2012) 'What's the use of the 2012 Food Assistance Convention?', available at http://www.odi.org/ opinion/6656-food-assistance-convention-hunger-food-price.

Clay, E., Dhiri, S. and Benson, C. (1996) *Joint Evaluation of European Union Programme Food Aid. Synthesis Report*, London: Overseas Development Institute.

Clay, E. and Schaffer, B. (eds.) (1984) *Room for Manoeuvre. An Exploration of Public Policy in Agriculture and Rural Development*, Heinemann Studies in Development and Society, London: Heinemann Educational Books.

Clay, E. and Stokke, O. (2000) 'The changing role of food aid and finance for food', in: Clay, E. and Stokke, O. (eds.) *Food Aid and Human Security*, London: Frank Cass.

Coates, J., Rogers, B. L., Webb, P., Maxwell, D., Houser, R. and McDonald, C. (2007) *Diet Diversity Study*, ODAN, Emergency Needs Assessment Service, Rome: World Food Programme.

Cohen, S. (2001) *States of Denial. Knowing about Atrocities and Suffering*, Cambridge: Polity.

Collins, R. (2008) *A History of Modern Sudan*, Cambridge: Cambridge University Press.

Collins, S. (2001) *How Bad Does It Have To Get? The Nutritional Status in N Darfur in the Spring of 2001*, Al-Fashir: Save the Children-UK.

Corbett, J. (1988) 'Famine and household coping strategies', *World Development*, 16 (9): 1092–1112.

Cosgrave, J., Goyder, H. and Hoogendoorn, A. (2010) *Sudan EMOP 10760.0: Food Assistance to Populations Affected by Conflict: An Operation Evaluation*, Rome: WFP.

Crawford, N. and Pattugalan, G. (eds.) (2013) *Protection in Practice: Food Assistance with Safety and Dignity*, Rome: WFP.

Cutler, P. (1984) 'Famine forecasting; prices and peasant behaviour in Northern Ethiopia', *Disasters*, 8 (1): 48–56.

Cutler, P. (1991) 'The political economy of famine in Ethiopia and Sudan', *Ambio*, 20 (5): 176–178.

Darfur Development and Reconstruction Agency (2011) *Trade and Market Bulletin North Darfur*, Volume 1. Number 1. Boston: DRA and Feinstein International Center. Tufts University.

Darfur Development and Reconstruction Agency (2012) *Trade and Market Bulletin North Darfur*, Volume 2, Number 1, Boston: DRA and Feinstein International Center, Tufts University.

Darfur Development and Reconstruction Agency (2014b) *Trade and Market Bulletin. North Darfur*, Volume 4, Number 2, DRA and Feinstein International Center at Tufts University.

Darfur Development and Reconstruction Agency (2014a) *Trade and Market Bulletin. North Darfur*, Volume 4, Number 3, Boston: DRA and Feinstein International Center at Tufts University.

Davies, S. (1996) *Adaptable Livelihoods. Coping with Food Insecurity in the Malian Sahel*, Basingstoke: Macmillan Press Ltd.

De Waal, A. (1986) *Free Food Distribution in Darfur 1985–7: For and Against*, Nyala: Save the Children-UK.

De Waal, A. (1989a) *Famine that Kills: Darfur, Sudan*, Oxford: Clarendon Press.

De Waal, A. (1989b) *The Sudan Famine Code of 1920. Successes and Failures of the Indian Model of Famine Relief in Colonial Sudan*, London: Action Aid.

De Waal, A. (1990) 'A re-assessment of entitlement theory in the light of recent famines in Africa', *Development and Change*, 21 (3): 469–490.

De Waal, A. (1997a) *Famine Crimes; Politics and the Disaster Relief Industry*, London: James Currey.

De Waal, A. (1997b) 'Sudan: 1972–1993. Privatising famine.', *Famine Crimes: Politics and the Disaster Relief Industry in Africa*, London: James Currey, 86–105.

De Waal, A. (2007a) 'Sudan: the turbulent state', in: De Waal, A. (ed.) *War in Darfur and the Search for Peace*, London: Justice Africa and Global Equity Initiative, 1–38.

De Waal, A. (ed.) (2007b) *War in Darfur and the Search for Peace*, London: Justice Africa and Global Equity Initiative.

De Waal, A. and Abdelsalam, S. A. (2004) 'Islamism, state power and jihad in Sudan', in: De Waal, A. (ed.) *Islamism and Its Enemies in the Horn of Africa*, Bloomington and Indianapolis: Indiana University Press, 71–113.

Dean, M. (2010) *Governmentality. Power and Rule in Modern Society*, 2nd edition, London: Sage Publications.

Deng, L. (2002) 'The Sudan famine of 1998. Unfolding of the global dimension', *IDS Bulletin*, 33 (4): 28–38.

Development Initiatives (2003) *Global Humanitarian Assistance 2003*, Wells: Development Initiatives.

Development Initiatives (2009) *Global Humanitarian Assistance Report 2009*, Wells: Development Initiatives.

Development Initiatives (2010) *Sudan Aid Factsheet 1995–2009. Trends in Overseas Development Assistance*, Wells: Development Initiatives.

Development Initiatives (2011) *Global Humanitarian Assistance Report 2011*, Wells: Development Initiatives.

Devereux, S. (2007) 'Sen's entitlement approach. Critiques and counter critiques', in: Devereux, S. (ed.) *The New Famines. Why Famines Persist in an Era of Globalisation*, London: Routledge, 66–89.

DFID (1997) *Report on Sudan Emergency Food Distributions*, London: Department for International Development.

DFID (2009) *The Neglected Crisis of Undernutrition: Evidence for Action*, London: Department for International Development.

DFID (2011) *Saving Lives, Preventing Suffering and Building Resilience: The UK Government's Humanitarian Policy*, London: Department for International Development.

Diraige, I. (1994) *Summary of WFP Relief and Development Activities in Darfur Three States in 1994 and Recommendation for 1995*, Al-Fashir: World Food Programme.

Dixon, M. (2014) 'The land grab, finance capital, and food regime restructuring: the case of Egypt', *Review of African Political Economy*, 41 (140): 232–248.

Donovan, K. (2013) *Infrastructuring Aid: Materializing Social Protection in Northern Kenya*, CSSR Working Paper No. 333, Cape Town: Centre for Social Science Research. University of Cape Town.

Dorosh, P. and Subran, L. (2009) 'Food aid, external trade and domestic markets: implications for food security in Darfur', *International Association of Agricultural Economists Conference*, Beijing: IFPRI and World Bank.

Duffield, M. (1990a) 'From emergency to social security in Sudan – Part I: The problem', *Disasters*, 14 (3): 187–203.

Duffield, M. (1990b) 'From emergency to social security in Sudan – Part II: the donor response', *Disasters*, 14 (4): 322–334.

Duffield, M. (1992) 'Famine, conflict and the internationalisation of public welfare', in: Doornbos, M. (ed.) *Beyond Conflict in the Horn: Prospects for Peace, Recovery and Development in Ethiopia, Somalia and the Sudan*, The Hague: Institute of Social Studies.

Duffield, M. (1994a) 'The political economy of internal war: asset transfer, Complex Emergencies, and International Aid', in: Macrae, J. and Zwi, A. (eds.) *War and Hunger. Rethinking International Responses to Complex Emergencies*, London: Zed Books, 50–69.

Duffield, M. (1994b) 'Complex emergencies and the crisis of developmentalism', *IDS Bulletin*, 25 (4): 37–45.

Duffield, M. (2002a) 'War as a network enterprise: the new security terrain and its implications', *Cultural Values*, (6): 153–165.

Duffield, M. (2002b) 'Social reconstruction and the radicalization of development: aid as a relation of global liberal governance', *Development and Change*, 33 (5): 1049–1071.

Duffield, M. (2002c) 'Aid and complicity: the case of war displaced Southerners in Northern Sudan', *Journal of Modern African Studies*, 40 (1): 83–104.

Duffield, M. (2007) *Development, Security and Unending War; Governing the World of Peoples*, Cambridge: Polity Press.

Duffield, M. (2013) *Disaster-Resilience in the Network Age Access-Denial and the Rise of Cyber-Humanitarianism*, DIIS Working Paper 2013:23,

Copenhagen: Danish Institute for International Studies.

Duffield, M. (2015) 'Becoming remote... living in the ruins. Toward a critique of digital humanitarianism', *Relaciones* Internationales, 30, available at http://www.relacionesinternacionales.info/ojs/article/view/659.html.

Duffield, M. (2016) 'The resilience of the ruins: towards a critique of digital humanitarianism', *Resilience*, DOI: 10.1080/21693293.2016.1153772

Duncan, J. (2014) *The Reformed Committee on World Food Security and the Global Governance of Food Security*, PhD in Food Policy, City University: London.

Edkins, J. (2000) *Whose Hunger? Concepts of Famine, Practices of Aid*, Borderlines, Mineapolis and London: University of Minnesota Press.

El-Basri, A. (2014) 'We can't say all that we see in Darfur', available at http://foreignpolicy.com/2014/04/09/we-cant-say-all-that-we-see-in-darfur/.

El-Mekki, A. (2007) *Displacement and Political Change in Darfur: The Dynamics of Leadership and Representation*, Al-Fashir: Civil Affairs Division, UNAMID.

Elbashir, A. and Ahmed, A. (2005) *Study on Food Security Policies in Sudan. Study Prepared for the World Food Programme in Khartoum, Sudan*, Khartoum: World Food Programme.

Eldridge, E., Salter, C. and Rydjeski, D. (1986) 'Towards an early warning system in Sudan', *Disasters*, 10 (3): 189–196.

ENN (2003) *Community Based Approaches to Managing Severe Malnutrition. ENN Report on the Proceedings of an Inter-agency Workshop*, Dublin: Emergency Nutrition Network.

ENN (2005) *Operational Challenges of Implementing Community Therapeutic Care. ENN Report on an Inter-Agency Workshop Community Therapeutic Care*, Washington, DC: ENN.

ENN (2008) *Integration of Community-Based Management of Acute Malnutrition, Workshop Report*, Washington, DC: Emergency Nutrition Network.

ENN (2011) *Conference on Government Experiences of Community-based Management of Acute Malnutrition and Scaling Up Nutrition Conference Report*, Addis Ababa. Emergency Nutrition Network.

Essex, J. (2014) 'From the global food crisis to the age of austerity: the anxious geopolitics of global food security', *Geopolitics*, 19 (2): 266–290.

EU (2012) *EU Approach to Resilience: Learning from Food Crises*, Brussels: EU.

Evans, B. and Reid, J. (2013) 'Dangerously exposed: the life & death of the resilient subject', *Resilience: International Policies, Practices & Discourses*, 1 (2): 83–98.

FAO (1974) 'Report of the Council of FAO. Sixty-Fourth Session. Rome, 18–29 November 1974', available at http://www.fao.org/docrep/meeting/007/F5340E/F5340E03.htm#ch2.4.

FAO (1996) 'Rome Declaration on World Food Security', available at http://www.fao.org/docrep/003/w3613e/w3613e00.HTM.

FAO (2003) *International Workshop. Food Security in Complex Emergencies: Building Policy Frameworks to Address Longer-term Programming Challenges*, 23–25 September 2003, Tivoli, Italy: FAO.

FAO (2008) *High-Level Task Force on the Global Food Crisis. Comprehensive Framework for Action.*, Rome: Food and Agriculture Organisation.

FAO (2009) *Declaration of the World Summit on Food Security*, Rome: Food and Agriculture Organisation.

FAO (2010) *High Level Task Force on the Global Food Security Crisis. Updated Comprehensive Framework for Action*, Rome: Food and Agriculture Organisation.

FAO (2012a) 'Global Information and Early Warning System', available at http://www.fao.org/giews.

FAO (2012b) 'Low-Income Food-Deficit Countries (LIFDC) – list for 2012', available at http://www.fao.org/countryprofiles/lifdc.asp.

FAO (2012c) 'FAOSTAT', available at http://faostat.fao.org/site/485/default.aspx#ancor.

FAO (2012d) *High Level Expert Forum on Addressing Food Insecurity in Protracted Crisis, Report*, 13–14 September, Rome: Food and Agricultural Organisation.

Federal Ministry of Health (2014) *Report of a Simple Spatial Surveying Method (S3M) Survey in Sudan*, Khartoum: Federal Ministry of Health.

Federal Ministry of Health and Central Bureau of Statistics (2012) *Sudan Household Health Survey 2010. National Report*, Khartoum: Government of Sudan.

Ferguson, J. (1990) *The Anti-politics Machine. 'Development', Depoliticisation, and Bureaucratic Power in Lesotho*, Cambridge: Cambridge University Press.

Flint, J. (2009) *Beyond 'Janjaweed': Understanding the Militias of Darfur*, Geneva: Small Arms Survey.

Flint, J. and De Waal, A. (2008) *Darfur. A New History of a Long War*, African Arguments. London: Zed books.

Foucault, M. (1977). *Discipline and Punish: The Birth of the Prison* (translated by A. Sheridan), London: Penguin Books.

Foucault, M. (1980) 'Truth and power', in: Gordon, C. (ed.) *Power/Knowledge: Selected Interviews and Other Writings* (translated by Gordon, C., Marshall, L., Mepham, J., Soper, K.), New York: Pantheon Books, 109–133.

Foucault, M. (1981) 'Questions of method: an interview with Michel Foucault', *Ideology and Consciousness*, 8: 3–14.

Foucault, M. (1984) 'Nietzsche, Genealogy, History ', in: Rabinow, P. (ed.) *The Foucault Reader*, London: Penguin Books, 76–87.

Foucault, M. (1991) 'Governmentality', in: Burchell, G., Gordon, C. and Miller, P. (eds.) *The Foucault Effect: Studies in Governmentality*, London: Harvester Wheatsheaf, 87–104.

Foucault, M. (2000) 'The subject and power', in: Faubion, J. (ed.) *Power* (translated by Robert Hurley and others), New York: The New Press.

Foucault, M. (2007) *Security, Territory, Population. Lectures at the College de France 1977–78*, (translated by Burchell, G.), Basingstoke: Palgrave.

Foucault, M. (2008) *The Birth of Biopolitics. Lectures at the College de France. 1978–1979* (translated by Burchell, G.), Basingstoke: Palgrave.

G8 (2009) *'L'Aquila' Joint Statement on Global Food Security. L'Aquila Food Security Initiative (AFSI)*, L'Aquila, G8, available at http://www.g8.utoronto.ca/summit/2009laquila/2009-food.html.

Gallab, A. (2008) *The First Islamist Republic. Development and Disintegration of Islamism in the Sudan*, Aldershot: Ashgate.

George, S. (1976) *How the Other Half Dies. The Real Reasons for World Hunger*, London: Penguin Books.

Gillespie, S., Haddad, L., Mannar, V., Menon, P., Nisbett, N. and the Maternal and Child Nutrition Study Group (2013) 'Maternal and Child Nutrition 4. The politics of reducing malnutrition: building commitment and accelerating progress', *Lancet*, 382: 552–569.

Gillespie, S. and Harris, J. (2016) 'How nutrition improves. Half a century of understanding and responding to the problem of malnutrition', in: Gillespie, S., Hodge, J., Yosef, S. and Pandya-Lorch, R. (eds.) *Nourishing Millions: Stories of Change in Nutrition*, Washington, DC: International Food Policy Research Institute.

Gordon, C. (1991) 'Governmental rationality: an introduction', in: Burchell, G., Gordon, C. and Miller, P. (eds.) *Studies in Governmentality, with Two Lectures by and an Interview with Michel Foucault*, Chicago: The University of Chicago Press.

Government of Sudan (2010) *Darfur: Towards New Strategy to Achieve Comprehensive Peace, Security and Development*, Khartoum: Government of Sudan.

Gramizzi, C. and Tubiana, J. (2012) *Forgotten Darfur: Old Tactics and New Players*, HSBA Working Paper 28, Geneva: Small Arms Survey.

Guha-Sapir, D. and Degomme, O. (2005) *Darfur: Counting the Deaths. Mortality Estimates from Multiple Survey Data*, Brussels: Centre for Research on the Epidemiology of Disasters.

Gupta, A., Schuftan, C., Valente, F., Rundall, P. and Holla, R. (2012) 'Ready to use therapeutic food is not the solution to malnutrition [letter]', *World Nutrition*, 3 (4): 168–171.

Gupta, A., Jonsson, U. and Rundall, P. (2013) 'Is it enough to declare conflicts of interest? A response to the Lancet Series on maternal and child nutrition', *Lancet*, 382: 1150.

Haldrup, S. and Rosen, F. (2013) 'Developing resilience: a retreat from grand planning', *Resilience*, 1 (2): 130–145.

Hamid, A. R., Salih, A. A. A., Bradley, S., Couteaudier, T., El Haj, M. J., Hussein, M. O. and Steffen, P. (2005) *Markets, Livelihoods and Food Aid in Darfur: A Rapid Assessment and Programming Recommendations*, Khartoum: EU, FAO and USAID.

Hamid, G. (n.d.) *Localising the Local: Reflections on the Experience of Local Authorities in Sudan*, Riyadh: Arab Urban Development Institute.

Hancock, G. (1989) *Lords of Poverty*, London: Macmillan.

Hardy, J. (1985) *Nutritional Surveillance and Drought Monitoring Project. Report on Project Activities October–December 1985*, Nyala: Oxfam.

Harir, S., Hødnebø, K. and Tvedt, T. (1994) 'A chronology of the Sudan. 1972–1992', in: Harir, S. and Tvedt, T. (eds.) *Short Cut to Decay. The Case of the Sudan*, Uppsala: The Scandinavian Institute of African Studies.

Harrell-Bond, B. (1986) *Imposing Aid. Emergency Assistance to Refugees*, Oxford: Oxford University Press.

Harrison, C. and Wagabi, C. (2011) *Operational Review of ODS Voucher Programme in Sudan*, Khartoum: World Food Programme.

Harrison, G. (2013) 'Solving malnutrition through business and science?', available at http://progressivedevelopmentforum.wordpress.com/2013/07/08/solving-malnutrition-through-business-and-science/.

Harriss, B. (1986) *Booklet for the course on: Food Policy and Planning*, London: Nutrition Policy Unit, London School of Hygiene and Tropical Medicine.

Harvey, D. (2005) *A Brief History of Neoliberalism*, Oxford: Oxford University Press.

Harvey, P. (2007) *Cash-based responses in emergencies*, HPG Report 24, London: Overseas Development Institute.

Harvey, P. and Lindt, J. (2005) *Dependency and Humanitarian Relief; A Critical Analysis*, HPG Report 19, London: Overseas Development Institute.

Harvey, P., Proudlock, K., Clay, E., Riley, B. and Jaspars, S. (2010)

Food Aid and Food Assistance in Emergency and Transitional Contexts: A Review of Current Thinking, HPG Commissioned Report, London: Overseas Development Institute.

Haver, K. and Carter, W. (2016) *What It Takes: Principled Pragmatism to Enable Access and Quality Humanitarian Aid in Insecure Environments*, Secure Access in Volatile Environments. Humanitarian Outcomes.

Hedlund, K., Majid, N., Maxwell, D. and Nicholson, N. (2012) *Final Evaluation of the Unconditional Cash and Voucher Response to the 2011 12 Crisis in Southern and Central Somalia*, Report, Nairobi: UNICEF.

Hoddinott, J. and Yohannes, Y. (2002a) *Dietary Diversity as a Food Security Indicator*, Food Consumption and Nutrition Division Discussion Paper No. 136, Washington, DC: IFPRI.

Hoddinott, J. and Yohannes, Y. (2002b) *Dietary Diversity as a Food Security Indicator*, Washington, DC: Food and Nutrition Technical Assistance Project. Academy for Educational Development.

Hossain, N., Brito, L., Jahan, F., Joshi, A., Nyamu-Musembi, C., Patnaik, B., Sambo, M., Shankland, A., Scott-Villiers, P., Sinha, D., Kalita, D. and Benequista, N. (2014) '*Them Belly Full (But We Hungry)': Food Rights Struggles in Bangladesh, India, Kenya and Mozambique. Synthesis Report from DFID-ESRC Research Project Food Riots and Food Rights*, Brighton: Institute of Development Studies.

Howe, K., Stites, E. and Chudacoff, D. (2015) *Breaking the Hourglass: Partnerships in Remote Management Settings – The Cases of Syria and Iraqi Kurdistan*, Boston: Feinstein International Center, Tufts University.

Human Rights Watch (1998) *Famine in Sudan, 1998. The Human Rights Causes*, New York: Human Rights Watch.

Human Rights Watch (2011) *Darfur in the Shadows. The Sudanese Government's Ongoing Attacks on Civilians and Human Rights*, New York: Human Rights Watch.

Humanitarian Aid Commission (2009) *Humanitarian Situation in Sudan*, Khartoum: Ministry of Humanitarian Affairs.

Hussain, M. N. (1991) 'Food security and adjustment programmes: the conflict', in: Maxwell, S. (ed.) *To Cure All Hunger. Food Policy and Food Security in Sudan*, London: Intermediate technology publications, 85–113.

IBFAN (2012) *The Scaling Up Nutrition (SUN) initiative and IBFAN's Concern about the Role of Business*, IBFAN Discussion Paper, November 2012, London: IBFAN.

Ibrahim, F. (1998) 'The Zaghawa and the Midob of North Darfur – a comparison of migration behaviour', *GeoJournal*, 46: 135–140.

Ibrahim, I. (2011) *Study Report. Causality Study on Causes of Persistent Acute Malnutrition in North Darfur (Kabkabyia). 2010–2011*, Khartoum: Word Food Programme.

ICISS (2001) *The Responsibility to Protect. Report of the International Commission on Intervention and State Sovereignty*, Ottawa: International Development Research Centre.

ICRC Resource Centre (2014) 'ICRC hopeful to resume activities as soon as possible', available at http://www.icrc.org/eng/resources/documents/news-release/2014/02-02-sudan-activities.htm.

International Crisis Group (2007) *Darfur's New Security Reality*, Africa Report Number 134, Brussels: International Crisis Group.

International Crisis Group (2014) *Sudan's Spreading Conflict (III): The Limits of Darfur's Peace Process*, Africa Report No. 211, Brussels: International Crisis Group.

Jackson, A. (2014) *Negotiating perceptions: Al-Shabaab and Taliban Views of Aid Agencies*, HPG Policy Brief 61, London: Overseas Development Institute.

Jackson, T. (1982) *Against the Grain. The Dilemma of Project Food Aid*, Oxford: Oxfam.

Jaspars, S. (2000) *Solidarity and Soup Kitchens: A Review of Principles and Practice for Food Distribution in Conflict*, HPG Report 17, London: Overseas Development Institute.

Jaspars, S. (2010) *Coping and Change in Protracted Conflict: The Role of Community Groups and Local Institutions in Addressing Food Insecurity and Threats to Livelihoods. A Case Study Based on the Experience of Practical Action in Darfur*, HPG Working Paper, London: Overseas Development Institute.

Jaspars, S. (2015) 'Sudan's permanent food emergency: A historical analysis of food aid, governance and political economy', in: Christoplos, I. and Pain, A. (eds.) *New Challenges to Food Security. From Climate Change to Fragile States*. London: Routledge.

Jaspars, S. and Maxwell, D. (2008) *Targeting in Complex Emergencies: Somalia Country Case Study*, Boston: Feinstein International Center, Tufts University.

Jaspars, S. and O'Callaghan, S. (2008) *Challenging Choices. Protection and Livelihoods in Darfur; A Review of DRC's Programme in Eastern West Darfur*, HPG Working Paper, London: Overseas Development Institute.

Jaspars, S. and Shoham, J. (1999) 'Targeting the vulnerable; the necessity and feasibility of targeting vulnerable households', *Disasters*, 23 (4): 359–372.

Jaspars, S. and Young, H. (1995a) *General Food Distribution in Emergencies; from Nutritional Needs to Political Priorities*, RRN Good Practice Review 3, London: Overseas Development Institute.

Johnson, D. (2003) *The Root Causes of Sudan's Civil Wars*, Oxford: James Currey.

Kahn, C. (2008) *Conflict, Arms and Militarization: The Dynamics of Darfur's IDP Camps*, Geneva: Small Arms Survey.

Karadawi, A. (1999) *Refugee Policy in Sudan. 1967–1984*, Refugee and Forced Migration Studies, Volume 1, New York and Oxford: Berghahn Books.

Karim, A., Duffield, M., Jaspars, S., Benini, A., Macrae, J., Bradbury, M., Johnson, D., Larbi, G. and Hendrie, B. (1996) *Operation Lifeline Sudan. A Review*, Birmingham: University of Birmingham.

Keen, D. (1991) 'Targeting emergency food aid: the case of Darfur in 1985', in: Maxwell, S. (ed.) *To Cure All Hunger. Food Policy and Food Security in Sudan*, London: Intermediate Technology Publications, 191–206.

Keen, D. (1992) *Refugees: Rationing the Right to Life. The Crisis in Emergency Relief*, London: Zed Books.

Keen, D. (1994) *The Benefits of Famine. A Political Economy of Famine and Relief in South Western Sudan 1983–89*, Oxford: James Currey.

Keen, D. (2008) *Complex Emergencies*, Cambridge: Polity Press.

Keen, D. (2014) '"The camp" and "the lesser evil": humanitarianism in Sri Lanka', *Conflict, Security & Development* 14. (1): 1–31, available at http://dx.doi.org/10.1080/14678 802.2013.856176.

Kelly, M. (1992) 'Entitlements, coping mechanisms and indicators of access to food: Wollo Region, Ethiopia, 1987–88', *Disasters*, 16 (4): 322–338.

Kelly, M. and Buchanan-Smith, M. (1994) 'Northern Sudan in 1991: food crisis and the international relief response', *Disasters*, 18 (1): 16–34.

Khalid, M. (2009) 'Darfur. A problem within a wider problem.', in: Hassan, S. andRay, C. (eds.) *Darfur and the Crisis of Governance in Sudan. A Critical Reader*, Ithaca and London: Cornell University Press, 35–42.

Khalifa, A. (2006) *Operation Lifeline Sudan. Is it a Horse to Help or is it a Trojan Horse? A Critical Study of Operation Lifeline Sudan*, Khartoum: International Africa University, DIMARSI (in Arabic).

Kothari, U. (2001) 'Power, knowledge and social control in participatory development', in: Cooke, B. and Kothari, U. (eds.) *Participation. The New Tyranny?*, London and NewYork: Zed Books, 139–152.

Lang, T. (2010) 'Crisis? What crisis? The normality of the current food crisis', *Journal of Agrarian Change*, 10 (1): 87–97.

Lautze, S. and Raven-Roberts (2006) 'Violence and complex humanitarian emergencies: implications for livelihoods models', *Disasters*, 30 (4): 383–401.

Leader, N. (2000) *The Politics of Principle: The Principles of Humanitarian Action in Practice*, HPG Report 2, London: Overseas Development Institute.

Leroy, J., Ruel, M., Frongillo, E., Harris, J. and Ballard, T. (2015) 'Measuring the food access dimension of food security: a critical review and mapping of indicators', *Food and Nutrition Bulletin*, 36 (2): 167–195.

Levine, I. (1997) *Promoting Humanitarian Principles: The Southern Sudan Experience*, RRN Network Paper 21, London: Overseas Development Institute.

Levine, S. and Mosel, I. (2014) *Supporting Resilience in Difficult Places. A Critical Look at Applying the 'Resilience' Concept in Countries where Crises are the Norm*, HPG Commissioned Report, London: Overseas Development Institute.

Levine, S., Pain, A., Bailey, S. and

Fan, L. (2012) *The Relevance of 'Resilience'?*, HPG Policy Brief 49, London: Overseas Development Institute.

Leys, C. (1996) *The Rise and Fall of Development Theory*, Oxford: James Currey.

Lipton, M. (1983) *Poverty, Undernutrition and Hunger*, World Bank Staff Working Papers, Number 597, Washington, DC: World Bank.

Loeb, J. (2013) *Talking to the Other Side. Humanitarian Engagement with Non-state Actors in Darfur, Sudan, 2003–2012*, HPG Working Paper, London: Overseas Development Institute.

Macrae, J., Bradbury, M., Jaspars, S., Johnson, D. and Duffield, M. (1997) 'Conflict, the continuum and chronic emergencies: a critical analysis of the scope for linking relief, rehabilitation and development planning in Sudan', *Disasters*, 21 (3): 223–243.

Macrae, J. and Zwi, A. (1994b) 'Famine, complex emergencies and International Policy in Africa. An overview', in: Macrae, J. and Zwi, A. (eds.) *War and Hunger. Rethinking International Responses to Complex Emergencies*, London: Zed Books, 6–36.

Mahoney, L. (2013) 'Chapter 4. Food, political power and protection in Darfur', in: Crawford, N. and Pattugalan, G. (eds.) *Protection in Practice: Food Assistance with Safety and Dignity*, Rome: WFP, 77–90.

Mahoney, L., Laughton, S. and Vincent, M. (2005) *WFP Protection of Civilians in Darfur*, Rome: World Food Programme.

Marriage, Z. (2006) 'The comfort of denial: external assistance in southern Sudan', *Development and Change*, 37 (3): 479–500.

Martinez, J. C. and Eng, B. (2016) 'The unintended consequences of emergency food aid: neutrality, sovereignty and politics in the Syrian civil war, 2012–15',

International Affairs, 92 (1):
153–173.

Masefield, G. B. (1967) *Food and
Nutrition Procedures in Times of
disaster*, FAO Nutritional Studies
No. 21, Rome: FAO.

Maxwell, D., Sim, A. and Mutonyi,
M. (2006) *Review of WFP Food
Assistance Programming Practices in
Southern Sudan*, Boston: Feinstein
International Center, Tufts
University.

Maxwell, D. (2011) *The Politicization
of Humanitarian Food Assistance:
Using Food Aid for Strategic,
Military, and Political Purposes*,
Boston: Feinstein International
Center, Tufts University.

Maxwell, D., Vaitla, B. and Coates,
B. (2014) 'How do indicators of
household food insecurity measure
up? An empirical comparison from
Ethiopia', *Food Policy*, 47: 107–116.

Maxwell, S. (1989) *Food Insecurity
in North Sudan*, Discussion
Paper 262, Brighton: Institute of
Development Studies.

Maxwell, S., Swift, J. and Buchanan-
Smith, M. (1990) 'Is food security
targeting possible in Sub-Saharan
Africa? Evidence from North
Sudan', *IDS Bulletin*, 21 (3):
52–61.

McKeon, N. (2014) *The New Alliance
for Food Security and Nutrition:
Coup for Corporate Capital?*, TNI
Agrarian Justice Programme
Policy Paper, Amsterdam:
Transnational Institute.

Middle East and African Studies
Centre (2013) *The Foreign
Organizations in Sudan. The Hidden
Agenda and the Real Objectives*,
Sudanese Studies Papers 10,
Khartoum: Middle East and
African Studies Centre.

Morris, S., Cogill, B. and Uauy,
R. (2008) 'Maternal and Child
Undernutrition 5. Effective
international action against
undernutrition: why has it proven
so diffi cult and what can be done
to accelerate progress?', *Lancet*,
371: 608–621.

Morrow, N., Mock, N., Bauer, J. and
Browning, J. (2016) 'Knowing
just in time: use cases for mobile
surveys in the humanitarian world ',
Procedia Engineering, 159: 210–216.

MSF-Holland (1997) *Report of an
Inter-agency Workshop on Food
Security Assessments in Emergencies*,
December 1997, Amsterdam:
Medecins Sans Frontieres.

National Population Council
General Secretariat, Ministry of
Wellfare and Social Security and
Government of Sudan (2010)
*Sudan Millennium Development
Goals Progress Report 2010*,
Khartoum: Government of Sudan.

New Alliance for Food Security and
Nutrition (2014) 'New Alliance
for Food Security and Nutrition',
available at http://new-alliance.org/
about.

Niblock, T. (1987) *Class and Power in
Sudan. The Dynamics of Sudanese
Politics 1889–1985*, Albany: State
University of New York Press.

Norris, M. (1983) 'Local government
and decentralisation in Sudan',
*Public Administration and
Development*, 3 (3): 209–222.

Nutriset (2015) 'Nutrisets timeline',
available at http://www.nutriset.
fr/en/about-nutriset/nutriset-
timeline.html.

O'Brien, J. (1983) 'The formation
of the agricultural labour force in
Sudan', *Review of African Political
Economy*, 26: 15–43.

O'Brien, J. (1985) 'Sowing the seeds
of famine: the political economy of
food deficits in Sudan', *Review of
African Political Economy*, 33: 23–32.

O'Fahey, R. (2008) *The Darfur
Sultanate. A History*, London:
Hurst.

O'Fahey, R. and Tubiana, J. (2007)
*Darfur. Historical and Contemporary
Aspects*, Bergen: Centre For
Middle Eastern and Islamic
Studies, University of Bergen.

O'Malley, P., Weir, L. and Clifford,
S. (2006) 'Governmentality,
criticism, politics', *Economy and
Society*, 26 (4): 501–517.

Ockwell, R. (1999a) *Thematic Study on Recurring Challenges in the Provision of Food Assistance in Complex emergencies*, Rome: World Food Programme.

Ockwell, R. (1999b) *Food Security and Food Assistance among Long Standing Refugees. Issues Relating to Assessments, Targeting, Self-reliance, and Determining When and How to Phase Down and Out Food Assistance among Refugees in Ongoing 'Care and Maintenance' Situations*, Rome: World Food Programme and UN High Commissioner for Refugees.

ODI (2015) *Doing Cash Differently. How Cash Transfers can Transform Humanitarian Aid. Report of the High Level Panel on Humanitarian Cash Transfers*, London: Overseas Development Institute.

OECD (2005) *The Development Effectiveness of Food Aid. Does Tying Matter? Preliminary Version*, Paris: OECD.

OECD/DAC (2008) *Concepts and Dilemmas of State Building in Fragile Situations. From Fragility to Resilience*, Paris: OECD.

OECD/DAC (2010) *Ensuring Fragile States are not left behind. Summary report*, Paris: OECD.

Office of Foreign Assets Control (2013) *Sudan Sanctions Program*, Washington, DC: Office of Foreign Assets Control. U.S. Department of the Treasury.

Osman, E. F. (1993) 'Targeting realities of food aid: the experience of Darfur State', *SCF Food Aid Meeting*, Nairobi: Save the Children-UK.

Oxfam (2001) *Report of an Inter-agency Workshop to Discuss Minimum Standards for Food Security in Disaster Response*, 8 November 2001, Oxford: Oxfam.

Oxfam (2014) *Moral Hazard? 'Mega' Public–Private Partnerships in African Agriculture*, Oxfam Briefing Paper 188, Oxford: Oxfam.

Oxfam GB (c1995) *Registration and Distribution*, Working in Emergencies, Practical Guidance from the Field, Oxford: Oxfam GB.

Oxfam International (2005) *Food Aid or Hidden Dumping? Separating Wheat from Chaff*, Oxfam Briefing Paper 71, Washington, DC: Oxfam International.

Pacey, A. and Payne, P. (1985) *Agricultural Development and Nutrition*, London: Hutchinson and Co by arrangement with the FAO and UNICEF.

Pantuliano, S., Jaspars, S. and Basu Ray, D. (2009) *Where to Now? Agency Expulsions in Sudan: Consequences and Next Steps*, London: Overseas Development Institute.

Pantuliano, S. and O'Callaghan, S. (2006) *The 'Protection Crisis': A Review of Field Based Strategies for Humanitarian Protection in Darfur*, HPG Discussion Paper, London: Overseas Development Institute.

Pantuliano, S. and Young, H. (eds.) (2011) Famine. *Disasters* themed issue, available at http://onlinelibrary.wiley.com/journal/10.1111/(ISSN)1467-7717.

Parotte, J. (1983) 'The Food Aid Convention: its history and scope', *IDS bulletin*, 14 (2): 10–15.

Patel, M. (1994) 'An examination of the 1990 91 famine in Sudan', *Disasters*, 18 (4): 313–331.

Patel, R., Bezner Kerr, R., Shumba, L. and Dakishoni, L. (2015) 'Cook, eat, man, woman: understanding the New Alliance for Food Security and Nutrition, nutritionism and its alternatives from Malawi', *The Journal of Peasant Studies*, 42 (1): 21–44.

Patey, L. (2010) 'Crude days ahead? Oil and the resource curse in Sudan', *African Affairs*, 109 (437): 617–636.

Pattugalan, G., Bonsignorio, M. and Goublet, L. (2012) *Case Study on the Effects of Voucher Transfers on WFP Beneficiaries Safety And Dignity, Gender and Social Dynamics*, Khartoum: WFP Sudan.

Payne, P. (1990) 'Measuring malnutrition', *IDS Bulletin*, 21 (3): 14–30.

PAX (2016) *Sudan Alert. The EU's Policy Options for Sudan*, Utrecht: PAX.

Pearson, R. (1986) *Lessons Learnt from Famine in Sudan (1984–1986)*, Khartoum: UNICEF.

Pelletier, D. and Jonnson, U. (1994) 'The use of information in the Iringa Nutrition Programme. Some global lessons for nutrition surveillance', *Food Policy*, 19 (3): 301–313.

Prato, S. and Bullard, N. (2014) 'Editorial: re-embedding nutrition in society, nature and politics', *Development*, 57 (2): 129–134.

Protein-Calorie Advisory Group of the United Nations (1977) *A Guide to Food and Health Relief Operations for Disasters*, New York: United Nations.

Provost, C., Ford, L. and Tran, M. (2014) 'G8 New Alliance condemned as new wave of colonialism in Africa', available at http://www.theguardian.com/global-development/2014/feb/18/g8-new-alliance-condemned-new-colonialism.

Prunier, G. (2008) *Darfur. A 21st Century Genocide*, 3rd edition, Ithaca, NY: Cornell University Press.

Radio Dabanga (2013a) 'Darfur farmers threatened by armed herdsmen grazing livestock', available at https://www.dabangasudan.org/en/all-news/article/darfur-farmers-threatened-by-armed-herdsmen-grazing-livestock.

Radio Dabanga (2013b) 'Herders beat, rob 1,000 displaced in Tawila, North Darfur: Sheikh', available at http://allafrica.com/stories/201307110103.html.

Radio Dabanga (2013c) 'Herders torch crops, militia assaults farmers in West Darfur', available at https://www.dabangasudan.org/en/all-news/article/herders-torch-crops-militia-assaults-farmers-in-west-darfur.

Radio Dabanga (2013d) 'Hunger in Central Darfur camps', available at https://www.dabangasudan.org/en/all-news/article/hunger-in-central-darfur-camps.

Radio Dabanga (2013e) 'Militiamen impose 'protection fees' on Central Darfur farmers', available at https://www.dabangasudan.org/en/all-news/article/militiamen-impose-protection-fees-on-central-darfur-farmers.

Radio Dabanga (2013f) 'Sudan official to ask clerics advice on Darfur blood money issue', available at https://www.dabangasudan.org/en/all-news/article/sudan-official-to-ask-clerics-advice-on-darfur-blood-money-issue 27 March 2013.

Radio Dabanga (2014a) 'Darfur society critical of officials praising Rapid Support Forces', available at https://www.dabangasudan.org/en/all-news/article/darfur-society-critical-of-officials-praising-rapid-support-forces.

Radio Dabanga (2014b) 'Sudan presidency to provide East and South Darfur with 10,000 tons of sorghum', available at http://allafrica.com/stories/201405190728.html.

Radio Dabanga (2014c) ''Sirba camps for the displaced are now quasi-towns'': West Darfur HAC officials', available at https://www.dabangasudan.org/en/all-news/article/sirba-camps-for-the-displaced-are-now-quasi-towns-west-darfur-hac-officials.

Rangasami, A. (1985) 'Failure of exchange entitlements' theory of famine. A response', *Economic and Political Weekly*, 41: 1747–1751.

Refugee Studies Programme (1991) *Responding to the Crisis among Refugees: The Need for New Approaches. Report of the International Symposium*. Oxford: Refugee Studies Programme.

Relief and Rehabilitation Commission (1991) *Emergency Relief Policy for 1991*, Khartoum: Government of Sudan.

Reshaur, K. (1992) 'Concepts of solidarity in the political theory of Hannah Arendt', *Canadian Journal of Political Science*, 25 (4): 723–736.

Reuters (2014) 'Sudan expels two senior U.N. officials: sources', available at http://www.reuters.com/article/2014/12/25/us-sudan-un-expulsions-idUSKBN0K30IC20141225 .

Riley, B. (2004) *US Food Aid Programmes. 1954–2004. A Background Paper*, Paris: OECD.

Ruel, M. (2002) *Is dietary diversity an indicator of food security or dietary quality? A review of measurement issues and research needs*, FCND Discussion Paper No. 140, Washington, DC: Food Consumption and Nutrition Division. International Food Policy Research Institute.

Ruel, M. and Alderman, H. (2013) 'Maternal and Child Nutrition 3. Nutrition-sensitive interventions and programmes: how can they help to accelerate progress in improving maternal and child nutrition?', *Lancet*, 382: 536–551.

Ryle, J., Willis, J., Baldo, S. and Madut Jok, J. (eds.) (2011) *The Sudan Handbook*, Oxford: James Currey.

Sathyamala, C. (2016) 'Nutritionalizing food: a framework for capital accumulation', *Development and Change*, 47 (4): 818–839.

SC-UK (1991) *Agreement between the Relief and Rehabilitation Commission and Save the Children Regarding Assistance for the 1991 Food Relief Programme*, Khartoum: Children-UK, Save the Children-UK.

SC-UK (1993) *Review of the 1991–93 Relief Programme and Strategy for Relief Programme in Darfur State for 1994*, Khartoum: Save the Children-UK.

SC-UK (1997) *Targeted Food Aid, 1996*, Al-Fashir: Save the Children-UK.

SC-UK (c1986) *The Development of SCF's Programme in Darfur*, Khartoum: Save the Children-UK.

SC-UK Darfur (1991) *Summary Report on Food Security. May 1991*, Al-Fashir: Save the Children-UK.

Scaling Up Nutrition Movement (2014) *An Introduction to the Scaling Up Nutrition Movement*, available at *http://scalingupnutrition.org/about-sun*.

Schaffer, B. (1984) 'Towards responsibility: public policy in concept and practice', in: Clay, E. and Schaffer, B. (eds.) *Room for Manouvre. An Exploration of Public Policy in Agriculture and Rural Development*, London: Heinemann Educational Books, 142–190.

Schofield, C. (2013). 'Social nutrition as part of MSc Human Nutrition Course', email message to S. Jaspars, 16 January 2013.

Schuftan, C. and Holla, R. (2012) 'Two contemporary challenges: corporate control over food and nutrition and the absence of a focus on the social determinants of nutrition', in: Right to Food and Nutrition Watch (ed.) *Who Decides About Global Food and Nutrition? Strategies to Regain Control*, Brot fur die Welt, FIAN International, ICCO.

Scott-Smith, T. (2016) 'Humanitarian dilemmas in a mobile world', *Refugee Survey Quarterly*, 35: 1–25.

Seaman, J. (2000) 'Making exchange entitlements operational: the food economy approach to famine prediction and the RiskMap computer programme', *Disasters*, 24 (2): 133–152.

Sen, A. (1981) *Poverty and Famines. An Essay on Entitlement and Deprivation*, Oxford: Clarendon Press.

Sen, A. (2000) *Development as Freedom*, Oxford: Oxford University Press.

Sharp, K. (1998) *Between Relief and Development: Targeting Food Aid for Disaster Prevention in Ethiopia*, RRN Paper 27 London: Overseas Development Institute.

Shaw, J. (1967) 'Resettlement from the Nile in Sudan', *Middle East Journal*, 21 (4): 462–487.

Shaw, J. (1970) 'The mechanism and distribution of food aid. Multilateral food aid for economic and social development', *Journal of World Trade Law*, 4 (2): 207–237.

Shaw, J. (2001) *The UN World Food Programme and the Development of Food Aid*, Basingstoke: Palgrave.

Shaw, J. (2011) *The World's Largest Humanitarian Agency*, Basingstoke: Palgrave Macmillan.

Shoham, J. (2005) *Food Security Information Systems Supported by Save the Children UK. A Review*, London: Save the Children-UK.

Shoham, J. and Clay, E. (1989) 'The role of socio-economic data in food needs assessment and monitoring', *Disasters*, 13 (1): 44–60.

Sidahmed, A. S. (2011) 'Islamism and the State', in: Ryle, J., Willis, J., Baldo, S. andMadut Jok, J. (eds.) *The Sudan Handbook*, Oxford: James Currey, 94–107.

Singer, H., Wood, J. and Jennings, T. (1987) *Food Aid. The Challenge and the Opportunity*, Oxford: Clarendon Press.

Slim, H. (2015) *Humanitarian Ethics. A Guide to Morality of Aid in War and Disasters*, London: Hurst and Company.

Sorbo, G. (1985) *Tenants and Nomads in Eastern Sudan. A Study of Economic Adaptations in the New Halfa Scheme*, Uppsala: Scandinavian Institute of African Studies.

SPLM, SRRA and OLS (1998) *Joint Targeting and Vulnerabilities Task Force in SPLM Controlled Areas of Bahr El Ghazal*, Lokichokkio: Operation Lifeline Sudan.

Stiglitz, J. (2002) *Globalisation and its Discontents*, London: Penguin Books.

Stoddard, A., A., H. and Renouf, J. (2010) *Once Removed. Lessons and challenges in remote management of humanitarian operations for insecure areas*, London: Humanitarian Outcomes.

Stoddard, A., Harmer, A. and DiDomenico, V. (2009) *Providing Aid in Insecure Environments: 2009 Update*, HPG Policy Brief 34, London: Overseas Development Institute.

Stoddard, A., Harmer, A. and Haver, K. (2006) *Providing Aid in Insecure Environments: Trends in Policy and Operations*, HPG Report 23, London: Overseas Development Institute.

Street, A. (2015) 'Food as pharma: marketing nutraceuticals to India's rural poor', *Critical Public Health*, 25 (3): 361–372.

Sudan Council of Ministers (2008) *Agriculture and Articulate a Future Vision and Action Plan for Agricultural Revival. Executive Programme for Agricultural Revival*, Khartoum: Council of Ministers General Secretariat.

Sudan Tribune (2012) 'Government suspends seven aid groups in Eastern Sudan', available at http://www.sudantribune.com/spip.php?article42773.

Sudan Tribune (2013) 'Sudan urged to renew residence permits of UN humanitarian staff in Darfur', available at http://www.sudantribune.com/spip.php?page=spipdf&spipdf=spipdf_article&id_article=47567&nom_fichier=article_47567.

Sudan Tribune (2017) 'Riyadh making efforts to achieve full lift of U.S. sanctions on Sudan: envoy', available at http://sudantribune.com/spip.php?article62510

Sudan Vision (2014) 'N. Darfur provides humanitarian aid to affected localities', available at http://news.sudanvisiondaily.com/details.html?rsnpid=234771.

TAFAD (2006) *Proposals for a renewed Food Aid Convention,*

Ottawa: Trans-Atlantic NGO
Food Aid Policy Dialogue.

Tanner, V. (2002) *Save the Children
(UK)'s Response to Drought
in North Darfur 2000–2001*,
Evaluation, Save the Children-UK.

Tanner, V. (2005) *Rule of Lawlessness.
Roots and Repercussions of the
Darfur Crisis. Interagency Paper*,
Khartoum: Sudan Advocacy
Coalition.

Tanner, V., Tubiana, J. and Adam
Abdul-Jalil, M. (2012) *Traditional
Authorities' Peacemaking Role in
Darfur*, Washington, DC: United
States Institute of Peace.

Taylor, A. and Seaman, J. (2004)
Targeting Food Aid in Emergencies,
ENN Special Supplement Series
No. 1, Oxford: Emergency
Nutrition Network.

Taylor, N. (1985) *Nutritional
Surveillance and Drought
Monitoring Project. Report on Project
Activities March–May 1985*, Nyala:
Oxfam, UNICEF and Darfur
Regional Government.

Terry, F. (2002) *Condemned
to Repeat? The Paradox of
Humanitarian Action*, Ithaca and
London: Cornell University Press.

The Sphere Project (2004)
*Humanitarian Charter and
Minimum Standards in Disaster
Response*, 2004 edition, Geneva:
The Sphere Project.

Toole, M. J., Nieburg, P. and
Waldman, R. J. (1988) 'The
association between inadequate
rations, undernutrition prevalence
and mortality in refugee camps:
case studies of refugee populations
in eastern Thailand, 1979–1980,
and Eastern Sudan, 1984–1985',
Journal of Tropical Pediatrics, 34:
218–224.

Traub, J. (2010) *Unwilling and Unable:
The Failed Response to the Atrocities
in Darfur*, Occasional Paper Series,
New York: Global Centre for the
Responsibility to Protect.

Tubiana, J. (2011) *Renouncing
the Rebels: Local and Regional
Dimensions of Chad–Sudan

Rapprochement*, Geneva: Small
Arms Survey.

Tvedt, T. (1994) 'The collapse of
the state in Southern Sudan
after the Addis Ababa Agreement.
A study of internal causes and
the role of NGOs.', in: Harir, S.
and Tvedt, T. (eds.) *Short Cut
to Decay. The Case of the Sudan*,
Uppsala: Nordiska Afrikainstitutet,
68–103.

UKAID, Children's Investment
Fund Foundation and Federal
Government of Brazil (2013)
'Global Nutrition for Growth
Compact', available at https://
www.gov.uk/government/uploads/
system/uploads/attachment_data/
file/248760/Endorserscompact_
update7_10_2013.pdf.

UN General Assembly (1991)
*Strengthening of the Coordination
of Humanitarian Emergency
Assistance of the United Nations*, A/
RES/46/182, 78th Plenary Meeting,
New York: United Nations.

UN OCHA (1999) *OCHA
Orientation Handbook on Complex
Emergencies*. New York: UN
Office for the Coordination of
Humanitarian Affairs.

UN OCHA (2012) *OCHA on
Message: Humanitarian Principles*,
New York: UN Office for the
Coordination of Humanitarian
Affairs.

UN OCHA (2014a) *Darfur: New
Humanitarian Needs and Aid
Delivery Factsheet*, Khartoum: UN
Office for the Coordination of
Humanitarian Affairs.

UN OCHA (2014b) *2014 Revised
Strategic Response Plan*, Khartoum:
UN Office for the Coordination of
Humanitarian Affairs.

UN OCHA (2015) *2016
Humanitarian Needs Overview*,
Khartoum: UN Office for the
Coordination of Humanitarian
Affairs.

UN OCHA (2016) *Humanitarian
Response Plan*, Khartoum: UN
Office for the Coordination of
Humanitarian Affairs.

UN OCHA (2017) *Darfur Humanitarian Overview*, Khartoum: UN OCHA.

UN SCN (1988) *Nutrition in Times of Disaster. Report of an International Conference held at the World Health Organization Headquarters*, World Health Organization Headquarters, Geneva: WHO and UNHCR.

UN SCN (1992) *Symposium Report. Nutrition Policy Discussion Paper No.12. Nutritional Issues in Food Aid*, Rome, 24–25 February, Geneva: United Nations Standing Committee on Nutrition.

UN SCN (1994) *Report of a Workshop on the Improvement of the Nutrition of Refugees and Displaced People in Africa*, University of Nairobi, Machakos, Kenya: UN Administrative Committee on Coordination/Standing Committee on Nutrition.

UN Security Council (2014) 'Security Council Report. Monthly forecast', available at http://www.securitycouncilreport.org.

UNDP (1994) *Human Development Report*, United Nations Development Programme, available at http://hdr.undp.org/en/reports/global/hdr1994/.

UNDP and Darfur Regional Authority (2013) *Developing Darfur: A Recovery & Reconstruction Strategy*, Khartoum: United Nations Development Programme.

UNHCR (1995) *Report of a Workshop on Tools and Strategies in Needs Assessment and the Management of Food and Nutrition Programmes in Refugee and Displaced Populations*, Addis Ababa: United Nations High Commissioner for Refugees.

UNHCR, WFP and ENN (1999) *Food Security Assessments, Self-reliance, Targeting and Phasing Out in Ongoing Refugee Situations. A Summary Report of an Inter-agency Workshop.* Rome: UNHCR, WFP, Emergency Nutrition Network.

UNICEF (1990) *Strategy for Improved Nutrition of Children and Women in Developing Countries*, New York: United Nations Children's Fund.

UNICEF (2013) *Bridging the Nutrition Security Gap in Sub-Saharan Africa: A Pathway to Resilience and Development*, Paris: United Nations Children's Fund.

Upton, J., Denno Cisse, J. and Barrett, C. (2016) 'Food security as resilience: reconciling definition and measurement', *Agricultural Economics*, 47 (Supplement): 135–147.

US Department of the Treasury (2009) *Report to Congress January 2009. Effectiveness of U.S. Economic Sanctions with Respect to Sudan*, Washington, DC: US Department of the Treasury.

US Embassy in Khartoum and Sudan Ministry of Foreign Affairs (1958) *Agreement on Economic, Technical and Related Assistance*, Khartoum: US Government and Sudan Government.

US Government (1955-57) 'United States policy objectives in the Sudan', available at http://digital.library.wisc.edu/1711.dl/FRUS.

US Government (2010) *Feed the Future Guide*, Washington, DC: US Government.

US Government (2012) 'Food security and the G8 Summit', available at http://feedthefuture.gov/article/food-security-and-g8-summit.

USAID (1986) *Evaluation of the African Emergency Food Assistance Program 1984-85. Synthesis Report*, Washington, DC: USAID.

USAID (2012) *Building Resilience to Recurrent Crisis. USAID Policy and Programme Guidance*, Washington, DC: USAID.

USAID (2014) *Multi-Sectoral Nutrition Strategy 2014–2025*, Washington, DC: USAID.

Uvin, P. (1992) 'Regime, surplus and self-interest', *International Studies Quarterly*, 36 (3): 293–312.

Vercillo, S., Kuuire, V., Ato Armah, F. and Luginaah, I. (2015) 'Does the New Alliance for Food Security and Nutrition impose biotechnology on smallholder farmers in Africa?', *Global Bioethics*, 26 (1): 1–13.

Victora, C., Adair, L., Fall, C., Hallal, P., Martorell, R., Richter, L. and Sachdev, H. (2008) 'Maternal and Child Undernutrition 2. Maternal and child undernutrition: consequences for adult health and human capital', *Lancet*, 371: 340–357.

Vincent, K. and Cull, T. (2011) 'Cell phones, electronic delivery systems and social cash transfers: recent evidence and experiences from Africa', *International Social Security Review*, 64 (1): 37–51.

Walker, J. and Cooper, M. (2011) 'Genealogies of resilience: from systems ecology to the political economy of crisis adaptation', *Security Dialogue*, 42 (2): 143–160.

Walker, P. (1988) 'Famine relief amongst pastoralists in Sudan: a report of Oxfam's experience', *Disasters*, 12 (3): 196–202.

Walkup, M. (1997) 'Policy dysfunction in humanitarian organizations: the role of coping strategies, institutions, and organizational culture', *Journal of Refugee Studies*, 10 (1): 37–60.

Weiss, T. (2000) 'Governance, Good Governance and Global Governance: Conceptual and Actual Challenges', *Third World Quarterly*, 21 (5): 795–814.

Welsh, M. (2014) 'Resilience and responsibility: governing uncertainty in a complex world', *The Geographical Journal*, 180 (1): 15–26.

Were Omamo, S., Gentilini, U. and Sandström, S. (eds.) (2010) *Revolution: From Food Aid to Food Assistance. Innovations in Overcoming Hunger*, Rome: WFP.

WFP (1969) *Interim Evaluation; WFP Assistance to Three Land Settlement Projects at Khasm el Girba in the Sudan*, WFP Intergovernmental Committee, 16th Session, Rome: World Food Programme.

WFP (1970) *Khartoum Green Belt. Terminal Report*, WFP Intergovernmental Committee, 17th Session, Rome: World Food Programme.

WFP (1972) *Interim Evaluation Report. Afforestation and Wood Processing Operations in the Blue Nile and Kassala Provinces*, WFP Intergovernmental Committee, 22nd Session, Rome: World Food Programme.

WFP (1974) *Terminal Report. Resettlement of Refugees in the Gedaref District*, WFP Intergovernmental Committee, 26th Session, Rome: World Food Programme.

WFP (1975a) *Interim Evaluation Report. Scheme for Sawmilling and other Forestry Operations in Bahr El Ghazal Province*, WFP Intergovernmental Committee. 28th Session, Rome: World Food Programme.

WFP (1975b) *Interim Evaluation Report. Assistance to Primary, Secondary and Vocational Schools*, WFP Intergovernmental Committee, 28th Session, Rome: World Food Programme.

WFP (1976) *Interim Evaluation Report. Rural Development of the South*, WFP Committee on Food Aid Policies and Programmes, 1st Session, Rome: World Food Programme.

WFP (1983) *Project Summary. Restocking of the Gum Belt*, WFP Committee on Food Aid Policies and Programmes, 15th Session, Rome: World Food Programme.

WFP (1986) *Lessons Learnt from the African Food Crisis: Evaluation of the WFP Emergency Response*, WFP Committee on Food Aid Policies and Programmes, 21st Session, Rome: World Food Programme.

WFP (1988a) *Progress Report. Dairy Development in Khartoum Area*,

WFP Committee on Food Aid Policies and Programmes, 25th Session, Rome: World Food Programme.

WFP (1988b) *Project Sudan 3709: Assistance to Rural Works in Drought Prone Areas*, Committee on Food Aid Policies and Programmes, 26th Session, Rome: World Food Programme.

WFP (1997) *Progress Report on WFP's Development Portfolio*, Executive Board, Resumed Second Regular Session, Rome: World Food Programme.

WFP (1998a) *From Crisis to Recovery*, Executive Board, Annual Session, Rome: World Food Programme.

WFP (1998b) *Development Project Sudan 5745.0. Improved Water Access in Semi-arid Areas*, Executive Board, Second Regular Session, Rome: World Food Programme.

WFP (2000) *Food and Nutrition Handbook*, Rome: World Food Programme.

WFP (2002) *Food Aid in Conflict Workshop, Report*, Rome: World Food Programme.

WFP (2003) *Food Aid and Livelihoods in Emergencies: Strategies for WFP*, Policy Issues, Rome: World Food Programme.

WFP (2006) *A Report from the Office of Evaluation. Full Report of the Evaluation of EMOP 10339.0/1: Assistance to Populations Affected by Conflict in Greater Darfur, West Sudan.*, Rome: World Food Programme.

WFP (2008a) *WFP Strategic Plan 2008–2013*, Rome: World Food Programme.

WFP (2008b) *Emergency Operation (EMOP) Sudan 10760.0 (for 2009)*, Rome: World Food Programme.

WFP (2009a) *Humanitarian Assistance in Conflict and Complex Emergencies. June 2009 Conference Report and Background Papers*, Rome: World Food Programme.

WFP (2009b) 'International Food Aid Information System', available at http://www.wfp.org/fais.

WFP (2009c) *Emergency Food Security Assessment Handbook*. 2nd edition, Rome: World Food Programme.

WFP (2012a) *WFP Humanitarian Protection Policy*, Executive Board First Regular Session Rome, 13–15 February 2012, Rome: World Food Programme.

WFP (2012b) *Nutrition at the World Food Programme. Programming for Nutrition-Specific Interventions*, Rome: World Food Programme.

WFP (2013a) *WFP Strategic Plan (2014–2017)*, Executive Board Session, Rome, 3–6 June 2013, Rome: World Food Programme.

WFP (2013b) *Sudan: An Evaluation of WFP's Portfolio 2010–2012. Vol. I – Evaluation Report*, Country Portfolio Evaluation, Rome: World Food Programme.

WFP (2014a) *Darfur Comprehensive Food Security Assessment. Sudan, 2012–2013*, Khartoum: World Food Programme.

WFP (2014b) *North Darfur, Sudan. Food Security Monitoring, May 2014*, Khartoum: World Food Programme.

WFP (2015a) *IDP Profiling Results. Geneina Town Camps, West Darfur*, Khartoum: WFP.

WFP (2015b) *Protracted Relief and Recovery Operations – The Sudan 200808*, Executive Board Annual Session Rome, 25–28 May 2015, Rome: World Food Programme.

WFP (2016) *Mobile Vulnerability Analysis and Mapping*, Rome: WFP.

WFP, Darfur States Ministries of Agriculture and North Darfur State Ministry of Health (2011) *Comprehensive Food Security Assessment in Darfur*, Khartoum: World Food Programme.

WFP and FAO (2010) *The State of Food Insecurity in the World. Addressing Food Insecurity in Protracted Crises*, Rome: Food and Agriculture Organisation.

WFP, Government of Sudan and UNICEF (2007) *Emergency Food*

Security and Nutrition Assessment in Darfur, Sudan 2006. Final Report, Khartoum: World Food Programme.

WFP, Government of Sudan and UNICEF (2008) Food Security and Nutrition Assessment of the Conflict-affected Population in Darfur, Sudan, 2007. Final Report, Khartoum: World Food Programme.

WFP, Government of Sudan (HAC and MoA) and FAO (2009) 2008 Darfur Food Security and Livelihood Assessment. Final Report, Khartoum: World Food Programme.

WFP and UNICEF (2005) Emergency Food Security and Nutrition Assessment, Rome: World Food Programme.

WFP and UNICEF (2014) The Case for Investment in Nutrition in Sudan, Khartoum: WFP and UNICEF.

WFP Sudan (2010) Emergency Operation Sudan: EMOP 200151 (for 2011), Rome: World Food Programme.

WFP Sudan (2011) Food Vouchers, Khartoum: World Food Programme.

WFP Sudan (2012) Emergency Operation (EMOP) Sudan 200457 (for 2013), Khartoum: World Food Programme.

WFP Sudan (2013) United Nations World Food Programme Country Strategy for WFP in Sudan (2013–2015), Khartoum: World Food Programme.

WFP Sudan (2014) WFP Sudan Vouchers Standard Operating Procedure, Khartoum: World Food Programme.

WFP Sudan (2015) Food Security Monitoring North Darfur, Sudan, November 2015, Khartoum: Word Food Programme.

WFP Sudan (2016) Darfur Food Security Monitoring. November 2016, Sudan, Khartoum: Word Food Programme.

WHO (1995) Physical Status: The Use and Interpretation of Anthropometry.

Report of a WHO Expert Committee, Geneva: World Health Organization.

WHO, UNHCR, IFRC and WFP (2000) The Management of Nutrition in Major Emergencies, Geneva: World Health Organization.

Wiesmann, D., Bassett, L., Benson, T. and Hoddinott, J. (2008) Validation of Food Frequency and Dietary Diversity as Proxy Indicators of Household Food Security Report. Submitted to: World Food Programme, Rome: World Food Programme.

Williams, C. (1986) Nutritional Surveillance and Drought Monitoring Project. Darfur. Report of March:April Survey 1986, Nyala: Oxfam.

Williams, P. and Bellamy, A. (2005) 'The Responsibility To Protect and the crisis in Darfur', Security Dialogue, 36: 27–47.

Williams, T. (1992) 1991 Sudan Relief Programmes Evaluation, Oxfam GB.

Wilson, K. (1992) 'Enhancing refugees' own food acquisition strategies', Journal of Refugee Studies, 5 (3/4): 226–246.

Woodward, P. (1990) Sudan, 1898–1989. The Unstable State, Boulder: Lynne Reiner Publishers.

World Bank (1986) Poverty and Hunger Issues and Options for Food Security in Developing Countries, A World Bank Policy Study. Washington, DC: World Bank.

World Bank (1989) Sub-Saharan Africa. From Crisis to Sustainable Development. A Long Term Perspective Study, Washington, DC: World Bank.

World Bank (2002) Governance and Development, Washington, DC: World Bank.

World Bank (2009) Sudan: The Road Toward Sustainable and Broad-Based Growth, Washington, DC: World Bank.

World Bulletin (2014) 'ICC shelves Darfur case for lack of UN support', available at https://www.africanglobe.net/africa/icc-shelves-darfur-case-lack-support/.

World Food Conference (1974) 'Universal Declaration on the Eradication of Hunger and Malnutrition', available at http://www.ohchr.org/EN/Professional Interest/Pages/radication Of HungerAndMalnutrition.aspx.

Yongo-Bure, B. (2009) 'Marginalization and war: from the south to Darfur', in: Hassan, S. and Ray, C. (eds.) *Darfur and the Crisis of Governance in Sudan. A Critical Reader*, Ithaca and London: Cornell University Press, 68–83.

Young, H. (1992) 'A case study of the Chadian refugees in Western Sudan: the impact of the Food Assessment Mission', *Journal of Refugee Studies*, 5 (3/4): 327–355.

Young, H. (1999a) 'Public nutrition in emergencies: an overview of debates, dilemmas and decision-making', *Disasters*, 23 (4): 277–291.

Young, H. (ed.) (1999b) Special Issue: *International Public Nutrition and Emergencies: The Potential for Improving Practice. Disasters Journal* 23 (4). Overseas Development Institute.

Young, H. (2007) 'Looking beyond food aid to livelihoods, protection and partnerships: strategies for WFP in the Darfur states', *Disasters*, 31 (S1): S40–56.

Young, H., Borrel, A., Holland, D. and Salama, P. (2004) 'Public nutrition in complex emergencies', *Lancet*, 364: 1899–1909.

Young, H. and Jaspars, S. (1995) *Nutrition Matters: People, Food and Famine*, London: Intermediate Technology Publications.

Young, H. and Jaspars, S. (2009) *Review of Nutrition and Mortality Indicators for the Integrated Food Security Phase Classification (IPC).*

Reference Levels and Decision-making, Rome: UN Standing Committee on Nutrition.

Young, H. and Maxwell, D. (2009) *Targeting in Complex Emergencies: Darfur case study*, Boston: Feinstein International Center, Tufts University.

Young, H. and Maxwell, D. (2013) 'Participation, political economy and protection: food aid governance in Darfur, Sudan', *Disasters*, 37 (4): 555–578.

Young, H., Osman, A., Aklilu, Y., Dale, R., Badri, B. and Fuddle, A. (2005) *Darfur – Livelihoods under Siege*, Boston: Feinstein International Center, Tufts University.

Young, H., Jacobson, K. and Osman, A. M. (2009a) *Livelihoods, Migration and Conflict: Discussion of Findings from Two Studies in West and North Darfur, 2006–2007*, Boston: Feinstein International Center. Tufts University.

Young, H., Osman, A. M., Abusin, A. M., Asher, M. and Egemi, O. (2009b) *Livelihoods, Power and Choice: The Vulnerability of the Northern Rizeigat, Darfur, Sudan*, Boston: Feinstein International Center, Tufts University.

Young, H., Sadler, K. and Borrel, A. (2012) 'Public Nutrition in Humanitarian Crisis', in: Erdman Jr, J., MacDonald, I. and Zeisel, S. (eds.) *Present Knowledge in Nutrition*, 10th edition. Edited by John W. Erdman Jr, Ian MacDonald and Steven Zeisel, Oxford: Blackwell Publishing Ltd.

Zetter, R. and Henry, J. (eds.) (1992) *The Nutrition Crisis Among Refugees.* Journal of Refugee Studies 5. Oxford: Refugee Studies Programme.

Index

Also available in the series Politics and Development in Contemporary Africa

Mobility between Africa, Asia and Latin America: Economic Networks and Cultural Interactions
EDITED BY UTE RÖSCHENTHALER AND ALESSANDRO JEDLOWSKI

'Empirically rich and conceptually astute, this volume gives the reader unparalleled insight into the lives of mobile traders crisscrossing the Global South. Essential reading for anyone interested in contemporary globalization and its historical roots.'

Neil Carrier, University of Oxford

'This important collection offers compelling accounts of geopolitical histories, personal trajectories, and unexpected cultural outcomes. The volume is recommended to anyone interested in Africa's diverse transnational connections.'

Heidi Østbø Haugen, University of Oslo

Agricultural Reform in Rwanda: Authoritarianism, Markets and Zones of Governance
BY CHRIS HUGGINS

'A very informed, nuanced analysis of agriculture in Rwanda, spanning zones of governance, compliance and resistance in a "developmental" state. As always, only some citizens and communities benefit. This book shows us why.'

Timothy M. Shaw, University of Massachusetts Boston

'An extraordinary study of the state-directed commercialization of Rwandan agriculture. In this nuanced account, Huggins reworks the contemporary agrarian question.'

Philip McMichael, Cornell University